Foreign Bonds:
An Autopsy

Foreign Bonds: An Autopsy

By

MAX WINKLER

BeardBooks

Washington, D.C.

CONTENTS

To Beatrice, Howard and Bobby

ACKNOWLEDGMENT

Thanks are hereby extended to the following for aid
rendered in connection with the compilation of material for this study: George W. Edwards, Howard C. Green and Bernhard Ostrolenk, of the
Department of Economics, College of the
City of New York; I. G. Rudkowsky and
Charles Evers of the American Council
of Foreign Bondholders; Joseph Lilly
of the World-Telegram; Murray
W. Kline, formerly of the Port
of New York Authority, and
Vaso Trivanovich of the
National Industrial Conference Board.

FOREWORD

An adequate study of the causes, effects and remedies of defaults on governmental obligations, which are rapidly approaching the staggering total of twenty-five billion dollars (exclusive generally of intergovernmental war debts), is no mean task. Nor is it of small importance not merely to the world, but more especially to the citizens of the United States, who in the wild scramble to gain the supposedly substantial profits of foreign investments now find themselves "holding the bag" filled with uncollectable promises to repay many billions of dollars.

The huge sums in default have affected and will continue to affect vitally the domestic and international affairs of many nations, and above all those of the United States. Among items involved are international trade, tariffs, investments, foreign exchange, the merchant marine, the recognition of governments, inflation, the domestic financial situation, and the balancing of budgets, and even the seeds of war and revolution.

The work of preparing an adequate study of these defaults is so enormous that there are few who have both the capacity and inclination to undertake it. The American public is fortunate in having this analytical study by a man of such outstanding reputation and ability as Dr. Winkler.

The subject matter is of very great importance. The treatment makes it highly interesting, not only because of its painstaking accuracy, but because of the sympathetic and witty manner in which it is presented. Under the skilled pen of Dr. Winkler, dry statistics have become living, interesting, and not infrequently amusing things.

That there is nothing new under the sun is shown again by his historical survey (going back 2500 years) covering previous defaults, inflation, depressions, war debts, and the like.

Dr. Winkler quotes with misgiving the Hegelian dictum that "We learn from history that we learn nothing from history."

Let us hope that the present study will open the eyes of at least the American investor so that he will use fully such remedies as are available to handle the present situation and safeguard himself against similar difficulties in the future.

THOMAS H. HEALY, PH.D.,
Assistant Dean,
Georgetown School of Foreign Service

INTRODUCTION

ECONOMIC phenomena, despite the assertions of professional economists, do not readily lend themselves to reliable diagnosis, and still less to accurate prognosis. The number of intangible elements is too great to justify any implicit faith in prognostications, irrespective of the repute of the prophet. The remedies prescribed may prove beneficial or futile, and in all probability they will, except by pure accident, prove of little or no value if they are based solely or even largely upon the various mechanical devices and implements manufactured in the countless economic laboratories and statistical workshops.

Those who feel called upon to hazard a diagnosis of an economic ailment are as a rule groping in the dark. They may hit or miss. To perform physical postmortems is a relatively simple task: the corpse can be dissected and the various agents responsible for the demise studied minutely. This method is merely the procedure of following the line of least resistance. While it may prove of no avail to those who have already succumbed, it may be of some help to those countless potential victims, present and future, who are ready to be preyed upon when a suitable opportunity presents itself.

Had an honest attempt been made to examine the various governmental borrowings, running into billions, at the time transactions were effected, and had the findings of such an examination been made public, few would have taken them seriously. After the damage has been done and the autopsy performed, the findings can no longer be ignored. The task may not be a pleasant one, but whenever the deceased is suspected of having fallen a victim to unnatural causes a postmortem is obligatory. Foreign bonds, that is, obligations sold on behalf of foreign governments, states and municipalities, come within this classification, and, in an attempt to contribute in a measure to the promotion of public welfare, an autopsy seems in order. Hence the present study: *Foreign Bonds—an Autopsy.*

Twenty-two billion, three hundred million dollars of contractual obligations of governments, states, and municipalities, will be in default at the beginning of 1934.* Interest due and unpaid will total well over 12½ billions, and is accumulating at the rate of more than one billion dollars a year, equivalent to over two thousand dollars a minute.

The hugeness of these figures is apparent when we consider that the amount in default is equivalent to about $12 for each man, woman and child living, regardless of race and color and creed, including cattle-breeders from Abyssinia, tin miners from Bolivia, nitrate workers from Chile, coffee planters from Haiti, shippers from Kwantung, dairymen from Lithuania, silver miners from Mexico, guano workers from Peru, copper miners from Rhodesia, rice growers from Siam, pearl fishers from Tahiti, cotton planters from

---

* The difference between these figures and those by a Washington Bureau which has recently completed a compilation of statistics relative to governmental defaults is due to the fact that the Bureau has confined its study only to issues sold in the United States and that it has omitted the defaults of Russia, China, and Mexico. It is apparent that if other countries were left out, the sum would be even smaller than that furnished by the Bureau in question.

Uganda, merchants from Xanthos, sisal planters from Yucatan, and herdsmen from Zululand.

The amount in default is only slightly less than the total expenditure of the United States Government from its foundation, about a century and a half ago, to the outbreak of the Great War. It is equal to almost three and a half times the total expenditure of Great Britain in connection with the Napoleonic conflict, covering a quarter of a century.

It is equal to fifteen times Great Britain's outlay in connection with her South African War. It is equal to thirty-two times the annual income of all the Balkan countries; fifty times that of the Scandinavian Kingdoms; one hundred and fifteen times that of the Baltic countries; and four hundred and fifty times the annual income of all the Central American Republics. It is equal to the aggregate wealth of fourteen States, including Arizona, Arkansas, Delaware, Florida, Idaho, Maine, Montana, Nevada, New Hampshire, New Mexico, North Dakota, Rhode Island, Utah and Vermont.

These gigantic figures bind the respective countries for all time and eternity. They can never pay them. They never expect to pay them.

It is the investor in foreign bonds, especially the American investor—that docile and often incomprehensible person—of whom the present study will treat at length. It will show that had there been a proper diagnosis at the time foreign bonds were sold by the billions, to millions of investors, defaults would be occurring today with less distressing frequency. It will examine the governments and the various political subdivisions that are withholding payments on contractual obligations.

It also attempts to throw light upon the reasons for the collapse of the credit of nations and upon the effects of suspension of payments upon their economic and financial structure. It presents a résumé of governmental defaults through the ages, going back as far as twenty-five hundred years ago, when Dionysius of Syracuse debased the country's currency in order to reduce its outstanding indebtedness. It tells of the defaults in ancient Rome, of defaults in the Middle Ages, and finally of defaults and repudiations in modern times.

It describes the transformation of the United States from a debtor nation to the world's most powerful creditor country, with investments abroad aggregating more than seventeen billion dollars all made within a decade and a half.* It endeavors to point out how

---

*Details of America's stake abroad as of January 1, 1933, compared with 1932 and 1914, are given hereunder (in millions of dollars):

Region	1933	1932	1914
Europe	5,159	5,765	350
Canada	4,547	4,601	750
South America	3,077	3,079	100
Central America	3,009	3,015	1,200
Australasia	895	1,012	175
Miscellaneous	476	495	50
	17,163	17,967	2,625

The distribution of America's stake abroad by countries is given in the subjoined table (in thousands of dollars):

EUROPE

Country	1933	1932
Austria	127,557	129,500
Belgium	250,055	259,125
Czechoslovakia	54,112	55,500
Denmark	165,217	172,101
France	294,500	362,500
Germany	1,285,000	1,661,785
Great Britain	745,000	755,893
Hungary	127,650	138,000
Italy	509,295	536,102
Jugoslavia	94,497	94,500

the investor was prevailed upon to succumb to the impressive statements contained in prospectuses descriptive of foreign loans; how he was forced to discover that the idol he had been taught to worship not

Country	1933	1932
Netherlands	142,500	165,000
Norway	206,500	215,000
Poland	190,750	192,000
Rumania	102,500	105,000
Spain	127,700	164,000
Sweden	271,500	289,486
Miscellaneous	464,700	470,038
	5,159,033	5,765,530

Detailed figures for South American and Central American republics are as of January 1, 1932, and comprise statistics relative to portfolio investments—that is, bonds and shares publicly and privately placed with American investors, and direct investments—that is, foreign plants and properties acquired by American interests without the flotation of securities:

SOUTH AMERICA	Direct Investments	Portfolio Investments	Total Investments
Argentina	$ 355,364,000	$ 499,980,800	$ 855,344,800
Bolivia	61,619,000	61,104,000	122,723,000
Brazil	222,748,000	401,624,000	624,372,000
Chile	331,835,000	327,367,000	659,202,000
Colombia	140,494,000	200,402,800	340,896,800
Ecuador	11,777,000	10,726,000	22,503,000
Paraguay	12,615,000	150,000	12,765,000
Peru	126,530,250	102,881,000	229,411,250
Uruguay	27,904,000	81,977,300	109,881,300
Venezuela	240,970,100	......	240,970,100
Total South America	$1,531,856,350	$1,686,212,900	$3,218,069,250
CENTRAL AMERICA			
Costa Rica	$ 22,166,000	$ 9,400,000	$ 31,566,000
Cuba	1,026,314,500	206,320,500	1,232,635,000
Dominican Republic	69,322,000	19,684,000	89,006,000
Guatemala	69,979,000	4,775,000	74,754,000
Haiti	14,191,000	16,015,000	30,206,000
Honduras	71,485,000	1,250,000	72,735,000
Mexico	725,063,900	162,296,300	887,360,200
Nicaragua	13,002,000	2,646,700	15,648,700
Panama	28,584,000	19,866,000	48,450,000
Salvador	29,466,000	12,880,300	42,346,300
Miscellaneous Latin America*	60,000,000	......	60,000,000
Total Central America	$2,129,573,400	$ 455,133,800	$2,584,707,200
GRAND TOTAL, LATIN AMERICA	$3,661,429,750	$2,141,346,700	$5,802,776,450†

* Includes the Guianas, Jamaica, and other West Indies.
† Inclusion of currency issues in the figure presented in another table accounts for the apparent discrepancy.

only had feet of clay, but was entirely compounded of clay. It further tells how he became an easy prey to the liberal yield offered by foreign bonds, backed by countries whose past fiscal record he was led to believe to be perfect; why he failed to appreciate the fact that prospectuses were prepared to sell and not to inform; how he discovered that the budget of a borrowing country was "balanced"—as if balancing a budget were not merely a proper distribution of red and black ink! It endeavors to explain why he was not informed how the "balance" was brought about. It throws light upon the loan of a Latin American city which, according to the circular descriptive of the bonds, had "for twenty years promptly met its debts" —largely because it had not borrowed in twenty years. It tells of a loan to a South American province which owes about $1,750,000, but which has received only a small part of this amount; of a loan to a Latin American republic of $3,800,000, which netted the borrower the impressive sum of $190,000; of another of $10,000,000, which yielded $3,200,000; and of one which netted the borrower about forty cents on the dollar.

It also shows that governments rarely resort to repudiation when treated fairly and honorably, and that defaults are inevitable when attempts are made by lenders to take advantage of temporarily embarrassed borrowers by exacting all sorts of concessions and imposing all sorts of impossibly harsh terms.

And it finally tells of how little the investor has learned from the past experiences of earlier creditors, thus proving once again the truth of the Hegelian dictum that "We learn from history that we learn nothing from history."

CHAPTER I

THE UNITED STATES, BANKERS TO THE WORLD

On a summer day in 1914, in the streets of Sarajevo, a Serbian youth, driven by we know not what homicidal impulse, fired a shot at an Austrian Archduke, killing the nobleman and his morganatic wife. The eruption that followed unleashed the panting Furies of War. One set of belligerents, known later as the Allies, was sufficiently far-sighted to turn to the United States for financial accommodations. America was rediscovered. Large loans were underwritten on behalf of England and France, which loans, thanks to a sympathetic and understanding press, met with a cordial reception on the part of the liberty- and democracy-loving American investing public. The latter apparently regarded it as a rare privilege to be able to contribute to a war which was fought, as they were led to believe, for the sole purpose of ending wars; which was to ensure the self-determination of nations; and which was, above all, to make the world safe for democracy. Eventually the United States was also drawn into the cataclysm and given the opportunity to participate in the struggle for "lofty ideas and ideals." With the United States in the fray, the war had to be fought to a successful conclusion.

America's contribution to the cause in man power

was considerable, but her accommodation in funds was enormous. To be sure, most of the money advanced to the Allies was expended within the United States for all sorts of war materials, and accounted, in a large measure, for the prosperity which prevailed at that time and thereafter. When the carnage was over, it was found that the damage caused by four years of warfare had to be made good. This led to a continuation of loans to European countries, not only to those that had been the Allies during the war, but also to the erstwhile belligerents, known as the Central Powers.

It appears sadly ironical, to consider, that it was American funds which were largely instrumental in bringing about the collapse of the Central Powers, and that it was almost exclusively with American funds that the Central Powers were rehabilitated. The cynic will, of course, remind us that these were banking transactions, and that there was a handsome commission in the one which was designed to destroy, as well as in the other designed to rebuild.

Such was the beginning of a New Golden Age, so similar to that *aurea ætas*, of which Ovid sang so eloquently in his *Metamorphoses*. Millions, millions mounting to billions of dollars, were poured into foreign countries, many of which the American investing public had never heard of before. The desire to lend was in direct proportion to the ignorance concerning the borrower. One is almost tempted to remark that bond issues of non-existent borrowers would probably have sold with more pronounced success than obligations of *bona fide* debtors whose geographical boundaries could be traced on the larger and more dependable maps.

How was it possible to emerge, within a relatively short period of time, as the world's banker after having been indebted to the rest of the world to the extent of about five billion dollars as recently as 1914? How was it possible to interest hundreds of thousands of Americans, who euphemistically call themselves investors, and to whom the mere term "foreign" was anathema, in bonds and shares of practically every country, state, city, and corporation throughout the world? How was it possible and what means did underwriters of foreign issues employ, to convert the American investor? By what magic did this transformation occur in the investor, who still clung tenaciously to the Jeffersonian philosophy that "we have a perfect horror at everything like connecting ourselves with the policies of Europe," and who was a loyal adherent to Washington's summary of the essential principles of American government, including "peace, commerce and honest friendship with all nations, entangling alliances with none"—the American investor, that incomprehensible person whom tradition has taught to view as inferior everything beyond the confines of his own land; to whom even today Czechoslovakia is the same as Jugoslavia; who still confuses Bucharest with Budapest; who places Carlsbad in Germany; who sells Latvian bonds because of his distinct antipathy to Latin American loans; who regards Porto Alegre as a suburb of Berlin; and to whom Santa Catharina (a province in Brazil) is a former Muscovite empress whom posterity has canonized because of her piety and virtue?

And it is this same incomprehensible person who gradually discovered the world about him. He willingly heeded the call when invited to invest in Abyssinia and Albania; to help finance coffee plantations in Colombia, cotton-growers in Ceará, banks in Iceland, mines in Montenegro, public utilities in the Canary Islands, power companies in Mallorca, silver mines in Greece, oils in Mesopotamia, railroads in Persia, telephones in China, light companies in Taiwan, mortgage banks in Bulgaria, sugar and rubber plantations in Java and Sumatra, quebracho developments in Paraguay, and babassu nuts in Brazil. The paraphrased lines of a European bard eminently fit the situation:

> Who counts the nations, names the name
> Of those who here to borrow came?

America has been referred to as the land possessed of a record, or superlative, complex. If she does not hold the record in one particular field, she will set out to acquire it. As a creditor nation, England ranked first. To America this was unbearable. Hence, the feverish haste with which foreign investments were made. Their desirability was rarely questioned. The principal object, on most occasions, was the extent of the *ad hoc* profit.

The consequences of such policy did not concern America's bankers. The investor resided in a fool's paradise, relieved of the burden of thinking for himself. The banker was doing it for him, or any of the numerous investment advisory institutions engaged in the rather profitable business of thinking for their fellow-men. That such policies did not concern the politicians in the borrowing countries, from Abyssinia to Zanzibar, should occasion little surprise. The position they occupy or the office they hold is ephemeral. Their philosophy of life is *carpe diem*, enunciated by Horace two thousand years ago. They rarely think of the morrow. Tomorrow they may be swept out of office. Today they can live only by yielding to the multiple undertaking of expenditures, proposed by themselves and their temporary adherents, who violate with silent complicity the weak sense of decency and exchange favors by the misuse of the public treasury. In order to enjoy the present they cheerfully mortgage the future, and in order to win the favor of the voter they launch costly and often sterile public works which exceed the taxable possibilities of the country.

"*Après moi le déluge,*" exclaimed a King of France who saw a flood coming which, according to Luzatti, was a necessary catastrophe as an atonement for all the ignominy which the monarchy had produced. "*Après moi le déluge,*" said the Siles and the Leguias, the Irigoyens and the Ibáñez, the Machados and the Luiz, and the flood they invoked has already come with national bankruptcy and default. Realizing that their days are counted and their acts not weighed while they are still in power, many of these Latin American rulers did not hesitate to expend public funds, without restraint either of decency or patriotism. When subsidies were requested they were readily made, and those who furnished the funds rarely cared to inquire into their use. Nor did anyone volunteer the information.

So long as the golden stream was flowing in, respect and gratitude filled the hearts of Argentineans and Brazilians, Bolivians and Peruvians, Chileans, Colombians and Uruguayans, and of the residents of many states and statelets on the European continent, for the manifestation of goodwill and confidence on the part of the United States. Thousands of young men from those countries came to the United States, presumably to learn its language and commercial methods. They apparently overlooked the fact that the American himself needed considerable education along these lines, else American manufacturers would not ship snow shovels to Panama, where it has never snowed as far as records go, and where it is not likely ever to snow; or umbrellas to Antofagasta, where it has not rained in centuries and where rain is not likely to fall in the years to come. Presidential pilgrimages were in style. Executives of the United States exchanged visits with rulers of Latin American republics who, only shortly after they had been eulogized by America's president, were overthrown by revolutions and, in many instances, thrown into gaol where they had ample time to ponder over the compliments paid them by their more powerful colleague north of the Rio Grande.

America's leadership in the field of international finance was undisputed. The center had moved to the banks of the Hudson from the banks of the Thames, whither it had moved a century earlier after the Napoleonic wars. Wall Street took the place of Lombard Street. So, at least, many persuaded themselves into believing. Americanization and American methods were the goal of every nation across the Atlantic and south of the Rio Grande, in the Far East and on the isles of the Pacific. Americans were openly proclaimed the chosen children of God, immune against the vicissitudes of fate and fortune. It was suddenly discovered that the United States abounded in experts in practically every field and was at all times ready to lend these wizards of economics and finance to whoever was anxious to borrow them. Apparently it did not occur to the American investor that each time an expert was dispatched to a foreign land, he began to be prepared for a loan to the country in question. The expert's advice was almost invariably accompanied or followed by the flotation of bond issues on behalf of the nations whom he had been "invited" to advise. The investor had no time to consider these relatively irrelevant matters. Nor did those who were "qualified" to consider them for him. The New Era was fast approaching. It was short-lived. The results are still being felt keenly. The American investor is now learning what his cousin across the ocean experienced half a century earlier— non-payment of interest on contractual loans, but multiple explanations for such policy on the part of the debtor.

CHAPTER II

DEFAULT AND REPUDIATION

A BORROWER'S failure to pay interest, or failure to meet sinking fund payments or maturing obligations on a stipulated date, constitutes a violation of agreements and is regarded in financial language as default or bankruptcy. A government or any political subdivision is guilty of default if it violates the rights of creditors in failing to meet obligations in whole or in part, with or without an express announcement to that effect. Etymologically, the word "default" is derived from the Latin *de*, which is in this case merely a prefix of intensive force, and *fallere*, meaning "to deceive," or "to cheat." Default then means a thorough and complete deception of the creditor by the debtor.

"Repudiation" also traces its origin to the Romans. Its component parts are *re*, indicating repetition, and *pudere*, "to be ashamed of." Originally it meant to be ashamed of something or someone. The inference, however, in the use of the word in present financial language, is that the repudiator is to be ashamed only of himself.

Doctor Alfred Manes, in his classic treatise *Staatsbankrotte*, presents a number of definitions of the terms, and is surprised at the unanimity among scholars. There is no need for surprise. Regardless of terms and definitions, the practise of disregard for creditors is held in abhorrence everywhere. Governmental default, irrespective of classifications and erudite definitions, is briefly the repudiation by a government of a contractual debt owed by it either to domestics or foreigners, thereby rendering itself guilty of a breach of its obligations under domestic or international, and always moral, law.

Many years ago, when the United States was still a young nation and its constituent parts found it difficult to differentiate between right and wrong, the State of Pennsylvania defaulted with respect to its bonds, part of which were owned in England. A holder of such bonds addressed a letter[1] to the House of Representatives at Washington which reads as follows:

Your petitioner lent to the State of Pennsylvania a sum of money for the purpose of some public improvements. The amount, though small, is to him important and is a saving from a life income, made with difficulty and privation. If their refusal to pay (from which a very large number of English families are suffering) had been the result of war, produced by the unjust aggression of powerful enemies; if it had arisen from civil discord; if it had proceeded from an improvident application of means in the first years of self-government; if it were the act of a poor state struggling against the barrenness of nature, every friend of America would have been contented to wait for better times; but the fraud is committed in profound peace, by Pennsylvania, the richest state in the Union, after the wise investment of the borrowed money in roads and canals of which the repudiators are every day reaping the advantage. . . .

---

[1] See *Annals of the American Academy of Political and Social Science,* Vol. CXXXVIII, July 1928, p. 4.

In an article[2] published in the British press, the same gentleman said, in part: "I never meet a Pennsylvanian at a London dinner without feeling a disposition to seize and divide him. How such a man can set himself at an English table without feeling that he owes two or three pounds to every man in the company, I am at a loss to conceive. . . . If he has a particle of honor in his composition he should shut himself up and say, 'I cannot mingle—I must hide myself—I am a blunderer from Pennsylvania.' "

According to an eminent European scholar, governmental default is more pernicious than war, because war may be just, while default is never just. Furthermore, he says, it adds to the moral evil a material one. Even though one may find it difficult to subscribe unqualifiedly to this opinion, it is rather interesting as indicative of the views held by serious economists and students of finance concerning the problem of suspension of payment on contractual obligations.

It is disheartening for investors to discover that governmental default can be resorted to with impunity. It does not at all destroy the credit of a government, as some naïvely believe. On the contrary, it may often save the nation. The history of government loans is really a history of government defaults. Few, if any, nations of importance can boast of a perfect fiscal record, largely because we find none that have not at one time or another obtained loans. No one disputes the necessity of governmental borrowing. There is not one single reputable government or po-

---

[2] See *Annals, loc. cit.*

litical subdivision today which is not in debt. There may be differences of opinion regarding terms of loans, purpose of issue, interest rates, manner of amortization, extent of debt, or nature of security. Government loans are essential to the development of a nation's resources, and may be said to constitute a method of securing funds voluntarily rather than by force, that is through increasingly heavy taxes imposed upon nationals. Politicians do not cherish the latter; hence a tendency to over-borrow. It is for this reason that we always meet with the bitter complaint on the part of the people over the unbearably heavy debt with which the world is afflicted and over the fact that the debt burden, instead of growing lighter, is becoming more and more burdensome.

At the outbreak of the French Revolution the debts of European governments did not exceed two and one-half billion dollars. At the time the Treaty of Vienna was signed, a quarter of a century later, they had risen to three times that figure. By the middle of the past century they showed very little variation compared with the status in 1815. Towards the end of the century they totalled $30,000,000,000, and at the present time, the total indebtedness of the world may be placed at not less than $250,000,000,000, equivalent to $125 for each man, woman, and child living, including Abyssinians and Albanians, Chinese and Hindus, Bushmen and Burmese, Patagonians and Filipinos, Zulus and Zanzibars.

Since time immemorial the State appears to have been the most popular debtor. Its ability and capacity to meet payments were always regarded as superior to those of individuals or private corporations. The reason resides in all probability in the fact that corporate entities may disappear, in which case their obligations become valueless. The same is true of individuals. Governments, on the other hand, stay on forever. Political changes do not, as a rule, affect the status of obligations. The latter are generally based upon the "good faith and credit" of the people. It is on this basis that Russian bonds were placed with optimistic and hopeful investors who were told that "Russia, all her wealth and vast resources and the credit of the Russian people," were behind Russian bonds.

Public credit may prove highly beneficial or highly detrimental to a government, according to the manner in which it is used. Its value is determined by the applicability and the ultimate results of its employment. Nothing is more pernicious and dangerous than a credit contracted by a government which exceeds its budgetary capacity, or a credit employed for the purpose of waging wars or undertaking adventurous projects. Such loans are utterly unjustified. They almost invariably lead to disaster. The financial history of many a nation bears ample testimony to the correctness of this view. Of course, it is not always very easy to differentiate between so-called productive and non-productive loans. Nor is it very easy to determine in advance whether a loan contracted in time of peace is more productive than one secured in time of war. To begin with, what is productive? At the time a loan is floated, no one can determine with accuracy whether it is what is ordinarily regarded as productive. If a railway is to be constructed with the proceeds from the sale of a bond issue, we have apparently a loan of the productive type. If, however, the road turns out a complete fiasco, we are obliged to regard the loan as non-productive.

On the other hand, if a State borrows to wage war, we speak of a non-productive loan. If, however, the war is successful, and valuable territory is added to the land of the victorious power, the loan, at first glance non-productive, has turned out decidedly productive. To the loser, the borrowing has, of course, proved non-productive.

The last war affords an interesting illustration. The two principal belligerents on the European Continent were contracting loans for the purpose of waging what each hoped would be a successful conflict. What has happened to Germany, the loser? The subjoined table clearly illustrates the non-productivity of Germany's loans.

Except for the number of sheep, which shows an increase over the pre-war figure, Germany's losses were colossal. Whether this fact has something to do with the recent activities in the Reich, is problematical. The money she borrowed to wage the war has proved non-productive, as many holders of German war bonds would testify.

France's loans, on the other hand, both external and internal, contracted for the purpose of waging war, apparently destructive in character, have turned out rather productive. France was the victor. She acquired, *inter alia*, Alsace-Lorraine and, with it, vast tracts of land, yielding annually huge amounts of lumber; important manufacturing establishments of cotton goods, woolens, ribbons, machinery, ceramics and glass. She acquired iron ore reserves, estimated at 1,830,000,000

Germany's Losses through the War

	Position of Country in 1921	Position of Country Prior to the War	Decline in Per Cent
Area (square miles)......	181,909	208,780	12.86
Colonies (square miles)...	....	1,027,820	100.00
Population (home).......	61,000,000	67,812,000	10.04
Population (colonies).....	....	12,065,000	100.00
Coal reserves (tons)......	300,000,000,000	423,356,000,000	29.07
Potash reserves (tons)....	2,000,000,000	2,300,000,000	13.04
Mineral output (tons)			
Coal.................	136,210,000	191,511,000	28.87
Lignite..............	123,011,000	87,233,000	41.02
Coke................	27,921,000	32,167,000	13.19
Iron ore.............	7,500,000	28,607,000	73.78
Pig iron.............	7,500,000	16,764,000	55.26
Steel................	9,000,000	16,649,000	45.94
Beet-sugar output (tons).	1,153,000	2,730,000	43.11
Agricultural output (tons)			
Wheat..............	2,664,000	3,972,000	32.93
Rye.................	6,610,000	10,427,000	36.61
Barley..............	1,748,000	3,148,000	44.29
Oats................	4,717,000	9,038,000	47.81
Potatoes.............	26,821,000	45,569,000	41.14
Live stock (head) 1920			
Horses..............	3,581,000	4,516,000	20.70
Cattle..............	16,789,000	20,443,000	31.03
Sheep..............	6,139,000	5,476,000	12.11*
Swine..............	14,149,000	25,166,000	43.78
Foreign trade (tons)			
Exports.............	19,810,000	73,713,000	73.12
Imports.............	18,836,000	72,831,000	74.13
Total trade..........	38,646,000	146,544,000	73.63
Shipping (tonnage)......	680,000	5,108,000	90.17

* Denotes gain.

tons, which places France second only to the United States as a potential world producer of iron ore, and places her far in the lead in Europe. While prior to the war France's annual output of iron ore was 12 per cent of the world's total production, and Germany's output 20 per cent, as a result of the war France produces 23.5 per cent, while Germany's share has been reduced to only 4.2 per cent. France also acquired the potash mines of Alsace, covering an area of seven square miles, ranging in thickness from six to thirty feet. The potash reserves are estimated at 300,000,000 tons of pure potash and are valued at $3,500,000,000. Besides the iron ore of Lorraine and the potash of Alsace, France became for fifteen years the dominating factor in the Saar Basin, with coal reserves estimated at 16,500,000,000 tons and which in the last pre-war year produced 1,370,000 tons of pig iron, 2,000,000 tons of steel, and over 12,000,000 tons of coal. She also obtained over five hundred thousand square miles of territory, chiefly in Africa, and some twelve and a half million people.

On the basis of the foregoing, it is somewhat difficult to present a practical definition of what constitutes productive or unproductive borrowing at the time the loan is contracted. Here, as in most affairs of life, mass or individual, it is the result that counts.

Ever since borrowing has been in vogue, governments have been looked upon as preferred credit risks. *"Negocio com o Governo"* is to this day the most profitable occupation in Brazil. It is not less profitable in the United States or any of its political subdivisions. Employees of large cities bear sufficient testimony to the conclusion, regardless of the rank or position they hold. Be they ever so humble, they invariably profit so long as they remain on any of the municipal pay-rolls.

Poets and writers of antiquity all preach the doctrine of *"dulce et decorum pro patria mori."* If it is right to offer one's life for one's country, with the prospect of recovery rather slim, it should also be right to offer one's fortune, or at least a part of it, for one's country, with the hope of getting it back. Then again, a state in need of funds will, as was pointed out above, either tax its subjects or secure funds through forced loans unless voluntary subscriptions are forthcoming. The wise will choose the latter, lest they be compelled to accept the former.

Lending is as old as the records of history, and default, we imagine, came shortly after the first loan. Different kinds of governmental defaults are as many and various as the hues of the rainbow. A default may fall under any of the following classifications.

1. Reduction in the rate of interest.
2. Reduction in the amount of sinking fund or principal.
3. Delay in payment of interest.
4. Delay in the payment of sinking fund or principal.
5. Suspension of payment of interest.
6. Suspension of payment of sinking fund or principal.
7. Reduction in the rate of interest through the levy of taxes subsequent to the flotation of loans upon the interest.
8. Payment of interest in depreciated currency where the contract designates "gold" payment.
9. Payment of sinking fund or principal in depreciated currency where the contract calls for "gold" payment.
10. Payment of interest and/or principal in so-called blocked native currencies.
11. Payment of interest and/or principal in so-called scrip, that is interest or non-interest bearing certificates.
12. Forced conversion of loans.
13. Repudiation of interest.

14. Repudiation of sinking fund or principal.
15. Any number or all of the preceding categories together.

The fact that default is an ancient tradition of borrowers is seen in the oldest records. The psalmist sings of one "who sweareth unto his neighbor and disappointeth him not." Solon requests the Athenian who comes of age to take an oath that he will not violate lawful claims. The *Leges XII Tabularum* provide that the bodies of defaulters may be divided and distributed *pro rata* among the creditors. An ancient Germanic law, based presumably on the Roman code, provides that "the debtor when contracting an obligation pledges all his assets as well as his person as security." In the course of the Thirty Years' War provisions were made for payment in currencies at a fixed rate to protect investors against losses resulting from the depreciation of exchanges. From the 16th to the 19th century France ceased payments at least once every thirty years. In the course of the 19th century not one Latin American government escaped default, with some indulging in the practice as frequently as once every seven years.

An obligation ought to remain, in all conscience, an obligation, regardless of the entities of debtor and creditor. In each case the lender expects fulfillment of a contract, willingness and capacity to carry out agreements, and especially continuation of interest payment. Consequently there should be no difference between so-called public credit and private credit. However, there are many differences, with advantages and disadvantages on both sides.

If a private debtor fails to meet his obligation, the

lender proceeds against him with the aid of the law.
The debtor is brought into court and a verdict makes
it possible for the creditor to seize the debtor's property for the satisfaction of his claims. If a government cannot pay, or refuses to pay, particularly in
the case of a foreign obligee, there is nothing to be
done. At the inception of a private loan the prospective creditor has the opportunity of meeting the borrower, of inspecting his business, of judging his ability
to pay, of discovering the uses to which the money
will be put. In the case of a governmental loan the
lender knows all these things only from hearsay, from
the unguaranteed prospectus of a banking house which
is interested from the point of view of its own profit
in floating the loan. In the case of a private default
the lender can follow up the defaulter to his very fount
and origin, and discover for himself his prospect of
repayment. When a government defaults the creditor
must seek his way through myriad miles of tape of
all colors, must track and back-track across a road
obscured by the prints of a thousand red herrings,
before he can come even to the surface of the facts.

On the other hand a governmental loan has its decided advantages. A German authority on the subject
says: "The contractual obligation of a Government
which refuses or is unable to pay is, on careful analysis, less valuable than the note of a reputable and substantial private enterprise." While this is doubtless
true, it is equally true that the note of a private enterprise, which cannot pay, becomes worthless, whereas
that of a government which cannot pay, is not. Thanks
to the recuperative powers of a nation, its creditors
are justified in expecting that some day the govern-

ment will pay its just debts. One recalls the case of the Republic of Honduras which settled with its foreign creditors after having withheld payments fifty years. Incidentally the settlement, had it been reached one year later, would have synchronized with the centenary of Honduras' first default. No matter what political or economic upheavals may cause a government to suspend payment, the children of the borrowers, or the children's children, are likely to assume the obligation. This, in private loans, is rare. There are not many Sir Walter Scotts in this world.

One of the most important things to consider in making a loan is confidence. Demosthenes, in one of his orations, had this to say: "Furthermore, of the two boons which the city possesses, namely wealth and general confidence, confidence is by far the greater. If, however, any one believes that because we lack funds, we need not have a good name, he is very much in error. I for one pray to the Gods that we may be blessed with wealth, or if this is not possible for the moment, that we may continue to be regarded as dependable and worthy of confidence." Now, no matter how well a man may be regarded as a credit risk, he may die and leave his creditors at an impasse, their moneys unrecoverable. A State, on the other hand, with its government taking no matter what form, may continue to exist through the ages, and continues to hold out hope, however vain, of settlement of its debts.

From the foregoing it may be seen that governments have long been considered preferred credit risks, in spite of the fact that they may, with comparative impunity, suspend payments either from mere whim or from dire necessity. And thanks to this preferred status of the government we find no powers, and relatively few political subdivisions, which can boast a perfect fiscal record, for where there is a borrower, there is a potential defaulter.

CHAPTER III

HISTORICAL REVIEW

IT HAS already been pointed out that defaults are not new phenomena. One of the earliest instances which history has handed down to us is the default practiced by Dionysius of Syracuse. After having borrowed from his subjects against promissory notes maturing at a specified date, the Syracusan, when called upon to redeem or take up the notes, issued a decree to the effect that all money in circulation be turned over to the government. Those failing to adhere to the provisions of the decree were punishable by death. After he had obtained all the funds, he caused the coins to be reminted, by stamping at two-drachmae each one-drachma coin. With the money thus devalued or debased, Dionysius repaid all his outstanding indebtedness. One may rightly claim for the tyrant of Syracuse the epithet of Father of Currency Devaluation.

Another example is furnished by the Greek writer Polyaemus, according to whom Leukon enjoys the dubious distinction of having reduced the par value of the currency by fifty per cent. "Leukon needed funds," our informant tells us; "he therefore announced that he would cause other money to be issued and that outstanding money in circulation should be surrendered. They all brought what they possessed, but Leukon merely caused each coin to be stamped in such manner that the new coin contained twice the value of the old

one. In this way he made half of the amount collected
without harming the citizenry." Such a measure can
be adopted so long as the money is not required for
transactions abroad. Within the country any value
may be assigned to the monetary unit. Soviet Russia
and The Third Reich afford a concrete example. The
situation, however, assumes a different aspect when
foreign business is involved. Hence, Xenophon's remarks to the effect that "the merchants are obliged to
demand payment in kind in most cities, because the
money in circulation there is worth less outside."

Towards the end of the fourth century B.C. (377-
373), out of thirteen Greek municipalities belonging
to the AMA (Attic Maritime Association), which had
contracted loans with the Delos Temple, two were
guilty of complete default, while eight defaulted only
partially. It was because of this rather unpleasant experience that Delos, in the following century, gave
preference to private borrowers over governmental
bodies.

The province of Boeotia, according to the historian
Polybios, was in default on its contractual obligations
for nearly a quarter of a century.

In Ephesus the situation was somewhat more
serious and the steps taken by the Ephesians were
more revolutionary than those taken by their neighbors. According to one of the writings attributed to
Aristotle,[1] the budgetary deficit of Ephesus was covered through the sale of the jewels of the Ephesian
women from whom they had been confiscated, without allowing them any kind of compensation.

When the island of Chios found itself unable to

---

[1] Οἰκονομικά : *De cura rei familiaris.* II, 2, 19.

meet its debt, announcement was simply made that payments would have to cease until economic conditions improved and Chios would have regained its former prosperity.

An interesting case is presented by the financial transactions of Miletus, related by A. Andreades in his classic *Economic History of Greece*. Toward the end of the third century, in 282 B.C., Miletus secured a loan from Lysimachus, repayable in annual installments. The first payment was made on time. Difficulties arose in connection with the repayment of the second, aggregating twelve talents. Desirous of avoiding the stigma of default thrown against her, Miletus appealed to Cnidus for financial accommodations. Inasmuch as the finances of the latter were not sufficiently satisfactory to enable her to advance out of the treasury any sums to her neighbor, a public offering was resorted to, Cnidus officially encouraging her citizenry to subscribe to the issue. The bonds enjoyed the benefit of specific security in the form of a guarantee furnished by seventy-five citizens of Miletus selected by the city. Of the entire amount of 1,573,000 drachmæ, 18,000 drachmæ were taken by four Cnidians, on which no interest was to be paid for the first year, the rate thereafter to maturity, which was to be effected within three years, being 6 per cent per annum. The resolution passed by Cnidus on the occasion of the sale of the Miletus loan is of importance. "The People's Assembly of Cnidus has resolved to encourage all those who feel so inclined to grant a loan to the people of Miletus, by assuring to the lenders a certain measure of guaranty, giving public praise to those who subscribe and recording, in every respect, the readiness on the part of subscribers to help their neighbors, as well as their confidence in them." One is reminded of the campaigns in the United States at the time billions of dollars were underwritten on behalf of America's allies.

Towards the end of the century Miletus found herself once again in financial difficulties. Available records tell us that "owing to the existing economic depression and the resultant precarious state of public finance, borrowing seems the only way out of the difficulties." We are also informed that salaries of public officials were in arrears and that the introduction of a capital tax (εἰσφορά) was not being viewed with a great deal of optimism. The question arose as to how to arrange for a new loan when the credit standing of Miletus was not conducive to such transactions. The following method, original, to be sure, for that time, was adopted: Miletus requested publicly that all its inhabitants, female as well as male, should perform their patriotic duty by subscribing to a new bond issue in amounts of three thousand drachmæ and multiples thereof. Subscribers were asked to register at the office of the City Clerk, who recorded their names in the subscription list which was to remain open for an indefinite period. Of the amount subscribed, two-thirds were to be paid at once and turned over to the municipal revenue authorities. The remaining one-third was due at the end of the year. Interest at the rate of 10 per cent per annum was payable monthly. There appears to have been no fixed date of maturity, which would lead to the belief that we have here what was perhaps the first example of a perpetual *rente* sold on behalf of a government or a political subdivision. Some interesting provisions were put into effect in regard to the loan. The Assembly of Miletus decreed that the underwriters (in this case, the City Clerk or Municipal Audit Bureau) were strictly prohibited from making any deductions from the amount subscribed for. Nor was any one privileged even to propose that the service charges on the loan be not included in the municipal budget or that the creditors receive less than the amount advanced or stipulated in the loan contract or document descriptive of the obligation. In the event that anyone should introduce into the Miletus Assembly a motion to the above effect, and if the motion should be seconded and passed, having been read by the City Clerk and having been recorded by the City Recorder, the motion was to be invalid and the amount covering service charges on the loan included in the budget. On the other hand, each of the offenders—that is, those who introduced, seconded, and voted for the motion—as well as the City Clerk and Recorder, were to pay a fine of a thousand drachmæ and lose all civic right until the fine should be discharged in full.

As intimated above, currency debasement appears to have been the favorite form of default in ancient times. Antiquity preferred it to straight default and complete suspension, a method which, incidentally, played almost as important a rôle—if not a more important one—two thousand years later. Following the conclusion of the First Punic War (241 B.C.), Rome decreased the metallic contents of her monetary unit, the *as*, from twelve ounces to two and was in this manner placed in a rather enviable position to repay at one-sixth of the original value a staggering debt contracted in connection with the war against the Carthaginians. The masses, who were heavily in debt, do not appear to have protested against the proposal, which seems to have hit the wealthy classes the hardest.

In the course of the Second Punic War (218-201 B.C.), the debasement proceeded further, the metallic content being reduced to one ounce; while at the end of the Third Punic War (146 B.C.) another fifty per cent cut was adopted, leaving the metallic content of the Roman monetary unit at one-half an ounce or one-twenty-fourth the original par value of twelve ounces. Two thousand years later Germany improved on Rome's record. Her currency declined to one-trillionth of its original par value. In other words, a mark of 1913 could purchase one thousand billion marks of 1924.

While it is true that the above method, which is merely one of the numerous forms governmental default may assume, temporarily saved the Roman Empire, it had rather serious effects upon the entire economic and social life of the nation. It polluted the equity of her laws, corrupted the justice of her public officials to a much more marked degree than before, and destroyed the fortunes of thousands who had confidence in the honesty and integrity of their government as a whole, even though they thoroughly distrusted its numerous officials; it paralyzed commerce and trade; and, what was far worse, it seriously undermined the morale of the nation. What followed is a matter of historical record.

It may be of interest to compare the state of affairs in Rome, the scenes on the Forum Romanum and the Via Sacra, with that obtaining a little less than two thousand years later in the United States, following the depreciation of the American currency. In his *History of the American Revolution*, published in 1789, the evils of currency debasement are described briefly thus by David Ramsey: "That the helpless part of the community were legislatively deprived of their property, was among the lesser evils which resulted from the legal tender of the depreciated bills of credit. The iniquity of the laws estranged the minds of many of the citizens from the habits of love and justice. The nature of obligations was so far changed that he was reckoned the honest man who from principle delayed paying his debts. The mounds which government had erected to secure the observance of honesty in the commercial intercourse of man with man, were broken down. Truth, honor, and justice were swept away by the overflowing deluge of legal iniquity, nor have they yet [in 1789] assumed their ancient and accustomed seats."

Rome's recourse to currency debasement rather than outright default may possibly be explained on the basis of existing Roman laws. It will be recalled that the *Leges XII Tabularum* provide for the dismemberment of defaulters. It is not impossible that similar unwritten laws prompted the Germans to debase their currency. According to Heusler, the borrower in days gone by pledged as security for a loan contracted to the creditor "his whole self, with body and possessions."

The difficulties which arose in the Middle Ages in connection with meeting promptly contractual obligations were increased by the onerous burdens which borrowers were often required to assume. In 1121 Genoa was obliged to pay 25 per cent for money secured from

Roman banking houses. About half a century later, she was obliged to pay 100 per cent for a short-term loan. Nor were these loans contracted without the pledging on the part of the borrower of specific security. So long as funds were readily forthcoming, either in the form of increased revenues or new loans, payments were made. If neither of these could be obtained, default was resorted to regardless of the specific security or guaranty, the benefit of which many loans enjoyed.

Default during this period usually assumed the form of currency debasement, a method practiced several centuries earlier by the Roman Empire following the various Carthaginian wars, to which reference has been made. It should be borne in mind that borrowing in the Middle Ages was relatively limited, due, it seems, to the canonic laws prohibiting the payment of interest and based, it is believed, upon the interpretation of the famous *mutuum datis nil inde sperantes* (You may lend, but do not expect a return on the loan made).

It was for these reasons that many a medieval prince was unable to borrow from his Christian subjects who, despite all their loyalty, were not inclined to lend without a return. They were therefore obliged to offer hospitality to Jews who were in a position to lend and whose religion did not forbid charging interest to foreign princes. It is said that one of the Medici specifically exhorted his fellow-citizens to be kindly disposed towards the Jews who, by loaning money to their Christian neighbors, were keeping them from robbing and stealing and from committing equally heinous crimes to which they would doubtless resort if they were deprived of all facilities to borrow.

The Medici concluded that the Jews were doomed anyway.

The above soon received a new interpretation. *Mutuum datis nil (in) desperantes* was to be the new reading—that is, you may loan but need not despair in regard to anything. This, of course, meant that interest could be charged and it was in the course of this period that public credit developed and continued to expand. It was also in the course of this period that defaults were beginning to become more popular (with the borrower). Suspension of payment, reduction of interest and principal were frequent occurrences. One of the most commonly practiced methods was the transfer of debts by the states to private individuals, who subsequently refused payment. The stigma of default was thus removed from the debtor government and attached, to a certain extent, to the new debtor.

In the course of the 16th century Spain defaulted a number of times. In fairness to the country, it should be stated that it endeavored to avoid defaulting through an attempted sale of state assets. Failure to dispose of these decided Spain to exchange existing obligations into a 5 per cent bond which, almost immediately after authorization, declined to 25 per cent par. This did not, however, prevent Spain from carrying out her plan.

The Abbé Terray, French Minister of Finance during 1768-1774, had rather interesting views regarding debt payments. Each Government, the learned Frenchman maintained, should default at least once every hundred years, in order to restore equilibrium. Niebuhr[2] refers to him as the ideal man in a time of

---

[2] *Geschichte des Zeitalters der Revolution*, 1845, p. 134.

financial difficulties, "whose name will live through the ages, cursed and disgraced; a cleric of unlimited immorality; but a remarkable worker and unusually talented orator endowed with a distinct financial talent. . . . He tackled the government debt problem and arbitrarily reduced the rate of interest without regard for anybody; a measure prompted by necessity, against which there is less to be said than against many other financial manipulations resorted to at a time when other means fail to work."

One of the difficulties most frequently encountered, is the stipulated date of repayment. At maturity, conditions may be such as to make redemption impossible, or money rates may be so high as to render repayment through new borrowing prohibitive. In a study on "Government Credit" by a Russian statesman of the pre-revolutionary period who prefers to remain nameless, the following interesting point is brought out anent the above: "Whenever government bankruptcy is perfect and complete, which deprives the creditor of both interest as well as principal, disgrace is the outstanding characteristic of the nation in question and its credit will disappear for a long time. Whenever, on the other hand, the government stops at the edge of the abyss and, abhorring the pernicious consequences of complete bankruptcy, states emphatically that it is inability which prompts it to suspend payment, and invokes the aid of its creditors, gathering together all its strength; and if it succeeds by means of an absolutely free and voluntary agreement to exchange maturing obligations into perpetual bonds, it destroys at that very moment all dangers and doubts and, in place of pernicious baukruptcy, there enters governmental credit."

From the same authority we learn of Napoleon Bonaparte's attitude towards state borrowing: "It is odd to learn from history how the deep and comprehensive genius of Napoleon is no longer the same when the matter of credit is involved. He not only refuses to make use of the various means of borrowing, but opposes them systematically and bears a personal animosity against all credit operations and all those who occupy themselves with them. His secretary, Bourienne, was dismissed, because he had invested his funds in government bonds."

Napoleon's views concerning loans are known. "A well calculated borrowing system," the Corsican maintained, "is something which is both immoral and despicable. It taxes in advance coming generations; it sacrifices to the moment the dearest boon of humanity, the fate of the children; it undermines without being noticed the structure of the nation and condemns one generation to the curses of the coming ones." These lofty remarks did not apparently prevent Napoleon from leaving France with a debt of 759,-000,000 francs.

Defaults on the part of nations seem to occur either immediately preceding a boom or immediately following. As a rule, important governmental changes are followed or accompanied by repudiations. The attempt by Hungary, in 1869, to repudiate obligations contracted during the absolute régime; the refusal on the part of Prussia to recognize the debt of the Kingdom of Westfalia or Hesse, at the time these provinces became part of Prussia; the default of Italy following the creation of the new Italy; the defaults of Prussia following the far-reaching reforms undertaken by the Great Elector; the repudiation by Mexico of obligations contracted under Maximilian; and the repudiation by the Argentine Province of La Plata of a loan following a change in its political status, are instances of this fact.

One of Great Britain's eminent economists states, concerning governmental credit:

"The credit standing of a nation or a debtor in general is dependent upon the prompt payment of interest rather than the prospect of repayment of principal. For each has a right to sell one's chances to some one else, and so long as interest is being paid, to consider himself as having repaid the principal. . . . A declaration that repayment of principal is impossible even though such repayment may already have been promised, does not impair the credit as much as the slightest delay or disadvantageous change in the rate of interest."

The popularity of government loans in Great Britain seems especially marked. In connection with the sale of bonds by King Henry II in 1555, a contemporary historian points out that "God alone knows how the desire for a more liberal return was enticing the masses. Every one is anxious to invest his money in these bonds, including the servants who, too, brought their savings. The women sold their jewels, the widows surrendered their annuities to participate in the flotation. In short, each one rushed into it as if it were a conflagration."

Other rulers were equally successful in the securing of funds. The ease with which funds could be obtained led to the accumulation of debts appreciably in excess of the budgetary capacity of nations. Defaulted issues placed on behalf of Spain, France and Portugal amounted, in the early part of the 16th century, to as much as $500,000,000, an enormous figure for those days, especially if one takes into consideration that the world production of the precious metal during the second quarter of the century barely exceeded $30,000,000.

Defaults occurred rather frequently. Spain stands out above the other countries. She can boast of not less than six suspensions of payments. In 1557, she defaulted, emulating her neighbor in the North, the Kingdom of France. In 1575, she defaulted once more; and again twenty-one years later. In 1607, payments were suspended; the process was repeated in 1627 and in 1647, or one year before the conclusion of the Thirty Years' War. Spain's neighbor and ally, the Kingdom of Portugal, gave a rather satisfactory account of itself. Only one major default is recorded (1560). No account is taken of minor irregularities in regard to the nation's obligations towards foreign creditors.

It was not until the 17th and 18th centuries that export of capital began to assume a more important aspect. England and France appear to have been especially active in this direction. The Netherlands later on displaced these earlier creditor powers. Werner Sombart in his classic *"Der moderne Kapitalismus"* comments as follows on nations as lenders: "In the course of these early stages of capitalism, capitalistic interests still possessed nationalistic views which meant an appreciable gain in the power and prestige of the government. . . . However, the decisive step towards the internationalization of finance had not as yet been taken . . . the world of finance was still to a very large extent prompted by patriotic considerations. . . . It regarded itself as an integral part of the rising government, its own government. The rise to prominence depended primarily upon the debt of the State and the tax levying powers of the latter."

In the course of the 19th century, the policy of lending abroad made considerable progress, and we gradually begin to observe the development of internationalism in banking and finance. It was in the course of this period that defaults became more numerous. Five clearcut defaults are recorded in Germany. Of these, Prussia accounts for only two, which occurred in 1807 and 1813. Westfalia succumbed only one year earlier, in 1812. The Electorate of Hesse defaulted in 1814 and continued in default throughout the following year; and Sleswig-Holstein celebrated the middle of the 19th century by non-payment of her contractual obligations. Towards the end of the 17th century, Prussia experienced the thrills that come with non-payment. In 1683 the Great Elector suspended payments on practically all state debts. Between 1806 and 1811, default occurred on all external issues, while holders of internals had to wait until 1814.

Austria did not lag behind Germany. She, too, can boast of five full-fledged defaults in the course of the century. The first occurred in 1802. Three years later, the Hapsburg Empire defaulted again. In 1811 payments were once more suspended, and once again five years later. The record from here on is rather satisfactory for more than half a century, until 1868 when the Monarchy succumbed just once more.

Holland was guilty of only one default in the early part of the century, in 1814. The country has since met its obligations most meticulously and Holland's credit today ranks very high in the world's financial markets.

Spain continued to be the same poor credit risk throughout the century. No less than seven defaults are recorded. Starting in 1820, she repeated the performance in 1831, in 1834, in 1851, in 1867, in 1872 and in 1882.

Greece defaulted twice, in 1826 and in 1893, but the suspension was so complete that she more than made up for the infrequency of their occurrence. The State of Portugal improved upon its earlier record, defaulting four times in the century, in 1837, in 1841, in 1852 and in 1892.

Russia succumbed but once, in 1839. Turkey, three times, in 1875, again in the very next year, and for the third time five years later. Egypt defaulted in 1876. It was during this time that twelve Southern States in the United States defaulted with respect to interest or completely repudiated their obligations; and it was also at this time that each of the Latin American nations defaulted without exception, with a number of republics suspending payments more than once. One begins to appreciate the phrase often applied to 19th century finance, viz., The Age of Financial Pathology.

On many occasions default was not complete—that is, non-payment applied either to sinking funds or interest, or a mere reduction in the rate originally stipulated.

In the case of the Ottoman Empire, over-borrowing,

or rather over-lending, was to an appreciable extent responsible for the collapse of the country's credit. Between 1859 and 1875, about $1,000,000,000 was borrowed abroad, of which only about $500,000,000 was actually obtained by Turkey in the form of cash. It is authoritatively stated that hardly more than $100,000,000 was employed productively. Hence, the huge budgetary deficits reaching a climax in 1874 and resulting in bankruptcy the following year.

Zeitlin, the eminent economist and historian, was somewhat over-optimistic when he declared in 1906 that "complete repudiation is nowadays a rare occurrence in the case of governments." "Austria's bankruptcy," the Professor continues, "which occurred in 1811 may indeed be regarded as the last catastrophe of this character so far as a real world power is concerned; at the present time, complete bankruptcies may happily be looked upon as the dubious prerogative of a half or only quarter-civilized state." The learned professor adds, however, "provided there is no special reason for the action which the state in question takes."

Of considerable interest is also a remark of Baron von Freytag-Loringhoven to the effect that "For a government to go out of the way to retire outstanding obligations is today generally regarded as a serious political error. . . . Time has completely triumphed over the old theory of governmental parsimony, and it is fairly clear to most economists and students of finance why a nation weighed down by the heaviest debt burden may at the same time be the richest."

A method which governments often indulge in for the purpose of evading payments, is the so-called coupon tax, that is, a levy imposed upon interest due bondholders. In 1868, the Hapsburg Monarchy introduced a coupon tax of 16 per cent, which meant that an Austrian 5 per cent loan would in reality be a 4.2 per cent issue. London and Amsterdam immediately ordered the removal of the Austrian bonds from the British and Dutch Stock Exchanges.

Similarly, Spain introduced a 20 per cent coupon tax in 1898, although the country's obligations, sold sixteen years earlier, were said to be exempt from present and future Spanish taxation. It is of interest to call attention to the fact that foreign holders were not affected by this ruling.

In 1885 Russia introduced a coupon tax amounting to 5 per cent; while nine years later Italy ordered an increase in the coupon tax of 13.2 per cent to 20 per cent, to be applied to external as well as internal holders of various Italian obligations.[8]

In a number of instances, default was resorted to by governments on the grounds that undue advantage had been taken of a temporarily embarrassed nation and a loan granted on harsh and onerous terms. An interesting example is afforded once more by France's fiscal history. When Colbert became Minister of Finance in 1660 he ordered that an examination be made under the auspices of the *Chambres Ardentes,* a body created for that purpose, of the entire debt status of the nation. It was discovered that the lenders had made unjustifiedly large profits. Payment of interest was suspended, M. Colbert suggesting that

---

[8] To avoid defaults of this character, foreign bonds sold in the United States were said to be exempt from present and future taxation levied by the borrowing governments.

bondholders appeal to the bankers or those who had sold them bonds. His predecessor, Sully, had acted similarly, thus teaching his successors how to avoid giving the impression of insolvency.

Under date of November 29, 1596, Philip the Second of Spain decided to suspend payment on debts which, he said had been contracted at abnormally high rates. The monarch chose "the most suitable, the most modest and the most feasible method," that is, the destruction of all loan contracts or documents containing evidence of the nation's debts.

When Prussia annexed Silesia in 1763, following the Seven Years' War, she refused to recognize the latter's outstanding indebtedness, while the debt which, too, had become a part of Prussia was assumed only in part by the latter. She acknowledged only one-third of the indebtedness in 1824 and reduced the rate of interest.

The argument advanced for the repudiation of the Westfalian debt is most ingenious. Prussian officialdom maintained that the original subscribers had had an opportunity to dispose of their holdings at an earlier date, while those who had acquired bonds recently had no right to indulge in speculative ventures. A prominent German economist[4] comments on this quaint philosophy as follows: "Thus, the original subscribers are entitled to no consideration because they have not sold, while present owners are entitled to none because they have bought. If such sophistry were universally accepted, all states could easily rid them-

---

[4] Jacobsen: *Welche rechtlichen Ansprüche haben die Besitzer der Zwangsanleihen des ehemaligen Koenigreichs Westfalen herruehrenden Obligationen an die beteiligten Staaten?* Berlin, 1842.

selves of their obligations." And yet the above did not interfere with the declaration by both European economists and American authors of prospectuses that "even in the most trying days, Prussia paid her debts." Of course, repudiation following the collapse of the German mark is not interpreted as a default because the debt was payable in marks, the collapse of which may be said to have been beyond the country's control, having been the work of those charged with the fiscal policies of the whole country.

Defaults were occasionally resorted to when a new government was created, on the theory that "the old system must be liquidated in order to make room for the new one." Spain and Portugal, France and Mexico afford numerous examples of this type of default, of which Russia is the modern exponent *par excellence*. Oncken[5] is the author of the above view, to which Russia could readily refer and, which may perhaps be assumed to have served her in adopting the famous decree of December 1917, providing for the repudiation of all debts contracted by predecessor governments. The decree was published in the Russian newspaper *Pravda* under date of February 8, 1918, and is as follows:

1. All State loans concluded by the Governments of the Russian landlords and Russian bourgeoisie, enumerated in a special list, are hereby repudiated as from December 14, 1917. The December coupons of these bonds are not paid.

2. In the same manner are all the guarantees repudiated which the said governments gave to loans of various concerns and bodies.

---

[5] *Geschichte der Nationaloekonomie,* Leipzig, 1902, Vol. I, p. 446.

3. All foreign loans, without exception are absolutely repudiated.

4. Short term obligations and Treasury bonds remain in force. Interest on them is not paid, but the bonds will continue in circulation along with governmental credit notes.

5. Poor citizens who hold State bonds of internal loans of an amount of not more than 10,000 rubles (that is $5,000 at par of exchange) receive in exchange certificates, made out in their names, of a new loan payable in the new Russian ruble. The terms of the new loan will be determined at a later date.

6. Deposits in State savings banks and interest on them remain intact. All debentures of the annulled loans which belong to the savings banks are replaced by a book debt of the R.S.F.S.R. (Russian Socialist Federal Soviet Republics).

7. Cooperative organizations, local government bodies, and other democratic agencies or institutions of common utility holding debentures of the repudiated loans are to be given certificates in accordance with rules to be drawn up by the Supreme Economic Council in conjunction with representatives of these bodies, which must prove that the debentures were acquired by them previous to the publication of the present decree. (Note: The local organs of the Supreme Economic Council have to determine which of the bodies or agencies can be regarded as democratic or of common utility.)

8. The general direction of the liquidation of the State loans is entrusted to the Supreme Economic Council.

9. The work in connection with the liquidation of the loans is entrusted to the State Bank, which shall immediately begin the registration of all the debentures of State loans and other interest bearing securities in the hands of various holders which may or may not be subject to invalidation.

10. The Soviets, in agreement with the local economic councils, will appoint committees to determine what citizens are to be regarded as poor. These committees have the right to annul all savings not acquired by personal labor, even if they do not exceed the sum of 5,000 rubles (or $2,500).

Thus reads Soviet Russia's Decalogue. The country
has scrupulously adhered to the tenets contained
therein. She has paid nothing on the debt contracted
prior to the advent of Bolshevism and it would seem
that she has no intention of paying.

The fiscal history of Latin America, that stretch of
territory lying south of the Rio Grande and housing
about 110,000,000 people of various races and origins,
is replete with instances of governmental defaults.
Borrowing and default follow each other with almost
perfect regularity. When payment is resumed, the past
is easily forgotten and a new borrowing orgy ensues.
This process started at the beginning of the past century and has continued down to the present day. It
has taught us nothing.

A typical case which illustrates Latin American
financial policies is furnished hereunder and relates
to the sovereign Central American Republics of Guatemala:

1825   First loan of £163,000 to Central American Federa-
       tion contracted at 73 per cent, bearing interest at
       6 per cent per annum.

1827   Guatemala assumes 5/12th of debt, or £67,900.

1828–55 Default.

1856   Settlement on basis of loan and arrears being con-
       verted into £100,000 5's; Guatemala recognizes
       1/3rd of original debt, or £54,433. Interest in ar-
       rears estimated and cut down to £45,567. 50 per
       cent of customs given as security.

1863   Private loan of £11,300 for construction arranged in
       London.

1864   Loan of 1863 defaulted.

1869   Loan contracted for £500,000 at 70–½ per cent, bear-
       ing interest at 6 per cent per annum. Sinking fund

of 3 per cent per annum. Import duties given as security.

1876   All loans defaulted.

1878   1/3 interest due April 1, 1876 on 1869 loan, paid in November 1878.

1884   Settlement made. Because of political disturbances, agreement not carried out.

1887   Loans of 1856 and 1869 and back interest funded into new 4 per cent loan; sinking fund of ½ per cent applied to semi-annual drawings at par; secured on duties levied on each package of foreign merchandise that may be imported into country through any of ports, also on maritime revenues; payments made to a committee composed of representatives of foreign bonds, internal bonds and railways. Importers to pay pledged revenues to committee.

1888   Terms of 1887 accepted and £922,700 of 4 per cent loan created as follows: £100 of 1856 loan and back interest amounting to £62/1/8 exchanged for £144/14 new 4's; £100 of 1869 and £72/10 interest for £152/4; £100 of 1863 loan and £19/11/8 interest for £144/14 of new 4's. Internal debt settled on basis similar to foreign debt.

1894   All loans default and committee suspended.

1895   New arrangement: Internal and external debt exchanged into £1,600,000 new 4's; £100 of 1888 loan exchanged for £75 new bonds. Internals at rate of £80 ($500) for £75 new 4's; non-cumulative sinking fund of £15,000 to purchase bonds. Secured by special tax of 6s per quintal of coffee exported; proceeds paid to agents of bondholders.

1895–96 Negotiations for new loan of £658,500 with Hamburg bankers; secured on excess of coffee warrants after providing for external debt. These new terms were drawn up without consultation with Council.

1897 New arrangement with German bankers, again without consulting Council of Foreign Bondholders.

1898 Duty on coffee, which had been "irrevocably fixed" is reduced—new agreement reached providing for payment of interest on external debt at rate of 2 per cent in cash for 3 years, and 2 per cent in certificates which were to be exchanged for 4 per cent bonds after June 30, 1901.

1899 Coffee duty again reduced—subsequently raised.

1900 Contract of 1895 again violated.

1901–02 New agreement provides for payment of interest due December 1902 and June 1903 at rate of 1½ per cent and of later coupons at rate of 3 per cent. Arrears funded into new bonds; as security, all customs are pledged. Congress so mutilated terms that Committee did not submit it to holders.

1903 New agreement; as security Government gives 30 per cent of import duty, payable in gold. Agreement not ratified by Government; export duty on coffee changed again.

1904 New agreement provides for issuance of new bonds with interest at rate of 1½ per cent in 1905; 2 per cent in 1906; and 3 per cent thereafter. Government refuses to ratify agreement.

1903–08 Agreement reached with American Syndicate which made advances against coffee export duties and import duties payable in gold. Documents deposited with American Legation in Guatemala and holders given right to ask American Government for protection in case of violation of terms by Guatemala—thus, special security of 1895 is assigned to others.

1908 New agreement with American syndicate for $5,000,-000 loan.

1912 Coffee duty established at original rate.

1913 Arrangement of 1895 resumed on following terms:

Government to deliver to bondholders warrants for payment of coffee export duties enough to cover interest for 1913-14; in exchange for certificates of 1898, Government issues £29,656, 4's; for back coupons. Deferred certificates were issued with no interest. At end of 4 years, bondholders were to deal with Government regarding these certificates.

1917   Sinking fund not resumed as provided for in 1913 Agreement.

1919   Resumption of sinking fund.

1924   Railway loan of $3,000,000 contracted at 8 per cent.

1925   Additional tax imposed on coffee exported.

1927   Railway bonds issued to the amount of $1,950,000 at 8 per cent per annum.

1928   External loan of $2,515,000 issued at 8 per cent per annum. New 4 per cent external loan for £844,603 issued to take care of deferred interest certificates of 1913.

The above record of debt payment or rather non-payment is not unique in Central American financial history. It is the rule rather than the exception. But it did not interfere with America's liberal lending to Costa Rica, Salvador and Panama. Warnings were not heeded.

Under date of September 19, 1930, I released the following for publication. Part of it was published in the New York "Times" under date of September 21. The statement referred to the status of Latin American loans, with especial reference to Peru and Bolivia, which have since been declared insolvent. It read as follows.

Few there are who will question the desirability of prompt recognition by our Government of the Revolutionary regimes established in Argentina, Bolivia and Peru. These, and other countries, are privileged to work out their own salvation, so long as they do not endanger foreign life and property.

One may, however, question the wisdom of an official announcement that new loans to these governments "will receive prompt attention when placed before the Department of State."

Economic conditions in Latin America have been, and continue to be, distinctly unsatisfactory. It is also safe to assert that recent political upheavals are the result of adverse economic conditions. Many of the Latin American nations have doubtless over-borrowed or, what would seem to be more accurate, we have over-lent. We have been placing millions—tens of millions—hundreds of millions of dollars in Latin American enterprises. We have invested huge sums in oil and, in many instances, the result was—turmoil. We have placed large sums in Latin American bonds and, in some cases, the result for the borrower was—bondage. We have furnished substantial amounts to create booms in Latin America and the result in some cases was—boomerangs.

Neither Peru nor Bolivia is in a position to contract additional loans. Within ten years, the foreign debt of Peru has increased from about $5,000,000 to $112,000,000; whereas Peruvian revenues during the same period advanced from $30,000,000 to only $50,000,000. The total debt of Peru at the present time is about $145,000,000. A per capita debt of about $26 is not too heavy—so at least bond prospectuses tell us. However, of Peru's total population of 5,500,000, about half is composed of Indian serranos, who do not share the nation's debt burden; so that a per capita debt of $50 is perhaps nearer the truth, a figure which is doubtless a real hardship to a country like Peru, especially at this time.

Bolivia, with a total debt of about $70,000,000, of which over $60,000,000 is external, is another country which can hardly consider assuming additional burdens. Furthermore, Bolivia's annual revenues are about $15,000,000, resulting in chronic budgetary deficits. The status of her existing debt is precarious, as evidenced by the abnormally large yields, and great difficulties are encountered in obtaining funds necessary to meet debt charges. Recent payments were covered with the proceeds from the sale of the match monopoly to the Swedish Match combine, and it is reliably reported that arrangements have already been made to take care of the debt for the balance of this year by means of an internal loan contracted with local banks and bearing interest at the rate of 10 per cent per annum, with a 4 per cent sinking fund.

In view of these conditions, the statement emanating from Washington regarding the advisability of advancing money to the newly established governments of South America, is likely to be misunderstood by the majority of our investing public, who do not realize that the State Department does not supervise the making of loans abroad, but merely discusses such activities with the bankers in advance of the culmination of loan negotiations. The investing public, however, is likely to interpret the above statement as an unqualified endorsement of additional credits to South America.

CHAPTER IV

CAUSES OF DEFAULT

THERE are very few cases on record in which governments have defaulted willfully on legitimate obligations. A comprehensive study of the fiscal records of governments reveals that repudiation has rarely, if ever, been resorted to when borrowers were accorded fair and honorable treatment. When, however, lenders have tried to take advantage of temporarily embarrassed borrowers to exact concessions and have imposed impossibly harsh terms, debtors, not unnaturally, have refused to go out of their way to discharge their contractual obligations. They will meet payments as long as they possess the means to do so, and, when they lack funds, will try to borrow anew to pay their old debts; but if they fail in securing additional funds, they will have little compunction in ceasing payments altogether.

Another primary cause of defaults lies in unwise lending. During periods of prosperity, there is a tendency to extend loans for non-productive purposes or upon very dubious security, and at times even pressure has been brought to bear to induce foreign governments and municipalities to contract loans which they did not want or need. The demand for foreign bonds is reported to have been so pronounced at one time that the representative of a non-existent Latin American republic succeeded in interesting a group of London bankers in floating a loan on behalf of his "country."

In addition to the danger involved in unproductive individual investments, there is an even greater menace in the too liberal extension of credit during a boom period, even for so-called productive purposes, especially when followed, as boom periods usually are, by an abrupt reduction in the volume of available loans in a period of depression.[1] The recent financial history of a number of South American countries serves to illustrate this point. During the years 1924 to 1929, Great Britain and the United States made loans to South America of £50,000,000 and $1,200,000,000, respectively. As a result, boom conditions prevailed; railways were built and public enterprises carried out, imports were greatly increased, wages and prices were raised considerably, and there was a tendency toward over-expansion of production. In 1929 and 1930, when the steady flow of credit was cut off, these countries found themselves hard pressed to meet their interest and sinking fund obligations.[2] Their task was rendered more difficult by the severe decline in the commodity price level during the period in question. Like most debtor countries, they rely almost entirely upon the export of agricultural products and raw materials, and have suffered a severe loss in the exchange value of their national production.[3]

The same amount of wheat, coffee, sugar, rubber,

---

[1] Cf. H. F. Arendtz, *The Way Out of Depression* (New York, Houghton Mifflin, 1931), p. 38.

[2] Committee on Finance and Industry (MacMillan Committee), *Report* (London, H. M. Stationery Office, 1931), Cmd. 3897, pp. 79-84.

[3] Cf. *The Course and Phases of the World Economic Depression* (Geneva, Secretariat of the League of Nations, 1931), pp. 159-161.

silver or copper could not be exchanged for the same amount of dollars or for the same amount of manufactured goods as in former years. The situation demanded additional exports to meet outstanding obligations, but these added exports served to depress prices still further and thereby intensified the problem. Moreover, a fall in the general price level means that debts contracted in terms of gold prior to 1929 represent considerably more purchasing power than at the time of their arrangement. In other words, the burden of debts and accrued interest becomes much greater in terms of commodities or services than was originally intended, and the debtor countries are in reality being asked to repay more in both principal and interest than is consistent with the value they received.[4] The income of every government has been drastically decreased, although the debt charges remain stationary.

The unequal distribution of the world's gold supply is considered by many authorities to be another factor in increasing the number of defaults which have occurred during the last few years. The loan contract usually stipulates that repayments should be made in gold coin of a specific weight and fineness, but the fulfillment of this obligation has been rendered virtually impossible by the fact that the credit and monetary policy of the United States and other creditor countries has resulted in their obtaining the bulk of the world's gold supply.[5]

---

[4] Cf. Committee on Finance and Industry, *Report*, cited, pp. 91-92.

[5] According to the latest available figures (September, 1933), the distribution of gold among Central Banks of the leading countries of the world is approximately as follows: United States, $3,600,000,000; France, $3,200,000,000; Great Britain, $933,500,000; Switzerland, $351,500,000; Belgium, $375,500,000; Holland, $232,500,000; Italy, $367,500,000; and Germany, $73,500,000.

Several of the debtor countries have been forced to abandon the gold standard, while very few could afford to make substantial gold payments. In the view of many economists, the normal working of the gold standard has broken down in recent years because of the policy of the Federal Reserve Bank of New York and the Bank of France in deliberately sterilizing a large share of their gold holdings. Whereas the influx of gold into a country normally leads to inflation of credit, increased prices, and a consequent shifting in the balance of trade which reverses the flow of gold, it is charged that the practices of the central banks of France and the United States have prevented inflation from taking place, and thereby caused an unduly large share of the world's gold supply to lie idle in their vaults.[6] Matters were greatly complicated by the abandonment of the gold standard by the two principal creditor nations, Great Britain and the United States, in the Fall of 1931 and the Spring of 1933, respectively.

Aside from gold payments, and the possibility of securing new credits, debtor nations can meet their obligations only through the export of goods or by services. But, as is the case in regard to gold and credits, the policy of the United States and France, as well as other creditor nations, has tended to make repayment by these methods difficult.[7] Tariffs have

These eight nations possessed more than 80 per cent of the world gold supply, while France and the United States together possessed 60 per cent of the total world supply.

[6] *Ibid.*, pp. 96-97, cf. also Committee on Finance and Industry, *Report*, cited, pp. 68-69.

[7] Cf. Rogers, *America Weighs Her Gold*, cited, pp. 80-90, 183, 193 *et seq.*

been raised continually in the United States and abroad, with the avowed object of keeping out foreign goods as much as possible.

Moreover, the stringent restriction of immigration has caused a sharp decline in immigrants' remittance, which is one of the chief methods of payment by services.[8] Similarly, the subsidizing of the American merchant marine makes difficult the payment of obligations through shipping, and there are no other services of importance which are now performed largely by foreigners. With these methods of payment effectively blocked, it is not surprising that a number of countries have found it economically impossible to repay their obligations to the United States, and have been forced to default.

It is obvious that much of the responsibility for the present chaotic state of the international money market must be laid to the lack of effective supervision of any kind. Such supervision might be exercised directly by governments, by the central banks of the various countries, or by special organizations sponsored by the private banks. In general, there are two types of supervision needed which might be performed by different organizations. First, some control over the nature and volume of investments is needed. Loans should be offered only to borrowers whose economic and financial status is such as to offer acceptable guarantees of repayment, and the total amount of credit extended to foreign countries should be reasonably steady in volume. Second, the interests of the investor should

---

[8] Immigrant remittances have declined from $247,000,000 in 1922 to $223,000,000 in 1929, and $166,000,000 in 1930. (Ray O. Hall, *Balance of Payments of the United States,* revised as indicated.)

be amply protected both before and after purchasing foreign securities. Every prospective investor is entitled to full and impartial information regarding the financial status of the borrowing country, and every bondholder ought to be assured that all reasonable precautions are being taken to safeguard his investment. Similarly, the holders of defaulted bonds need some organization to look after their interests and to arrange, if necessary, for the funding of the unpaid obligations.

It is still an open question whether or not these ends could be achieved without strict state control over investments. It is evident, however, that the type of supervision exercised over foreign issues by the State Department in the past has been ineffective in safeguarding the investor,[9] and that some new method should be established. In a number of countries protection is obtained for the individual investor through private organizations which have been formed for the special purpose of looking after the interests of holders of foreign bonds. Probably the best known of these is the Corporation of Foreign Bondholders of London.

Professor Jenks[10] relates of a loan to the Republic of Colombia underwritten in Great Britain to the amount of $10,000,000, on which interest was to be paid at the rate of 10 per cent per annum, and from which interest and commission were deducted, leaving only about $3,200,000 for the Republic. In addi-

---

[9] For details concerning the policy of the United States Government toward foreign loans, cf. "Diplomatic Protection of American Investments Abroad," Foreign Policy Association *Information Service,* Vol. III, No. 3, April 13, 1927, p. 38.

[10] Jenks, L. H., The Migration of British Capital in 1875, pp. 46-47.

tion, the expenditure of this sum was entrusted to contractors who secured for the country "a toy navy and military stores." Even if these purchases represented full value, which they did not, Colombia was to pay well over 31 per cent for the privilege of being financed by European bankers.

The prize for doing a profitable business goes also to London interests, and pertains to a loan arranged on behalf of the Republic of Santo Domingo. The amount was for about $3,788,500. Interest was to be paid at the rate of 6 per cent per annum. The facts are as follows: The Government of Santo Domingo entered into a contract with a certain E. H. Hartmont, by which the latter agreed to provide $2,100,000 for the construction of roads and railways, of which $500,-000 was to be retained by him as compensation, the nominal amount of the loan to be fixed by the contractor. The Government undertook to pay for the service of the interest and the sinking fund, an annuity of $294,500 in half-yearly installments for 25 years, or a total of $7,362,500. Messrs. Peter Lawson & Co., acting for Mr. Hartmont, issued in London $3,788,500 in bonds, secured by a first charge on the customs duties of the ports of Santo Domingo and Puerto Plata, the guano royalties, and the revenues arising from the forests and mines of the Province of Samana. The bonds were redeemable in 25 years by a 1¾ per cent cumulative sinking fund. The issue price was 70, but at this price the loan received little support from the public and the bonds were subsequently disposed of at rates ranging from 55 to 50 per cent, to Messrs. Bischoffsheim & Goldschmidt and others, by whom they were later disposed of to the public. The

Government maintained that it had received only $190,000. Mr. Hartmont, however, contended that he tendered personally to the Government, $1,055,550, but that it was not accepted owing to negotiations for annexation in progress at that time with the United States. Interest on the loan was paid for three years, but it was stated that these payments were made by the Contractor and not by the Government. Upon default, the loan became the subject of a parliamentary inquiry.[11]

American investors remember rather vividly the impressive statement made in a prospectus descriptive of a loan on behalf of the City of Cordoba, Argentina. The amount involved was $4,669,500. Prospective buyers of the bonds were told, on page 1 of the circular, that the city "was founded in 1573" and that it "is the seat of the National University of Cordoba." This was destined to appeal to the American investor's appreciation of antiquity and higher learning. In order to facilitate the sale of bonds, the investor was told —also on page 1—that "for the past 20 years there has been no record of default in payment of either principal or interest on any debt of the City." The reason for this "impressive" record is contained on page 3 of the prospectus in a form which the average investor is not likely to comprehend. We learn that "following the so-called Baring crisis in 1890, all the political subdivisions of Argentina, following similar action on the part of the National Government and several other South American countries, suspended payment on the service of their external debt. At

---

[11] See Fifty-Fourth Annual Report of the Council of the Corporation of Foreign Bondholders, p. 378.

that time, payments were suspended on two sterling loans of the City of Cordoba which were then outstanding. A plan was sanctioned by the holders of these bonds in October, 1906, and carried into effect in 1907, whereby these loans were assumed by the Province of Cordoba." In other words, the City, which has a perfect record extending over a period of 20 years, has not borrowed in 20 years. It borrowed twice before and defaulted on both occasions. The Province had to take over the debt. Is not the above statement somewhat misleading, to say the least? Furthermore, what may be the meaning of the phrase ". . . in 1890 . . . several South American countries suspended payment"? Brazil was meeting her debt. So was Chile. So was even tiny Paraguay. Uruguay was contracting a loan of about $10,000,000, although bonds were not issued to the public. Ecuador had been in default. Colombia was settling a default, as was Peru. Bolivia had no debt. Which South American countries does the statement refer to? Perhaps the fortunate possessors of Cordoba bonds who paid $987.50 for a $1000 par value bond can give the answer.

The very severe crisis in Bolivia today is attributed by Dr. J. Santiago Aramayo, an eminent Bolivian engineer, to the wild borrowing and extravagant spending by the Siles government. Says Dr. Aramayo: "The fault was not entirely ours. The American bankers are as much to blame. In fact, much more so, because we have trusted them implicitly and placed our confidence in them. It was at their request that we created a Permanent Fiscal Commission despite the severe criticism directed against us by our neighbors. We turned over to them the control of the nation's income to assure the bondholders of the safety of their investments. Have the bankers or their representatives performed their duty honestly? Never!

"I can trace the activities of these unusual representatives who were charged with looking after the interests of hundreds of American investors who were prevailed upon to buy Bolivian loans. They invariably entrusted the preparation of reports to the Bolivian member of the Commission or to a minor employee. But they never failed to collect their rather substantial salary at the end of each month.

"Honesty rarely characterized their activities. To them, indeed, apply eminently the words from Julius Caesar (Act IV, scene 3):

CASSIUS

In such a time as this it is not meet
That every offence should bear his comment.

BRUTUS

Let me tell you, Cassius, you, yourself
Are much condemn'd to have an itching palm;
To sell and mart your offices for gold
To undeservers.

CASSIUS

I, an itching palm!
You know that you are Brutus that speak this,
Or, by the gods, this speech were else your last.

BRUTUS

The name of Cassius honours this corruption,
And chastisement doth therefore hide his head.

CASSIUS

Chastisement!

"The United States, the richest country the world has ever seen, can also boast, like Rome of old, of many a citizen with an 'itching palm.' " Dr. Aramayo traces his country's difficulties to the first Bolivian railroad loan contract entered into on the 27th of November 1906 with the National City Bank and Speyer & Company of New York. He also reminds us, in passing, that the United States Minister to Bolivia, the Honorable Wm. B. Sorsby, was instrumental in securing the contract for the American bankers.

CHAPTER V

CAUSES OF DEFAULT (*Continued*)

THIS chapter is to be an elaboration of the subheading of the preceding chapter, Unwise Lending. There is no question but that the major cause of default is the lending of money to unstable, undependable borrowers, and that original deception of the lender in regard to the status of the borrower goes directly to the hub of the whole dilemma. On March 3, 1926, long before the present disillusionment, I released the following for publication:

It is most amazing to find that so large a number of circulars, descriptive of foreign loans issued by prominent Banking and Financial Firms, contain statements which are either incorrect or decidedly misleading. The other day I happened to run across seven such circulars, and, strange though it may sound, no less than seven contained serious errors. To be sure, there is little to worry about for the moment. All new foreign loans are "over-subscribed" and foreign borrowers, taking advantage of this situation, contract and readily secure new credits before the proceeds of the earlier loan are fully expended. Our economists and financial writers, in a fashion typical of youth and, shall we say, lack of experience, place the best construction on all such financial transactions. Whether or not they will eventually cultivate the cynicism of old age, I am not in a position to state. Sorrows are bound to accrue, sooner or later, and then the glamour will begin to wane.

A. 1. Early in 1920 a prominent New York Banking firm offered in the New York market a block of Chilean External

5's of 1911. In the offering circular we read that "Chile has been borrowing for 95 years and has never defaulted on any of its loans."

2. In February 1921 a syndicate of American financial houses, including some of the foremost banking institutions, sold $24,000,000 worth of Chilean 8 per cent bonds in our market, advising in the circular descriptive of the loan that "The credit of the Republic of Chile has stood high with European investors since the flotation of the first external loan in London in 1822."

3. (a) In October 1921, a prominent investment banking house, in advertising the offering of $9,500,000 Chilean 8's, stated as follows: "Chilean credit has ranked high in European markets, the first external loan having been placed in London nearly 100 years ago, and we are advised that from the first days of the Republic the interest and sinking fund on the External Loans have been met promptly."

(b) In November 1921, the same firm sold an issue of Chilean 8 per cent bonds to the amount of $10,500,000. The circular descriptive of the loan contains the following statement: "Chilean credit has ranked high, the first external loan having been placed in London nearly 100 years ago, and we are advised that from the first days of the Republic the interest on the External Loans has been met promptly."

4. In 1922, a leading investment house advised, in connection with the sale of Chilean bonds, that "To our knowledge there has never been any default on Chilean Government bonds . . . since the first Chilean bonds were issued in 1822, a hundred years ago."

Inasmuch as every one of the foregoing statements is contrary to the facts, the question may well be raised as to whether the above banking firms, which are among the foremost and probably best equipped financial institutions in the world, should not have taken the trouble to ascertain the accuracy of such statements. I doubt very much whether they were familiar with the situation at the time they sold the bonds.

The facts are as follows: In 1822, Chile borrowed £1,000,000 in London. Bonds were offered at 67½ per cent, bearing interest at the rate of 6 per cent per annum, and enjoying the benefit of a yearly cumulative sinking fund of 1 per cent. As might have been expected, the obligation, costing the country well over 11 per cent, proved a heavy burden for the young nation. In 1826, Chile defaulted and it was only in 1840 that interest payments were resumed, all back interest having been capitalized and duly discharged.

From 1880 through 1883, during the War of the Pacific between Chile on the one side and Peru and Bolivia on the other, amortization on Chilean obligations was suspended. The service on subsequent Chilean obligations borrowings has been met promptly and punctually.

The foregoing clearly shows that statements made under A, 1, 3 (a) and (b), and 4, are absolutely contrary to fact, while statement made under 2 is decidedly misleading, because the credit of Chile could not have stood "high with European investors since the flotation of the first external loan in London in 1822." It could certainly not have stood high during the period 1826-1840, and probably did not stand high during 1880-1883.

B. The circular descriptive of the Province of Santa Fe (Argentina) $10,188,000 External 7's offered in 1925 by two prominent investment banking houses, contains the following statement: "The Government states that during each of the last twenty-five years all payments of interest on all bonds of the Province in the hands of the public have been promptly made when due." It is of interest to compare this statement with a report published recently in one of the most prominent Argentine financial weeklies as follows: "The Buenos Aires Corporation of Bondholders addressed a note to the Bolsa de Commercio (Stock Exchange), pointing out that the Province of Santa Fe . . . had not paid the matured coupons of its public debt and that there was nothing known officially as to whether anything was being done in the matter. . . ."

C. The circular descriptive of the Province of Lower Austria $2,000,000 Secured 7½'s, issued recently by two important New York firms, states that "The Province of Lower Austria has never defaulted on any of its obligations." That this statement is not entirely correct, is evidenced by the following: In 1911, the Province of Lower Austria contracted with a group of French bankers a loan of Fcs. 18,900,000, bearing interest at the rate of 4 per cent per annum and redeemable within 75 years by purchase or drawings, the Province having the option to call the bonds as a whole or in part, beginning in 1922. Interest on the loan defaulted on November 1, 1914 and it was only in 1924 (May 2nd) that an agreement was reached with the bondholders whereby the latter were to renounce the gold cause until October 31, 1936, interest payments to commence November 1, 1920, on a graduating scale, a moratorium to be declared covering the period November 1, 1920 to November 1, 1922. It was also stipulated that the Municipality of Vienna is to guarantee payments up to 50 per cent. On January 1, 1926, the above bonds were outstanding to the amount of Fcs. 18,346,500, which would seem to indicate that during a period of 14 years only Fcs. 551,500 have been retired, equivalent to less than 3 per cent of the total, whereas at least Fcs. 3,500,000 would have been retired during that period had the sinking fund been in operation in accordance with the loan contract.

It is needless to add that it is to the best interests of those identified with the distribution of foreign loans to examine more carefully the statements contained in prospectuses issued in connection with the sale of securities to the American investing public.

The following gem is contained in a special report published by Moody's Investors Service under date of July 30, 1925: "A few years ago, a certain Latin American province obtained a loan in the United States amounting to $1,500,000. Bonds bore interest at the rate of 8 per cent per annum and were redeemable within 18 years from the date of issue. The issue was sold at 85 per cent. Commission and expenses in connection with the flotation, and which were borne by the State, were said to have absorbed $243,000. In addition, the bankers deducted in advance interest for one year and sinking fund up to 1927, amounting to about $290,000. The State received in this way a total of $745,000, paying 8 per cent on $1,500,000, and annual amortization of about $60,000, a total of about $180,000 per annum. The State is thus paying [it pays no more] 25 per cent for the money borrowed in our market. Moreover, the bankers are reported to have paid the contractors who were to carry out certain works for which the above loan was floated, an amount of $485,000, so that there was hardly anything left for the State. . . ." It appears that the contractors were identified with the same institution which controlled the underwriting house, so that there is some question as to how productively the above sum of $485,000 was employed. Furthermore, it was stated at the time that in order to carry out the work, the State had to float an internal issue on which it paid interest at the rate of 10 per cent annually. Deducting the amount paid to the contractors, the actual cash received by the State could not have exceeded by very much interest and sinking fund payments for one single year. It is doubtless for this reason that bonds were not offered for public subscription. Little actual cash was required by the underwriters to effect the deal. When the period for which sinking fund payments had been provided expired, a strong demand for foreign bonds of all types was in evidence. This was especially true of Latin American issues. The above loan of $1,500,000 was therefore called for payment, through the issuance of a new loan of $1,750,000, bearing interest at the annual rate of 7 per cent. With the proceeds, the underwriters paid themselves back $1,500,000. It is not very difficult to figure out what became of the remainder. There was hardly any balance to speak of.

The above quotation from Moody's is preceded by the following observations:

Wisdom in making loans and consideration for the borrower are undoubtedly of the greatest importance, and as long as our bankers will heed both we shall have no difficulty in maintaining our recently gained position as the "world's leading banker." Unfortunately, there are still some, restricted in number to be sure, who are primarily interested in reaping unreasonable profits in their dealings with foreign borrowers, taking advantage of the pressing needs of the latter and their perhaps temporary fiscal difficulty.

We are quite confident that the rather small number of defaults on foreign issues would be even smaller if the methods employed by the bankers were less unethical. This, of course, does not apply to cases of outright repudiation as in Russia, for example.

The concluding observation is not less interesting:

If we ever expect to become international bankers who will command respect in the world's commerce and finance, we are treading on dangerous ground. If we feel that the credit of a nation is sound enough to justify our extending of credit to it, we ought to do it on decent terms. To demand the "last pound of flesh" is decidedly wrong economically as it is wrong on ethical and moral grounds.

It is financing of the above character and the inevitable

results which do infinite damage to the foreign securities markets, tending to bring into disrepute all foreign bonds irrespective of their investment merit.

Towards the end of 1929, a syndicate headed by a prominent New York banking house, and including one of Boston's leading investment firms, agreed to underwrite an $8,000,000 issue on behalf of the Province of Buenos Aires, which had previously been financed in the American market by the firms referred to above. Public offering was scheduled, but, on the very day on which the bonds were to be sold to the public, the Argentine Government abandoned the gold standard, with the result that Argentine exchange dropped precipitately, inducing the bankers to postpone the offering for the time being.

It is, however, possible that the engagements on the part of the Province were so urgent and that the bankers were so heavily involved in the situation, that they were obliged to grant a $4,000,000 six-months' credit to the Province. No public offering of this short-term note issue was made.

With the return of the enthusiasm on the part of American investors for bonds of all kinds, the bankers underwrote the above mentioned $8,000,000 issue, and offered it to the public, paying back to themselves, as one of the first steps, the $4,000,000 which they had apparently been obliged to advance. Bonds bore a 6½ per cent coupon and were offered at 95½, to yield 6.85 per cent, or appreciably below the yield on some already outstanding Province of Buenos Aires bonds.

Of particular interest is the fact that the circular descriptive of the bonds and the advertisement relative to the bond issue carried the following statement:

"For over thirty years, with the exception of two years during the World War, the Province has never failed to provide funds for the interest payments on its external debt. The Province funded the 1915 and 1916 interest payments at the time, and sinking fund payments were resumed in 1919 and 1920."

The above will doubtless convey the impression that, among borrowers, Buenos Aires occupies a very high position as regards its attitude towards creditors. One may to advantage compare the above statements with actual facts:

1. In 1891, the Province of Buenos Aires defaulted on all external obligations. In the same year, the Province defaulted on all obligations issued by the Mortgage Bank of the Province and responsibility for which the Province had assumed. Moreover, in addition to the default, the Province passed laws which were a distinct violation of the rights and privileges of the holders of those bonds. Even though it is true that these bonds were styled internal obligations, large amounts were held abroad, and one of the issues even carried a stipulation that payments are to be made in gold. The reason for believing that these bonds were widely held abroad resides in the fact that when the agreement was reached regarding settlement in 1906, it was done through the London firm of Baring Brothers.

2. In 1898, when the Argentine Government assumed the external obligations of the Province, bondholders were asked to convert their bonds, all of which bore interest at the rate of 6 per cent per annum, into an Argentine Government bond bearing interest at the rate of only 4 per cent per annum.

3. In 1906, when an agreement was made in reference to the bonds of the Mortgage Bank, all of which bore interest at rates varying from 6 to 8 per cent per annum, it was provided that the bondholders exchange their bonds for a new sterling loan bearing interest at the rate of only 3 per cent per annum, the rate increasing to 3½ per cent per annum after five years. With regard to principal, it was provided that about $40 par value of mortgage bonds were to be exchanged into the new issue at the rate of about $33 par value; while $40 of mortgage bank certificates were to be exchanged at the rate of $16.50 par value of new bonds.

4. In 1915, payment of interest and sinking fund on all external obligations was suspended once again, wholly or in part, with the exception of the 4½ per cent loan of 1910, which was originally underwritten by a syndicate headed by German bankers. Interest on the 3½ per cent loan due in 1915 was paid at the rate of 10 shillings in cash and £1/5/- in 5 per cent bonds. The interest due in 1916 was paid at the rate of 15 shillings in cash and £1/- in 10-year Province of Buenos Aires certificates. Interest on the other loans was funded into 5 per cent bonds at par, and the sinking fund was suspended for two years to January 1, 1917, inclusive.

5. In 1917, sinking fund payments were not resumed as provided in the 1915 agreement.

6. In 1918, the sinking fund on the 5 per cent Consolidation Bonds of 1915-16, scheduled to commence in 1918, was not resumed until November 1920. In the same year, interest was suspended on the 4½ per cent loan of 1910 referred to above and payments were

not resumed until May 1924, on which date sinking fund was also brought up to date.

7. In 1919, sinking fund payments on loans, the interest on which was funded into the 5 per cent Consolidation Loan, were resumed, with the exception of the 1910 Loan referred to above.

In view of the above "impressive" fiscal record of the Province of Buenos Aires, it is somewhat difficult to understand the statement made by a syndicate of prominent banking institutions in a circular descriptive of a new Province of Buenos Aires loan.

The above case is not the worst. Nonetheless, one might like to know whether statements in circulars mean anything, or whether their authors are rendered immune by the hedge clause given at the end of each prospectus, to the effect that information is not guaranteed, although derived from reliable sources?

One recalls the lurid literature descriptive of German and other Central European paper, known at the time as government, state, city, and corporation bonds, and as currency. One also remembers how huge were the transactions in these so-called securities, which American dealers and brokers, relatively unimportant to be sure, offered to the unsuspecting and gullible public as "long term" investments. They have turned out to be very long term investments. They are, one might say, permanent—nay, eternal—investments.

And while this almost fraudulent trade was carried on, no one raised his voice in protest, not even the wall paper concerns who must have felt the competition very keenly. Where were the McFaddens and the Johnsons then? Were the interests of the American public less dear and near to their hearts when millions of good American dollars were converted into paper which was destined to become absolutely worthless, except for whatever value it might possess to the collector of antiques or curios or souvenirs? The Honorable Louis T. McFadden might be interested to learn that among those who warned the investing public against speculation in marks, the late Paul M. Warburg ranked foremost.

Or is it possible that the gentleman from Pennsylvania and his colleagues farther west took seriously the assurance of a so-called specialist in German issues to his client, to the effect that a purchase of mark bonds would result in a profit of 2,500 per cent? Why did they keep silent when another "expert" advised his followers that "the purchasers of (such) bonds have the absolute knowledge that they are buying them at one-seventh the former price in dollars, and that they are in a position to make a large profit on the bonds that will in that event return them over 50 per cent per annum on their investment"? Another enterprising dealer felt that "German City bonds—universally considered the safest securities in the German market— are the greatest investment opportunity of the day. It is only because an American can buy temporarily marks as exceeding cheap that he is enabled to obtain these securities at such bargain prices." "Profits 150 to 1,200 per cent possible, account the present low foreign exchange rate," is the laconic recommendation of another.

Those who heeded the above enticing calls have today little except memories of what they optimistically called investments. They have not even fared so well as did the purchasers of a Russian loan, which has the distinction of being one of the first foreign loans to be admitted to the New York Stock Exchange. It is said that in connection with the listing, the Exchange was presented by the Russian Finance Minister with a most exquisite vase, which adorns today the Governor's Room of the Stock Exchange. On visiting day the holders of Russian bonds are presumably privileged to behold the gift. The dubious pleasure which may be derived from this sight, together with one-half of one per cent of the original cost of the investment, is all that has been left those who bought Russian bonds, despite warnings against investing in Russia, issued especially by European economists who directed attention to the unstable conditions in the country and who openly doubted the continuance of the service on Russian bonds.

These warnings, however, were more than neutralized by the impressive information given in prospectuses and circulars. The investor was told of the vastness of the country, the richness of the soil, and the smallness of the debt, reduced to a per capita basis. This method of computing debt figures is a favorite one with all those who design and prepare for general distribution and consumption foreign bond circulars. One recalls the prospectus descriptive of a loan sold on behalf of a Latin American republic, whose per capita debt was given as "less than one-twentieth" that of the United States. The prospectus did not, however, tell that about 90 per cent of the people of the country in question were living in hovels, paying an annual rental equivalent to about $2, and being about ten years in arrears on their payments. And yet the statement concerning the per capita debt made in the prospectus was accurate.

Philanthropy oozes from an announcement made in the American press on September 2, 1931, by a prominent New York banking house which had sold to the American public, on behalf of the Brazilian State of Pernambuco, a $6,000,000 loan at 97¾, bonds bearing interest at the rate of 7 per cent per annum. The announcement which was to cheer up the countless American investors who had purchased the bonds read as follows:

As Paying Agent for the above Loan, we regret to advise that funds for the payment of the interest due September 1, 1931, on these Bonds have not been received. Accordingly, we are obliged to refuse payment of the coupons due on that date.

In response to many demands by the Paying Agent for the remittance of funds, we received this morning a cable from the Secretary of Finance of the State of Pernambuco stating that a decrease in revenue compels the State to delay payment until conditions become normal.

Notice of any further developments of importance will be published in the New York Times by the Paying Agent for the information of Bondholders.

In the Spring of 1927, prior to the sale of these bonds, attention was directed to the fact that the State was not meeting, in strict accordance with the terms of the contract, the service on an external loan held largely in France, where the French Bondholders Association was endeavoring to bring about an adjustment. In connection with this fact, the suggestion was made that "the Bankers should think twice before selling bonds to the American public on behalf of a borrower who refuses to adhere to the provisions of the loan contracts." Treating one set of creditors in the manner in which they were treated by Pernambuco justified the belief that, in the event of difficulties, the State "might not hesitate to accord American investors the same treatment."

This suggestion was answered by the bankers who, under date of April 22, 1927, wrote that "The French Bondholders Association had not appeared in, or concerned itself with, the action which had been brought in the French courts by other French interests to enforce payment of certain coupons in gold." The letter adds that "inasmuch as the Association Nationale had been most active in protecting the interests of French bondholders in some cases, the fact that they had not taken action in this case warranted the inference that in their judgment the suit brought by these other parties was not well founded."

From the above, it was implied by the defending bankers that the French Bondholders Association regarded as unimpeachable the attitude on the part of Pernambuco towards the holders of its bonds referred to above. It is difficult to reconcile this interpretation by the Bankers with a letter addressed to them by the Association under date of March 25, 1927, or almost a month prior to the Bankers' letter of April 22, as follows:

We beg to call your attention to the judgment recently rendered by the Seine Tribunal against the Brazilian State of Pernambuco, copy of which you will find herewith.

This judgment formally recognizes the holders' right to demand payment on their coupons and of bonds drawn in pound sterling. We are moreover convinced that an examination of the circular descriptive of the issue or the terms and conditions set forth on the bond will convince you of the holders' claims.

We understand from telegraphic information which has reached Paris that you have signed with the State of Pernambuco a loan contract for the issuance on the New York market of a loan of six million dollars.

It appears necessary for us to draw your attention to the manner in which the government of this State seems to have treated its old creditors and we feel that it would be to the advantage of the eventual subscribers to the loan now under consideration that they be apprised thereof.

The fact that the Association is "convinced . . . of the justice of the holders' claims" would lead one, even if he were not a member of the august and venerable profession of banking, to conclude that it had "concerned itself with the action."

Be it as it may, the Pernambuco bonds no longer pay anything and are a long way from paying anything. Those who bought the bonds originally at 97¾ saw them decline in price to substantially less than 10 cents on the dollar. They have become investors in the true sense of the word.

From time to time, attention was called to the danger incident upon promiscuous lending. No one heeded the warning. Least of all those who should have heeded it most.

In the Spring of 1925 (March 12) when America was still young in the realm of international finance and when our knowledge of the world and of places therein was still restricted, the following statement of mine was published and may now bear repetition in view of what has taken place since:

There are two rather interesting cases which I believe deserve attention:

A. Several weeks ago a prominent New York Banking House offered for public subscription a large block of stock of a German concern. The price to the public was $13 per share, which appeared quite attractive on the basis of information contained in the circular and which was very impressive indeed. I questioned the accuracy of the figures, but was told that the firm had very carefully examined the situation, having had the aid and assistance of the German company. Somehow I refused to become convinced. I have just received a copy of one of the leading German papers wherein the circular distributed by the New York firm is somewhat closely examined under the caption of "A FALSE PROSPECTUS." The article says in part: ". . . in accordance with the information contained in the New York circular, the assets of the company are placed at about 196,000,000 marks (gold). The net profits for the year ending January 31, 1925, are estimated at $5,800,000, equivalent to 25,000,000 marks (gold). . . . Inasmuch as the data contained in this circular do not seem to be based upon actual facts and are apparently published in connection with the purchase by the New York House of a block of stock in the company, the management of the latter states emphatically that it has absolutely nothing whatsoever to do with the prospectus and, the information contained therein has no significance (*gegenstandslos*). At any rate, the prospectus was prepared and distributed in the United States without the knowledge or consent of the management of the company. Furthermore, the final figures for 1924 have not as yet been compiled for which reason it is impossible to state the results for the year in detail."

The above reminds me of an offering some three years ago by a leading firm of stock in a Scandinavian bank although it was generally known that the institution was on the verge of bankruptcy. Some two months after the offering, the bank actually collapsed and the stock was practically wiped out.

B. Two fairly prominent New York firms offered recently

"American" shares of a leading Austrian bank. These shares represented 5 Austrian shares and the price of the American share instead of being 5 times that of the Austrian share was about 8 times that price. A Viennese paper which obtained a copy of the circular descriptive of the offering comments on it about as follows: "The prospectus contains a brief excerpt of the Balance Sheet and a few very vague statements regarding the importance of the Bank, the size of its assets as compared with the book value of the stock and a list of enterprises affiliated with the institution. . . . No statement is made as to the rate of dividends, nor is there a profit and loss account. But we find, for example, 'current earnings excellent,' although every one knows that the Viennese banks had a very poor year in 1924 and that even today the earnings are still very far from excellent. Among the affiliated concerns mentioned, there are many which are no longer in existence (some, as a matter of fact, have not been in existence for decades); others are no longer affiliated with the bank, while some have never been connected with it. . . . It therefore appears advisable to add that the prospectus was prepared without the aid or even knowledge of the bank. Upon the request of the two New York firms, the bank sold to them 20,000 shares . . . not suspecting in the least that for such a small amount public propaganda would be made by the houses in question."

It may be of interest to point out that the bank is still in existence while the two American firms who sold the stock are no longer among the living.

Misleading or incorrect information contained in prospectuses distributed in the United States has, so far at least, not been taken seriously. What Great Britain thinks about it is best evidenced from the subjoined quotations from *The Law Times* of November 14, 1931, relative to the alleged falsification of prospectuses sponsored by Lord Kylsant, one-time powerful shipping magnate in Great Britain, and guiding genius of the Royal Mail.

The appellant, who had been the chairman of the R. M. S. P. Company, was charged (*inter alia*) that he, as a director of that company, published a prospectus, which he knew to be false in a material particular, inviting subscriptions to a debenture issue, with intent to induce persons to subscribe or advance money to the company, contrary to sect. 84 of the Larceny Act 1861. He was convicted on this charge at the Central Criminal Court and was sentenced . . . to twelve months' imprisonment in the second division. On other counts, which charged him with publishing accounts which he knew to be false in material particulars, he was acquitted. The prospectus, which was published in 1928, contained a statement of the capital issued and fully paid, of the existing debenture stock, of the reserve fund, and the insurance fund; and after setting out the history of the company and stating that the object of the issue was to provide additional capital for a new freehold building and for the general purposes of the company, it proceeded:

"The interest on the present issue of debenture stock will amount to £100,000 per annum. Although this company in common with other shipping companies has suffered from the depression in the shipping industry, the audited accounts of the company show that during the past ten years the average annual balance available (including profits of the insurance fund), after providing for depreciation and interest on existing debenture stocks, has been sufficient to pay the interest on the present issue more than five times over. After providing for all taxation, depreciation of the fleet, etc., adding to the reserves and payment of dividends on the preferred stocks, the dividends on the ordinary stock during the last seventeen years have been as follows":

and then it set out a table of the dividends paid for the year 1911 to the year 1927 inclusive, those dividends varying from

5 up to 8 per cent, and down, on one occasion in 1926, to 4 per cent, but in 1927 again rising to 5 per cent. *The prospectus did not state that for a number of years immediately preceding* it the company had sustained losses on its trading and investment income, after allowing for depreciation; or that the dividends for those years had ultimately been paid out of the earnings of the war period. It was conceded at the trial that every statement that appeared in the prospectus was true, and it was contended on behalf of the appellant (*inter alia*) that there was no evidence that the appellant had published a prospectus which was false in any material particular. The Court, however, held that a document could be false, where by a number of statements a false impression was intentionally conveyed, although each statement taken by itself might be true, applied to a criminal as well as to a civil case, and that the prospectus in the present case was accordingly false within the meaning of the section, because it put before intending investors, as materials upon which they could exercise a judgment on the existing position of the company, figures which apparently disclosed the existing position, but in fact concealed it.

The conviction was based on the British Larceny Act of 1861, as follows:

Whosoever, being a director, manager, or public officer of any body corporate or public company, shall make, circulate, or publish, or concur in making, circulating, or publishing, any written statement or account which he shall know to be false in any material particular, with intent to deceive or defraud any member, shareholder, or creditor of such body corporate or public company, or with intent to induce any person to become a shareholder or partner therein, or to intrust or advance any property to such body corporate or public company, or to enter into any security for the benefit thereof, shall be guilty of a misdemeanor. . . .

In giving the considered judgment of the Court, the

judge said that Lord Kylsant had been charged under section 84 of the Larceny Act, 1861, with, as a director of the Royal Mail Steam Packet Company, publishing, or concurring in publishing, accounts which he knew to be false in a material particular with intent to deceive or defraud the shareholders of the company, and, in a third count of the indictment, with publishing, or concurring in publishing, a prospectus inviting the public to subscribe to a Debenture issue of the company with intent to induce persons to entrust or advance property to the company. Lord Kylsant was acquitted on the charges dealing with the accounts, but he was convicted on that relating to the prospectus. In case there should be thought to be some inconsistency in the verdict, it was right to say that, with regard to the first two charges, the jury might have thought that existing shareholders in the company had some information from published accounts which the outside public had not, particularly in view of the fact that in the profit and loss accounts for the years in question (1926 and 1927) and in previous years there had been some indication of what was called "adjustment of taxation reserves," a somewhat abstruse expression which had given rise to considerable discussion during the case.

The material portions of the prospectus were the statement that the company's capital, issued and fully paid, was £8,800,000, the reserve fund £1,450,000, and the insurance fund £1,311,755, and the statement that although this company, in common with other shipping companies, has suffered from the depression in the shipping industry, the audited accounts of the company show that during the last 10 years the average annual balance available (including profits of the insurance fund), after providing for depreciation and interest on existing Debenture stocks, has been sufficient to pay the interest (£100,000 a year) on the present issue more than five times over.

There followed in the prospectus the dividends paid on the Ordinary stock of the company from 1911 to 1927, which, except in 1914, when no dividend was paid, and in 1926, when the dividend was 4 per cent, ranged from 5 per cent to 8 per cent.

One purpose for which the issue was made appeared to have been to pay off a £500,000 overdraft at the bank, which had been created in 1926 and renewed from time to time on the promise by the company that the Debenture issue in question would be made.

The grounds of the appeal were that there was no evidence that Lord Kylsant made or published, or concurred in making or publishing, a prospectus which was false in any material particular; that there was no evidence that he had made or published the prospectus knowing it to be false in any material particular; and that Mr. Justice Wright (who tried the case) misdirected the jury on various matters.

Mr. Justice Wright directed the jury that the words in the section "a statement . . . false in any material particular" were not limited to a case where one could point to an account or a statement and say: "Here are certain figures, here are certain words, which are false." That was unduly to narrow the words "in any material particular." To construe it otherwise would be to shut out a type of fraud in connection with written documents or accounts which might be of the utmost importance—namely, the type of fraud which might be found in a document which was fraudulent not in the sense of what it stated, but in the sense of what it concealed or omitted. This section covered the case of a written document which, as a whole, might be false, not because of what it stated, but because of what it did not state, and what it implied. The decision follows:

In the opinion of this Court those authorities are sufficient to support the summing-up of Mr. Justice Wright. It is true that those were civil proceedings, but we think that the opinions expressed are none the less applicable in the present case. Mr. Justice Wright, on more than one occasion, specifically called the attention of the jury to the distinction which they must bear in mind between possible civil liability and criminal liability.

In the opinion of this Court there was ample evidence on which the jury could come to the conclusion that this prospectus was false in a material particular and that it conveyed a false impression. The falsehood in this case consisted in putting before intending investors, as material on which they could exercise their judgment as to the position of the company, figures which apparently disclosed the existing position, but in fact hid it. In other words, the prospectus implied that the company was in a sound financial position and that the prudent investor could safely invest in its Debentures.

This implication arises particularly from the statement that dividends had been regularly paid over a term of years although times had been bad, a statement which was utterly misleading when the fact that they were paid, not out of current earnings, but out of funds which had been earned in the abnormal War period, is omitted.

The further question arises whether there was evidence on which the jury could properly find that Lord Kylsant knew that the document was false. If there was evidence that the document was false in the particulars already indicated, there was ample evidence on which the jury could find that Lord Kylsant knew of its falsity, knowing, as he did, of the means by which the dividends had been paid. And it is not, and cannot be, disputed that the prospectus was published with the intention of inducing persons to entrust or advance money to the company, which was sufficient to satisfy the requirements of the section.

In his summing-up Mr. Justice Wright told the jury that, before they could convict, they must find an intention to defraud, and he repeated that when, after they had retired, they sent a question to him. That direction was unduly favorable to Lord Kylsant, a mere intention to induce people to entrust money to the company being sufficient. In view of what occurred the jury must be taken to have found that what was done in this case was done with an intent to defraud.

In the result, we come, without hesitation, to the conclusion that in the summing-up, regarded as a whole, there was no misdirection, that there was ample evidence on which the verdict of the jury could be supported, and that the appeal must be dismissed.

In the light of recent unpleasant occurrences in the foreign securities market, it may not be amiss to refer to some warnings hazarded at the time when things were still running along smoothly and when defaults were still unknown to the American investor abroad. Prompted by the surprising accuracy of the forecasts, the writer cannot refrain from at least referring to some of them.

The following was published in the New York *Times* under date of July 24, 1926:

Warning against the purchase of bonds of three projected South American issues was issued yesterday by Dr. Max Winkler. . . . The loans involved are one of $3,000,000 for the Argentine Province of Mendoza; another of 5,000,000 gold pesos, or its equivalent in dollars, for the Argentine Province of Corrientes; and a third of $7,200,000 for the Brazilian State of Parana.

"Owing to the present apparent popularity of South American issues," Dr. Winkler said, "it is not unlikely that these loans will be concluded and that our investing public will be called upon to take up the bonds.

"In view of the decidedly unsatisfactory record of the prospective borrowers who are newcomers in the American market, I trust that for the benefit of our investors, the bankers will refrain from offering in this market bonds of the Province of Corrientes, which for more than seven years has been in complete default on its external debt; or of Mendoza which, while paying current interest on its foreign debt, is in default with respect to several years of interest and sinking fund. . . .

"Parana appears at present to be meeting the service of its debt promptly, but the State has in the past so frequently disregarded rights and privileges of its creditors that I feel the bankers ought to think twice before offering Parana obligations to the still inexperienced American investor who may be looking for bargains in the foreign field."

Of the above loans, only Corrientes did not come into the market because it was not possible to explain away the stubborn default of the Province with no apparent desire to remedy the situation. Mendoza succeeded in obtaining from American bankers, or, rather, the investing public, more than double what she had originally asked for; while Parana received less than $5,000,000.

The London *Evening Standard*, under date of August 9, 1926, was "glad to read that New York financial interests are advising the American public to have nothing to do with a loan to the Province of Corrientes which the Government of that Province is trying to raise. As investors in this country are

only too painfully aware, this Argentine Province has
been in default for several years, and although the
Council of Foreign Bondholders have made repeated
appeals to the National Government to take such steps
as may be in their power to put pressure on the Government to respect its obligations to foreign creditors,
there has been no result."

That the difficulties experienced by American investors in connection with German debts are not of
recent origin, may be gathered from the following
statement which appeared in the New York *Times*
under date of December 16, 1926:

Commenting on the intention of the German Government to
refuse further exemption from the existing 10 per cent coupon
tax on all German loans, Dr. Max Winkler . . . yesterday said
few persons realize that it was largely because of certain transactions between German borrowers and bankers, for the most
part American, that the decree was handed down.

"It is, of course, generally known," Dr. Winkler said, "that
relatively heavy borrowing on the part of the German States,
municipalities and corporations has been looked upon with a
certain degree of disfavor by German officials. It was for this
reason that the Advisory Bureau for Foreign Credits was
created to pass upon applications for loans to be contracted
in foreign markets. Whenever in the opinion of the bureau,
such loans were not likely to be of a productive character,
application was rejected and in that case internal borrowing
was resorted to.

"In several instances, however, municipalities and communal
districts have obtained foreign credits, largely on short term,
through the sale of internal treasury notes to foreign bankers
without the approval of the bureau or Government sanction.
In addition, certain loans, the flotation of which was restricted
expressly to the home market, had been turned over to foreign

bankers for sale abroad. The decision to levy a 10 per cent tax on all loans is therefore expected to put a halt to such operations, which, if they should increase in magnitude, may some day endanger the currency position of Germany, but will not preclude the granting of tax exemption to foreign loans which, in the opinion of the bureau, are of a distinctly productive character."

How much the above provision has accomplished, subsequent developments amply demonstrated. American bankers were definitely set on lending more and more. Nothing else mattered.

A week earlier, a mild warning was issued against the feverish haste to lend to Latin America. The Financial News of London, under date of December 8, 1926, reprints part of the warning as follows:

Among recent reports from our southern neighbors, the following may be mentioned:

1. Chilean cabinet forced out by militarists. New cabinet to be formed "to check communistic propaganda."

Note: Chile is now in complete default.

2. Mutinous troops in Rio Grande do Sul attack town of Santa Marta.

Note: Rio Grande do Sul is now in complete default.

3. Brazil Federal troops in town of Bage reported in revolt.

Note: Brazil is now in default on sinking fund payments and is meeting interest in scrip.

4. Brazilian Minister of Justice issues official statement regarding state of siege . . . censorship of Press and status of political prisoners.

5. Uruguay strengthens border patrols to prevent violation of Uruguayan territory.

Note: Uruguay is now in complete default.

6. Refusal by Nicaraguan liberals to lend support to new Conservative Government.

Note: Nicaragua is now in default with respect to sinking fund payments.

7. Possibility of landing U. S. marines in Nicaragua.

8. Mexico's alleged interference with internal affairs of Nicaragua.

9. Possibility of further complications of American negotiations with respect to Mexican oil and land laws.

Note: Mexico has been in complete default for years.

10. Costa Rica stirred by American recognition of new Nicaraguan regime.

Note: Costa Rica is now in complete default.

11. Rumors of unrest in Peru.

Note: Peru is now in complete default.

12. Continuation of Gomez dictatorship in Venezuela.

In the face of the above reports, American investors who have already placed substantial sums in South and Central American securities are going to be called upon in the near future to subscribe to large amounts of Latin American loans which are reported to be under negotiation with American banking houses.

. . . Past experience . . . as well as terms under which certain American issues have been and to a certain extent still are contracted, lead us to express the opinion that prior to the unqualified endorsement of securities of this type, more detailed information will have to be furnished the prospective buyer of these loans than is generally presented in circulars descriptive of such issues.

To be sure, no difficulties are bound to arise so long as events move along smoothly, that is, so long as holders of bonds continue to receive interest and sinking fund payments on their holdings promptly and regularly. In the event of default or repudiation, investors may reasonably be expected to carefully analyze the data on the basis of which they have purchased the bonds.

Under date of November 1, 1926, I made a statement in the New York *World* in connection with proposed loans to the Argentine province of Buenos Aires and the Argentine Government, as follows:

The financial situation in the Province of Buenos Aires would not seem sufficiently satisfactory to justify the unqualified endorsement of Buenos Aires obligations. The debt of the Province aggregates about 500,000,000 pesos, the service thereon absorbing about 50 per cent of the provincial revenues. The cost of the new financing will be rather heavy and the question may well be asked as to whether continuous borrowing at heavy costs is especially salutary. Proceeds from the sale of the Argentine Government loan are to be used for "productive" purposes. In view of rather frequent financing in this market in recent months by the Argentine Government, it is perhaps not entirely amiss to ask as to whether Argentina is not over-borrowing.

The New York *Tribune* of March 17, 1927 contains the following statement of mine:

Any one who has followed closely the various foreign offerings in this country within recent months could not help noticing the steady decline in the quality of such new loans.

The over-abundance of funds, together with the difficulty of finding the most profitable employment therefor at home, has contributed greatly to the pronounced demand for and the ready absorption of large foreign issues, irrespective of quality. The situation reminds one a great deal of conditions obtaining in England during the latter half of the nineteenth century when enormous sums of money were lost in the acquisition of many, but unsound, foreign investments.

The days of high interest rates are still fresh in the memory of our investing public. In consequence, they crave for high rates of interest and unreasonable profits on the investment of their capital, and these cravings are, as is to be expected, being taken advantage of by dishonest contrivances of promoters.

England has learned her lesson incurred by the British, the Dutch and the Swiss investor.

While high yield on a foreign bond does not necessarily indicate inferior quality, great care must be exercised in the selection of foreign bonds, especially today, when anything foreign seems to find a ready market. It is not too late yet. Foreign issues in default held by Americans are still few and far between. Promiscuous buying, however, is destined to prove disastrous.

The same warning appeared in the New York *Times* under date of March 17, 1927 and in the Financial and Commercial Chronicle on March 19.

Another evil from which the American foreign bond market suffered, was the senseless competition among underwriting houses whose representatives were crowding hotels and inns, pleading with governments, states and cities, as well as with corporations, to borrow American money. According to a special dispatch to the New York *Times*, dated Munich, December 18, 1931, Dr. Koepker-Aschoff, former Prussian Minister of Finance, stated that "the German authorities had been virtually flooded with loan offers by foreigners," adding that "during the years 1925 and 1926, not a week went by that a representative of a group of American banks came to see me in the Ministry for that purpose." It was remarked at one time that there were no more German bankers left in Germany, their places having all been filled by American financiers and their representatives. Whether or not a loan was actually needed, made little or no difference. It is reliably reported that an American house of issue succeeded in locating, in the northwestern part of

Bavaria, a hamlet which had up to that time escaped the notice of American agents. It was discovered that about half a million marks or about $125,000 was needed to improve the town's power station. How could a loan of so small an amount be offered to the American investor who had by now learned to "invest" by the tens and hundreds of millions? After much persuasion, the mayor of the town in question was convinced of the desirability of contracting a larger loan. The result was a $3,000,000 issue, successfully sold in the American market. After making the necessary additions to the power plant, the balance was employed towards the various projects which are ordinarily termed non-productive and which have inspired an American journalist to give vent to his feelings, which are pronouncedly anti-foreign, but not altogether without reason. One might, however, inquire whether funds obtained from abroad and employed towards the building of a gymnasium or a swimming pool are less productive than a loan made to a foreign country for the purpose of purchasing machine guns and other instruments of war. Of course, to some, swimming pools and bath houses are relics of barbarism and loans contracted for such purposes ought to be discouraged.

As regards competition among underwriters for foreign loans, the following statement published in the New York *Times* is of interest, particularly in the light of recent happenings:

American bankers were warned today against excessive competition for foreign loans by Max Winkler. . . . As evidence that this competition was rapidly becoming keener, he stated that the recently-offered City of Budapest $20,000,000 loan was in demand by thirty-six different houses, most of which were American.

Fourteen American banking houses are reported to be bidding for the new Belgrade city loan. Attention was also called to the fact that a bid of 94.25 per cent was made and, of course, accepted for an Argentine municipality 7 per cent loan offered the other day to be sold by bankers at not below 86.

The inevitable result of this competition is that the lender is obliged to make all kinds of concessions to the borrower, and the terms accepted are not always representative of the standing of the borrower. The biblical saying that "the borrower becomes a slave to the lender" is reversed, and the lender becomes a slave to the borrower.

Our bankers and particularly our investing public are getting a far less satisfactory deal than they would if there were more concerted action on the part of our bankers. Sooner or later, our bankers will recognize the futility of competition of this sort.

The above and similar warnings were hardly effective. On the contrary, they were greeted by an increase in the flotation of foreign loans, and decrease in quality.

In the Business Conditions Weekly, published by the Alexander Hamilton Institute under date of November 12, 1927, in connection with the listing of foreign shares on the New York market, one reads the following: "In the generally favorable or non-committal comment which has attended the announcement of foreign listing machinery, one word of warning has been heard. Dr. Max Winkler has indicated some of the less optimistic phases of the matter."

Under date of January 5, 1928, the following is part of an article which appeared in the New York *Telegram*:

While I shall . . . refrain from the hazards of assuming prophecies, I believe it within reason to state that, owing to the existence of a rather anomalous situation in our foreign securities market, certain opinions are likely to prove of interest. Furthermore, these opinions apply not only to the present situation, but also to conditions which existed about two years ago, as will be seen from a few concrete instances cited below:

In the course of 1925 the dollar bond of a certain European country was selling in New York to yield about 9 per cent. In the home market a loan was selling to yield 20 per cent on the basis of the rate of exchange prevailing at the time. A careful study of the situation conclusively showed that bonds were decidedly underpriced and that exchange was unjustifiedly low. Today (January, 1928) the same bonds have appreciated 200 per cent in price while exchange has risen over 56 per cent. To be sure, the dollar bonds have also risen, but the appreciation is considerably smaller.

At about the same time, a prominent local banking firm sold in this market an issue of bonds on behalf of a certain South American Republic, bearing interest at the rate of 6½ per cent and offered for public subscription at 97. Another bond of the same country, equally well secured, could be purchased on the European exchanges at 58, carrying a 6 per cent coupon.

Early in 1926, there was offered in this market a 7 per cent bond issue of a European corporation at fractionally below par. The company is of a substantial character and its loans are favorably regarded. However, an issue of the same company, traded in on the home market but payable as to principal and interest in United States currency, was selling at that time at 66 per cent, bearing a 6 per cent coupon.

The above article concludes with the following remarks: "The feverish haste with which American underwriters contract German loans has resulted oftentimes in the flotation of such loans on terms which, in my opinion, are not altogether justified on the basis of existing money conditions in Germany."

American bankers were endeavoring merely to transfer and apply to the rest of the world the installment selling system which had been flourishing in the United States. American bankers and manufacturers made the masses buy, regardless of whether or not they needed what was sold them, and irrespective of whether or not they would be able to repay.

One more quotation may throw additional light upon the attitude I had maintained for years. In the New York *Evening Telegram* of August 29, 1927, I had this to say:

If our position (as international bankers) is to become permanent, American investors and those charged with their guidance ought to be in a position to benefit from London's unique experience as an international market. There is much that we might learn. If we ever aspire to become international bankers who will command the respect of the world, we ought, in our foreign loan deals, to lay more stress upon value and less upon price.

Our financial journalists ought to discuss new offerings on the basis of their merit and not present a mere condensed statement of the information furnished in the prospectus. There ought to exist closer relations between American bankers and investors and the numerous Foreign Bondholders' Associations in Europe, with a view to preventing any foreign borrower from obtaining loans in any one market, if he has failed to adhere to terms of loan contracts in other markets.

We ought to refuse to be tempted by abnormally large profits. . . . The history of governmental defaults reveals that in a majority of cases, repudiations have their origin in the unusually harsh and onerous terms imposed by the lender.

When the nation's enthusiasm was aroused in connection with the proposed sale of German reparations bonds authorized by the so-called Young Plan which, although less than two years of age, has been showing signs of growing senility, the following views were expressed in an article published in the New York *Evening Post* in May, 1930:

Whatever mechanical devices may have been needed to pave the way for the Young Loan, seem to have been already perfected by our financial engineers. Whatever outward trimmings may have been deemed necessary to assure a cordial reception of the bonds, also seem to have been arranged by our financial embroiderers. The stage, in other words, is set and the debut of the offspring of the Young Plan is anxiously awaited by investors throughout the world. Most of the essential preliminaries have been attended to:

1. Low money rates prevail in practically every financial center and almost every week brings announcements of new reductions in the official rediscount rates.

2. The American portion of the shares of the B. I. S. (Bank for International Settlements) is understood to have been succesfully placed with about 100 banking institutions which were called upon to subscribe.

3. Germany continues to occupy first page in the world's press, thanks to her supremacy in the air. Brazil and Cuba declare holidays in honor of the arrival of the Zeppelin. Pernambucans are fined for keeping open shops while the dirigible is flying over their heads.

4. Washington is reported to have sanctioned the Young Loan, as it does other foreign issues in general, and Mr. McFadden's objections to the bonds, because of their alleged illegality, are either being toned down or are relegated to where similar objections raised on similar occasions are warehoused.

5. Surveys are being made and straw votes taken as to the probable response to the proposed loan on the part of the American investing public, and the results are reported as most satisfactory.

While we all believe in what is generally regarded as window-dressing, there is occasionally the temptation to overdress the newcomer. We have succeeded in creating a considerable degree of enthusiasm for the coming loan, but the enthusiasm seems cold and artificial. No doubt, the loan will be a success, irrespective as to whether it will yield 6 per cent or 5 per cent. The one hundred banks referred to above will be called upon to subscribe to the Young bonds, and they will in all probability heed the call. However, genuine success, that is the actual absorption of bonds by the investing public, will depend, above all, upon the relative attractiveness of the issue, especially when compared with other foreign, including German, bonds of similar quality.

Inasmuch as the proposed loan will be the first of a series of reparations bonds to be sold to the investing public here and abroad, it is highly desirable to make the first portion as attractive as possible, not merely in regard to security, but particularly in regard to the return on the investment. An old Oriental proverb is to the effect that one must not ask the physician, but the patient. The prospective investor, and not merely the banker, should be consulted. Consequently, it would seem much more desirable to underwrite the first tranche at a minimum profit, with the assurance that profits on the following reparations issues would more than compensate the syndicate, than to offer the bonds at a price which, comparing unfavorably with the quotation for similar issues, may not appeal to the investor. On the other hand, the genuine success of the first series will, without doubt, facilitate the successful placement of issues to follow. Unless the bankers are inclined to adopt the *après moi le déluge* attitude, the writer feels that they could, to advantage, give serious consideration to the points brought out in this essay.

"Playing with Matches" or "Kreuger & Toll— Truth vs. Fiction"

A quarter of a billion dollars may reasonably be estimated to represent America's stake in the Kreuger and Toll combine. The present value is probably less than one-tenth this amount. A rather expensive venture! Of the total, $115,500,000 represents what may euphemistically be termed investments in International Match, an American corporation with the majority of the board Americans. Present value of this "investment" is less than one-fifteenth this amount. The sum placed in Kreuger and Toll bonds and shares is also estimated at $115,500,000, whose present value is about $6,500,000. The balance is made up of miscellaneous "investments" in a number of enterprises directly affiliated with the late Ivar Kreuger.

Once more, America succeeded in creating a record. This time, it was the greatest financial scandal history boasts of. Not since the days of Rome, with her consuls and proconsuls, has the innocent and believing public been duped to such a tremendous extent. It is almost incredible to learn of the doings, or rather undoings, on the part of organizations, headed by men upon whom the public looks for guidance in matters financial and economic. And, curious though it may seem, all was done in strict accord with provisions of loan contracts, indentures, documents, agreements, and various other implements concocted in juridical laboratories and workshops.

The time is Spring, 1929. The place is the United

States, where dwell 126,000,000 potential buyers of
securities of all types and descriptions. The New Era
is at its height. Common stocks, also called equities
despite or because of the iniquities they subsequently
wrought, are eagerly desired by an ever-increasing
number of adherents of the New School of Economic
Thought. Stocks rise higher and higher. Further advances are confidently predicted. Bonds and fixed income securities are shunned, unless trimmed with
warrants, "rights," options and equally "promising"
privileges. The salesman who is bold enough to recommend bonds, is reported to the health authorities for
observation. A Treasury official is understood to have
been threatened with impeachment because he had
dared speak of bonds as desirable long-term investments. Never-ending prosperity is held out by the pro-
tagonists of the New School. Those who differ—and
they are decidedly restricted in number—are considered traitors. For, who but those who lack in patriotism could even dare believe in American stocks which
go down? Is not, they shout from the housetops, America the richest nation on earth? Is she not the mightiest
creditor power? Is she not the most perfectly self-
sufficient country in the world?

Amid such atmosphere, there descended upon the
American people, with the aid of the nation's mighty
monarchs of finance, a less than fifty-year-old Swede,
Ivar Kreuger by name. He had been in the match
business and had prospered. Contact with American
bankers may be assumed to have taught him that size
was prerequisite to everlasting fame. He yielded. And
thus began Kreuger's spectacular conquest. The cam-

paign was financed by American bankers who liberally furnished the people's millions.

With Ivar Kreuger gone, it is only natural that whatever irregularities and inconsistencies there may have occurred in connection with the various Kreuger transactions, will be blamed exclusively upon the late match manufacturer. He is not here to answer charges. Dead men tell no tales. Once again, the public will believe. Once more, it will be fooled. Herein lies the tragedy of man. He abhors the truth, because he cannot afford to listen to it. Especially in times of crisis. In boom times, he will not listen.

Of the $250,000,000 of good American money given by American bankers to Kreuger for whatsoever he was pleased to do with it, $50,000,000 represents an original investment in the so-called Secured Gold Debentures issued in March, 1929. Bonds were issued in accordance with an Indenture containing 84 pages of reading matter. From the viewpoint of vagueness and lack of protection as far as the investor is concerned, the Indenture is, in the opinion of the writer who is merely a student of economics, a masterpiece, and deserves to go down as such in the annals of financial writings.

The offering syndicate comprised America's finest. The price was 98, and the yield over 5⅛ per cent. Thus, price and yield denoted first-class quality. Legal matters in connection with the bonds were in the hands of equally high-grade firms at Boston and New York.

The loan was said to be specifically secured by pledge, under a Debenture Agreement, of the following securities:

Issue	Amount (Par Value)
Yugoslavia 6¼s, 1958	$ 7,000,000
Latvia 6s, 1964	6,000,000
Poland 7s, 1945	5,100,000
Ecuador 8s, 1953	1,986,900
Ecuador Mortgage Bank Gtd. 7s, 1949	1,000,000
Greece 8½s, 1954 (£979,902)	4,768,693
Rumania 7s, 1959	2,000,000
Rumania 4s, 1968 (£380,690)	1,852,628
France 3s and 4s (Fcs. 344,000,000)	13,477,576
Belgian National Rwy. Pfd. (Fcs. 80,000,000)	2,224,460
Prussian Mortgage Bank Gold 8s (RM 12,000,000)	2,858,400
Hungarian Land Reform Mortgage 5½s, 1979	12,000,000
Total	$60,268,657

It will be noted that the par value of the above aggregated well over $60,000,000. With the exception of Ecuadorian bonds and the possible exception of Latvian bonds, every one of the issues pledged or said to have been pledged was, in the Spring of 1929, regarded as a fundamentally secure investment. Many of the securities had a market or appraised value of or near par, while those issues which had no official market could, in those days, easily have been disposed of. At any rate, their value could readily have been determined. It may perhaps be added that Belgian National Railway stock, amounting to 80,000,000 francs, was quoted substantially above par in the Spring of 1929.

The syndicate was headed by Lee, Higginson and Company. The trustee was the Lee, Higginson Trust Company. The depository was the Skandinaviska Kredit A.B. of Stockholm. These facts are significant.

The Indenture provided that the ratio of the *par* value of pledged securities to the par value of outstanding debentures must always be 120 per cent. The same applied to the income from pledged securities. Failure to maintain such ratios would not constitute default, unless there was a default in the interest or sinking fund on the debentures, but provision was made for deposit of additional collateral to restore the ratios.

Pledged securities could be withdrawn provided the above ratios were maintained. There could also be substitutions. In case the latter took place, "eligible" securities must be put in place of pledged securities withdrawn. The following were "eligible":

a) Issues of sovereign countries or bonds of cities with more than 300,000 inhabitants. In other words, Russia, Mexico, China, Peru, and Bolivia would qualify, as would also Moscow and Leningrad. Even paper mark obligations of Germany could have been regarded as eligible, so that it would have been permissible to remove the above $60,000,000 par value of bonds and deposit in their stead, $60,000,000 par value of German Government Forced Loan of 1922, which could have been bought for $5.00 a million. That is to say, the above collateral could have been withdrawn, and other bonds deposited at an expense of only about $300. It is for this reason that one cannot subscribe unqualifiedly to reports that Kreuger had forged $100,000,000 worth of Italian bonds. Since the Indenture made it possible for Kreuger to obtain, without much ado, $60,000,000 worth of good bonds at a purely nominal expense, why should Kreuger have gone to the trouble and expense of having bonds forged? We made it possible to accomplish the same things with much less inconvenience.

b) Issues of Mortgage Banks.

c) Railway shares, dividends on which must be guaranteed by a sovereign government. The various Mexican railway issues, some hopelessly defaulted Latin American railway shares, would qualify under this provision, which says that dividends must be only guaranteed. Apparently, nothing is said about their having to be paid.

The circular contains four pages of material descriptive of the Kreuger and Toll Company, with particular reference to the Secured Debentures. Elaborate statistics, balance sheet figures, and earnings statements are presented. One looks in vain for the name of an accounting firm. It is not there. Is it not strange that a loan, involving tens of millions of dollars, is contracted merely on the say-so of one man who, even though he may have given the impression of honesty and integrity, was unable to furnish dependable information regarding so gigantic an enterprise? How much of their own money would the bankers have put up on Mr. Kreuger's statement? When, prior to his final act, he is believed to have approached the bankers for accommodations, which they would have had to supply out of their funds, how far did Mr. Kreuger get? The bankers apparently do not seem to have felt that way when other people's money was involved.

In this connection, it is of interest to quote from an article in the Svenska Dagbladet, written by Gustav Cassel, the renowned economist. Says Professor Cassel:

When such firms as Lee, Higginson and Company placed their names under Kreuger emissions, it was natural that we, in Sweden (and most certainly we in the United States) imagined that they had carefully examined the firm's position and that they exercised reliable and thorough supervision over its leadership. In this, we have been deceived. If abroad at this moment we are held responsible to a large degree for the Kreuger fiasco, we, too, to a lesser degree, may hold foreign interests responsible. . . . Year after year, they have given Kreuger and Toll tremendous moral backing without bothering to test the firm's position. Responsibility for this lies with these people, not with Sweden.

Late in March, there was released information regarding the nature of the collateral. The changes which had been made were sensational. With the exception of about Fcs. 74,000,000 of Rumanian Monopolies 7½ per cent bonds which are listed in Paris, not one issue said to comprise the collateral had a market. All marketable or reasonably sound securities had been taken out. The French bonds were gone. So was the Belgian National Railway preferred stock, on which the Belgian Government guarantees a minimum dividend of 6 per cent. So were the Greek 8½s; so were the Rumanian 7s, and the Polish 7s; and so were the Prussian Mortgage bonds. In their place, there were more Hungarians, in default, and more Yugoslavs on the verge of default.

The dates on which substitutions were made are also significant. According to the Trust Company which, as was stated above, was practically identical with the house of issue, information relative to substitutions had "been currently available" for debenture holders of the Trustee. However, debenture holders had complete faith in the bankers who had sold them the bonds, and it probably never occurred to them to inquire as to what collateral had been removed, and what issues put in their place. Even if they had obtained such information, to whom was it given out? The Trustee doubtless knew that the removal of French or Belgian bonds, and the pledging instead of Hungarians, changed the picture very radically. The market value of debentures secured by such pledged collateral became at once most seriously affected. Was some one using this information to his own advantage?

Considerable light was thrown on the entire situation in a number of hearings before the Senate Sub-Committee on Banking and Currency, at which the writer testified as an expert witness. In the course of the investigation, it was discovered that in a circular sent out by Lee, Higginson and Company, under date of October, 1931, the Kreuger and Toll Participating Debentures were "recommended," on the grounds that they were "at their present price . . . distinctly undervalued and afford an unusually attractive opportunity to make new commitments or to add to one's holdings." This recommendation was made at a time when the Participating Debentures, which were junior to the Secured Debentures, were selling around $9.00 (present price: zero).

In January, 1932, they were once again recommended as "an undervalued security" on the grounds that "taking into consideration facts alone and not general apprehension unsupported by facts, they represent, in our opinion, an interesting commitment from the standpoint of price in relation to intrinsic value."

The above recommendation also pointed out that "at their present market price, the equity issues of the Kreuger and Toll Company are selling for about $64,500,000." The authors of the above statement were silent as to how "the present market price" was arrived at. Furthermore, if they knew that there had been substitutions, they must have known that the value of the Secured Debentures was seriously reduced, leaving little, if anything, for the junior issues. Is it conceivable that they were knowingly advocating the purchase of practically worthless paper? Is it possible that a firm of the standing and reputation of Lee, Higginson and Company would go so far as to recommend the purchase of what was hardly more than a souvenir, at prices which indicated that what they were selling possessed "intrinsic value"?

Under date of January 28, 1932 they distributed a statement by Ivar Kreuger, according to which "the Company's holdings of foreign government bonds are *now* carried on the books at approximately $50,000,-000." It also pointed out that "the net assets . . . correspond to about $16 per Participating Debenture." Were they, one may ask, aware of substitutions on January 28? If so, why should not the holders of the Secured Debentures have been apprised of the changes?

A prominent house, with offices all over the United States and Canada, including Dallas, Philadelphia, Burlington, Plattsburg, St. Albans, Saranac Lake, Toronto, and Montreal, only shortly before Kreuger's death, published a special analysis of Kreuger and Toll, in which they recommended the Participating Debentures which "have an equity of around $16 for each Certificate." The report was concluded by advocating them as "an attractive purchase."

Another firm, in a special analysis prepared for its numerous clients, also recommended the purchase of the Certificates, that is, the Participating Debentures. "We can," the circular read, "see little or no point in disposing of the Participating Debentures at these levels and, in fact, we consider the American certificates attractive."

A reputable statistical organization whose records were "revised September 3, 1931" lists the collateral securing the Debentures as it was given in the original prospectus. The organization remains silent in regard to the method it applies in revising its records.

The whole picture was absolutely shocking. It shattered whatever faith the investor might have retained in those who were supposed to guide the financial destinies of the nation. Thanks to efforts of Senator Peter Norbeck, the whole truth came to light. A thorough investigation was ordered, because the Senator felt that little would be learned from the Committee formed immediately after the Kreuger suicide, under the auspices of the very firms which were responsible for the origination and distribution of the bonds, to "protect" the holders of Kreuger and Toll securities. Mr. Norbeck felt, and rightly so, that the Committee to "protect" the Secured Debenture holders was composed of six men, of whom five were connected with the houses of issue, and that merely for the sake of diversification the head of a New England textile mill had been added as a sixth member. One cannot, said the Senator, be plaintiff and defendant in one.

The investigation was very thorough. Pages of publicity. As to actual accomplishments, one is obliged to admit that there are none. The investor is precisely where he was before. He is ready for a second attack. Once again, the truth of the Latin saying is borne out:

"Mundus vult decipi—ergo decipiatur"—(The world wants to be deceived—Let it therefore be deceived).

Playing with Explosives—America's Invasion of Chile's Nitrate Fields

There are outstanding at present in the American market, mostly with what has been euphemistically referred to as American investors, Chilean Government and Municipal bonds to the amount of $289,000,-000—all the result of nine years of borrowing in the United States, or at the rate of more than $36,000,000 per annum.

Europe is not quite so fortunate. The total Chilean debt outstanding in Great Britain and on the Continent aggregates today less than $168,300,000, resulting from 46 years of borrowing covering the period 1885 to 1930, and representing transactions effected in the markets of London, Paris, Brussels, Zurich, Amsterdam, and Berlin. The above figure is equivalent to an annual rate of slightly more than $3,500,000, or one-tenth the annual average borrowing in the United States.

To what does the American investing public owe this particular privilege?

When, a little over a decade ago, United States bankers discovered the South American Republic of Chile, the American investing public was told of the very impressive fiscal record which the Republic south of the Rio Grande enjoyed. Circulars descriptive of Chilean obligations informed the innocent investor that Chile had contracted her first external loan in the London market more than a century ago, and that, throughout that period, there was no record of a default on any of the Republic's obligations, either external or internal.

I have been unable to find out why issuing houses should not have taken the trouble to ascertain the accuracy of statements they made, and on the basis of which they called upon the American public to invest funds.

To point out today that the depreciation in these securities is as marked as that in many domestic issues has no real foundation. I do not see the absolute necessity of an American investor traveling three thousand miles or more to lose his money. He could have done it at home, with much less inconvenience.

Impressed with the highly satisfactory record, even though such record seems to have existed primarily in the imagination of those identified with the origination and sale of Chilean bonds, the American investing public absorbed Chilean issues that continued to be brought out in ever-increasing amounts with a rapidity hardly encountered at any time in the history of borrowing governments.

Chile's principal wealth is based upon two products —Nitrate and Copper.

Chile's copper mines have for years been controlled by American interests, while the nitrate industry was largely in the hands of the British. In a desire to wrest from the British whatever could be wrested from them and to displace Great Britain—the classic center of international finance—American interests set out to acquire a controlling interest over Chile's total resources.

In 1924, the Chilean Government, in order to realize sufficient sums to cover the growing budgetary deficit, disposed, at auction, to an American group, some nitrate land known as the Coya Norte Properties, for about $3,500,000. This was the beginning of America's invasion into Chile's nitrate industry. Following the acquisition of the above properties, additional nitrate fields were acquired.

A proposal was made to the securities holders of the Anglo-Chilean Nitrate Railways Company, domiciled largely in Great Britain, to accept for their holdings, securities of a company organized in the United States, under the laws of Delaware, and known as the Anglo-Chilean Consolidated Nitrate Corporation. This enterprise created first mortgage bonds of £3,600,000; 7 per cent debentures of $16,500,000; and 1,756,750 shares of no par value common stock, the majority of which was owned by the sponsors of the entire enterprise. Before very long, these various securities had a market value of close to $100,000,000, most of which represented by the market value or quotation, rather, of the common stock. In this way, an original outlay of less than $3,500,000 showed a decidedly handsome profit over a short period of time.

It might perhaps be added that the American investing public was privileged to buy the 7 per cent debentures of $16,500,000 referred to above at the price of 100 cents on the dollar. He was, of course, also given, as an additional inducement to subscribe to the bonds, some shares of common stock with each debenture. It would be of interest to find out whether the individual investor was as successful in disposing of these additional common shares, as those who were in control of the situation are understood to have been.

In 1929, a syndicate of American bankers, comprising some of the foremost institutions of the country, sold to the American public $32,000,000 par value of bonds of another Chilean nitrate company. The price to the public was 99 per cent, and, thanks to very sympathetic treatment on the part of financial journalists and numerous foreign securities experts, the issue was a complete success—from the standpoint of the seller.

The company on behalf of which these bonds were sold, is the Lautaro Nitrate Company, Limited, said to be the largest producer of Chilean nitrate. The capital structure of this Company, after it had received attention from the American financiers, consisted—in addition to the issue of $32,000,000 referred to above —of an additional $10,000,000 of bonds payable in sterling; of about $40,000,000 par value of 7 per cent preferred stock, also payable in sterling; and of an authorized issue of $32,000,000 of 7 per cent preferred stock payable in dollars. There were also created 2,000,000 shares of common stock, all of which was to be owned by a new company, organized under the laws of Delaware, and known as The Lautaro Nitrate Corporation. This Company, being an American concern, naturally had to have more shares than any of its predecessor or affiliated enterprises. It consequently created 4,000,000 shares of common stock, of which more than half was turned over to the Anglo-Chilean, in which the Guggenheims owned substantially more than a majority.

The process of expansion went on, and, in March, 1931, an arrangement was made with the Chilean Government, whereby an enterprise was to be created that would absorb all the nitrate-producing properties of Chile—and thus there came into being the famous

Cosach, starting out as a concern comprising 36 Chilean nitrate-producing companies, and representing over 95 per cent of the nitrate productive capacity in Chile.

A revolution or, rather, a series of revolutions in the Republic changed it all—Cosach, Lautaro, Anglo-Chilean. Tens of millions of dollars worth of bonds and shares were reduced to levels representing what one might safely term souvenir value. Rather costly souvenirs, the cynic does not neglect to tell us!

Bribing a President's Son

One hundred million dollars is America's total stake in Peru. The present worth of this impressive amount is less than 10 million dollars. It would be of interest and of service to those who may, in the distant future, be called upon to place funds in the Land of the Incas, to refer to the attitude of American bankers towards Peru, especially its past fiscal record, as revealed before hearings conducted by the Senate Sub-Committee under the chairmanship of Peter Norbeck, and later, Duncan U. Fletcher.

According to one report by the South American expert for the banking house which later played a prominent part in Peruvian financing, "the condition of Government finances is positively distressing. Treasury obligations are almost impossible to collect. Government officials and employees are months in arrears in their salaries, and as one business man expressed it, the Government Treasury is 'flat on its back and gasping for breath.' With the small export trade continuing small, customs revenues are not of a large amount, and unless some sort of loan is forthcoming in the near future, I do not see how the Government can continue functioning on the basis of its present income."

An official of the banking house, at about the same time, had this to say in connection with a refusal to handle Peruvian loans: "As reasons for our declining the business, we cited the history of Peruvian credit, the political situation in Peru, and our feeling that the moral risk was not satisfactory. As far as the attitude of the banking house is concerned in connection with financing, it may be mentioned that the history of Peruvian credit, the political situation in Peru, and the company's feeling regarding the moral risk have hitherto caused them to avoid Peruvian financing."

Other comments made by officials and experts were along similar lines, as evident from the following:

"Peru has been careless in the fulfillment of contractual obligations. City of Lima 5 per cent loan coupons, due January 1, 1922, were not paid until the following May, 1922. The Peruvian 5 per cent gold bonds of 1920, due in January, 1922, were paid in September, 1922, and those due in July, 1922, were paid in October, 1922. The London *Times* in its issue of March 30, 1922, alluded to Peru's 'frequent unobservance of her undertakings to the Peruvian Corporation, her broken pledges over the Chimbote Concessions, and her flagrant disregard of guarantees given to the Northwestern Railway of Peru.' "

"Apparently the internal debt of Peru has not yet been placed on a satisfactory footing. The internal debt of 1918, which bears 7 per cent interest, had its 1922 and 1923 amortizations in arrears early in 1925, and apparently there are also some arrears in interest causing this issue to sell around 54 per cent to 56 per cent in Lima, which is almost as low as the amortizable debt of 1898, which bears no interest and sells around 50."

"As I see it there are two factors that will long retard the economic importance of Peru. First, its population of 5,500,000 is largely Indian, two-thirds of whom reside east of the Andes, and a majority consume almost no manufactured products. Second, its principal sources of wealth, the mines and oil wells, are nearly all foreign owned, and excepting for wages and taxes, no part of the value of their production remains in the country. . . .

"The country's political situation is equally uncertain. President Leguia, while not having the absolute power possessed by General Gomez in Venezuela, is the last word in all things political, and usually the first word as well. . . . I discussed political possibilities in the event of his death or retirement with many business and professional men during my stay in Lima. While some, including the United States Ambassador, were optimistic, the majority, even the President's political opponents and ill-wishers, believed a revolution or worse would result. . . ."

How, in the face of the above, American bankers found it necessary to pay a commission in excess of half a million dollars to Juan Leguia, favorite son of Peru's president, even the Senate Committee has been unable to ascertain.

The Case of Minas Geraes

In the interior of the United States of Brazil, south of Goyaz and Bahia, and north of Rio de Janeiro and

Sao Paulo, lies the State of Minas Geraes (General Mines), fifth in size, and first in population among Brazil's constituent provinces. A little over a quarter of a century ago (in 1907), the State contracted its first external loan, although authorization to borrow had been granted in September, 1904. A French banking house was privileged to handle the transaction. Twenty-five million francs, or five million dollars were involved. In 1915, sinking fund was suspended, and coupons paid partly in cash and partly in bonds.

Three years after the first loan was sold, Minas Geraes borrowed again. This time, the State was more ambitious, asking and securing 120 million francs, or about 30 million dollars. In 1911, another 50 million loan was contracted, bringing total borrowings, including the bonds issued to take care of defaulted interest, up to more than 211 million francs—all within a period of nine years, or at the rate of about 23½ million francs per annum.

In October, 1925, the *Association Nationale des Porteurs Français de Valeurs Mobilières* brought suit in the Civil Tribunal of the Department of the Seine against the State of Minas Geraes to enforce payment of coupons and drawn bonds of the 1907, 1910, 1911 and 1916 loans, in gold franc values. The memorandum prepared by the Association abundantly demonstrates that the State's refusal to maintain the service on its external debt on a gold basis, constituted a default in the performance of its obligations.

This type of default has lost a good deal of significance in the eyes of American bondholders due to the attitude of the United States Government toward creditors in respect of payment of interest and amortization on outstanding bonds in gold.

The State defaulted in appearance before the Seine Tribunal. Accordingly, the Paris Court, after hearing the Association's presentation of the matter, rendered a judgment against the State on October 22, 1925, as follows:

Whereas, both upon the face of the bonds and the coupon sheets of these loans, as well as in the notices and prospectuses of issue prepared and distributed by the issuing banks, it was expressly and positively stipulated that it was a question of gold loans, and that the repayment of principal and payment of interest were promised to be in gold. . . . For these reasons: Judgment is pronounced that the State of Minas Geraes in accordance with the obligations contracted by it is held liable to pay in gold the amount of coupons matured or to mature, and the principal amount of bonds drawn of this loan, 5 per cent gold of 1907, 4½ per cent gold of 1910, 4½ per cent gold of 1911, and 5½ per cent gold of 1916.

Furthermore, judgment is pronounced that in default of payment in gold the said State must pay in the notes of the *Banque de France* the amount corresponding to the gold value according to the rate of exchange on the day of payment of each coupon and of each bond drawn for redemption. In consequence, the State of Minas Geraes is sentenced to pay together with legal interest, etc.

After the rendition of this judgment, the State took an appeal to the Second Chamber of the *Tribunal Civil de la Seine* upon the ground that the Court below had no jurisdiction.

In view of the fact that such powerful creditor powers as the United States and Great Britain felt little if any compunction about ignoring completely so-called

gold clauses in loan agreements, one must not find
fault if a debtor state chooses to pay in "currency"
instead of "gold," as stipulated in the contract. What
is, however, significant is a statement made to bankers
identified with arranging financial accommodations for
the State by their South American expert, to the effect
that "It would be hard to find anywhere a sadder con-
fession of inefficiency and ineptitude than that dis-
played by the various State officials on these several
occasions."

This did not prevent the loan from being consummated. One of the officials of the issuing house took
exception to the following: "Prudent and careful administration of the State's finances has been axiomatic
with successive administrations in Minas," and pronounced the query: "In view of the extremely loose
way in which the external debt of the State was managed, do you think the statement quoted above would
be subjected to criticism?" It will be noted that in the
final draft of the prospectus the word "axiomatic" was
displaced by the word "characteristic."

A second loan was sold in the United States in 1929,
to the amount of 8 million dollars. Whereas London
participated in the first issue a year earlier, it refused
to subscribe to the second. The reasons are not far to
seek. In April, 1929, or about five months prior to the
public sale, representatives of a number of banking
firms, at a group meeting held at London, agreed that
"the prospect of a new government loan was most unfavorable; that the public was unwilling to invest in
bonds of any kind; and that the new loan would not
prove a success." Once again, London was right.

The War Debts—To Revise or Not to Revise—
Financing the Conflict Through Borrowing

No history of governmental defaults is complete without a reference to the so-called political debts to the United States, that is, loans and credits received during and immediately after the Great War by a number of European nations from the American Government, aggregating well over 11½ billion dollars. This is equivalent to about 92½ dollars for every man, woman and child living in the United States. It is equivalent to about one and one-quarter times the amount expended on all wars during a period of more than two and one-quarter centuries preceding the 1914-1918 cataclysm, and to slightly less than half the expenditure of the United States Government from its foundation in 1791 down to the last pre-war year, a period of a century and a quarter. The impressiveness of the figures is especially apparent if one considers that, during this long period, the United States fought England in 1812, Mexico in the 40's, the Civil War in the 60's, a number of Indian campaigns, and the Spanish War in the 90's.

How did these enormous debts originate? What renders them, in the eyes of economists and certain students of finance, different from other debts? Why do legislators and the American public in general refuse to accept this view? Why should there be so much talk of cancellation, postponement, or revision of payments? If these debts have actually been contracted in good faith, are not those who contracted them bound legally and morally to pay what they have agreed to pay? Will not cancellation, if approved by those to whom debts are payable, set a dangerous precedent, and destroy the sanctity of contractual commitments?

All these questions are being asked today, and have been asked for a decade and a half. The writer will endeavor to present, without any bias or embellishment, the history of the so-called political debts to the United States, in order to enable the readers intelligently to appraise the status of these debts, and the justification, or lack of it, as the case may be, of viewing political debts in a somewhat different light from commercial or private engagements.

When the war broke out in the Summer of 1914, Europe was not quite ready to bear the enormous financial burden imposed upon her by the outbreak of hostilities. She had to mobilize her resources, and, through them, the industries upon the immediate and proper functioning of which the success of the struggle invariably depends. Funds were obtained through the sale of American securities, largely by Great Britain, which had accumulated, over a period of years, huge amounts of rails and industrials. The selling was done on such a pronounced scale that the New York Stock Exchange authorities deemed it desirable to suspend trading.

Few of the belligerent nations had the courage of taxing their nationals to raise enough revenue to carry on the war. Great Britain's record in this respect is better than that of her Continental Allies. During the first two years, she raised, through various forms of taxes, a total of $2,047,000,000, and from loans $6,-154,000,000, or more than three times the amount obtained from taxation. In the last pre-war year, the nation's receipts aggregated $845,000,000.

France, who probably stood to lose more from defeat than any of her Allies, collected, by way of taxation, even less during the first two years of the war than she did in 1913. Whereas governmental revenue amounted, in the last pre-war year, to $860,000,000, it declined to $506,000,000 in 1915, and to $451,000,000 in 1916. During these two years, she borrowed a total of $5,023,000,000, or 5¼ times as much as she obtained from taxing her nationals.

Italy, which joined the Allies a year after hostilities started, also did not see her way clear to call upon her people to pay higher taxes than in time of peace. Borrowing proved more convenient. The nation's receipts, which amounted in 1914 to $458,000,000, fell to $424,-000,000 in 1915, and to $402,000,000 in 1916. Borrowing, however, increased from $507,000,000 in 1915 to $778,000,000 in the following year.

Russia met only about one-quarter of her wartime expenditure from revenue receipts. The remainder was derived from borrowing. Her income declined from $1,759,000,000 in 1913 to $1,391,000,000 in 1914, to $785,000,000 in 1915, and only $339,000,000 in 1916; while borrowing increased from $868,000,000 in 1914 to $3,037,000,000 in 1915, and to $4,231,000,000 in 1916—advances of 72 and 112 per cent, respectively.

Before the United States was drawn into the vortex, Europe succeeded in securing accommodations from her to the tune of several hundred million dollars. Great Britain borrowed a total of $1,065,000,000, while France was a fairly close second with about three-quarters of a billion. America also enjoyed the distinction of financing Russia to the extent of about $100,000,000—a mere bagatelle compared with what she was to do after deciding to throw in her lot with that of the Allied Powers, in an earnest endeavor to "make the world safe for democracy."

The markets of the United States, which remained neutral, were open to any nation who was willing and able to pay for goods furnished. However, by force of circumstances, and thanks to loans and credits obtained, American exports were chiefly to the Allies during the entire period of neutrality, because they succeeded in convincing America that they were fighting for justice and fairness, and that a German victory would spell disaster to the whole world, including the United States. What better reason could there be for supporting those whose mission it was to save the world, and, with it, western civilization?

When speaking of or discussing so-called political debts, one should bear in mind that loans extended to the Allies, whether by the United States Government, the American bankers or manufacturers, did not constitute the transfer of American funds to Europe. These loans were merely measured in terms of money. They were, in actuality, loans of absolutely essential commodities which the belligerents could not obtain at home. They were loans in clothing and food, in cotton and chemicals, in steel and copper, in ships and munitions. The money loaned stayed in the United States, and was used to pay for implements and engines of war.

The inevitable result was a most impressive gain in American exports to the Allies. In the twelve months ended June 30, 1915, United States exports of goods to Great Britain, France, Italy, and Russia, were valued at $675,000,000 in excess of shipments in the preceding twelve months. In the next fiscal year, exports to the Allies increased $1,882,000,000 over 1914, while sales from July 1, 1916 to June 30, 1917 showed a gain compared with the year ending June 30, 1914 of $3,125,000,000.

Inasmuch as the amount loaned to the Allies, or rather the credits arranged on their behalf, could not pay for all their purchases, it was necessary for them to dispose of their enormous holdings of American securities, which they had accumulated over a period of years, employing proceeds of the sales to settle accounts with American merchants and manufacturers.

In order to handle the steadily increasing demand for American goods, every industrial enterprise had to operate at full capacity. This meant that every one able and willing to work found ready employment. Labor grew scarce. It was aware of its position, and took advantage of it. Salaries and wages increased by leaps and bounds. Employers did not care. Their profits rose even more spectacularly. Prices of commodities advanced sharply. Farmers obtained higher prices than they had ever been able to secure before.

While Europeans were engaged in killing one another in the Ural Mountains in the East, or in the Vosges in the West, or in the Balkans and Carpathians in the South, America played the role of merchant in munitions, manufacturing and providing them in great quantities for the Entente Allies. The nation prospered as it had prospered never before. Every phase of the economic life of the country was steadily gaining. Whatever America owed Europe could now be repaid out of profits made in the dealings with the Old Continent. America ceased to be a debtor nation. She became a creditor power, without realizing the responsibilities which go with such role. And all this for two reasons: First, America was making it possible for the belligerents to buy from her a steadily increasing output; and, Second, she managed to remain neutral. Her President had been able to keep the nation out of war, something which must have had a very strong appeal at the time to the rank and file of the population, because it re-elected the President on the grounds that he had been able to stay out of the European fracas.

On the 6th of April, 1917, the United States ceased to be a merchant in munitions. Germany had managed to antagonize America. The long controversy in regard to Germany's methods of submarine warfare culminated in the Spring of 1917, and led to the United States taking a definite position on the side of the Allied Powers.

Of 423 representatives, 373—or more than 88 per cent—adopted the resolution declaring war against Germany. The Senate adopted it by a vote of 82 against 6, or more than 93 per cent. America's legislators were impressed with the remarks of President Wilson before the 65th Congress, which met at noon on April 2, 1917, that the United States "have no selfish ends to serve, we seek no conquest, no dominion, we seek no indemnities for ourselves, no material compensation for the sacrifices we shall freely make."

With the United States a full-fledged member of the Entente Allies, the American Government was now obliged to assume the task of financing them, which previous to America's entrance into the arena had been attended to by the financial community. Whether the enthusiasm for the Allied cause would have been as great as it was, had Americans realized what such enthusiasm would cost, is difficult to say. It meant that during the next three years, the United States Government would supply the Allies, with which she had now become definitely associated, with munitions of war of one form or another, valued at more than nine thousand five hundred million dollars. In exchange, America received unsecured promises of payment at indefinite dates in the future.

Five days after the declaration of war, Representative Kitchin of North Carolina introduced in the House of Representatives a bill authorizing a bond issue of $5,000,000,000, from the proceeds of which the Secretary of the Treasury, with the approval of the President, was authorized to extend credits not to exceed $3,000,000,000 to foreign governments. Within less than two weeks, the bill, which had been passed unanimously, became law. The sentiment was freely expressed in the course of the debate in the House that, as the United States was not prepared to fight her own battles, it was only right that she should finance the Allies, who were fighting America's battles along the battlefronts of Europe. Whether or not the loans were ever repaid was a minor consideration.

In September, 1917, Congress increased the appropriation for loans to foreign governments "then engaged in war with the enemies of the United States" by $4,000,000,000—bringing the total authorization for such loans up to $7,000,000,000. In April, 1918, the authorization was raised to $8,500,000,000, and in July, 1918, to $10,000,000,000. The method of handling the financial cooperation between the United States and her associates, worked out by Secretary of

the Treasury William Gibbs McAdoo, in consultation
with the financial members of the Commissions which
the Allies had sent to America for that purpose, were
as follows:

The United States Treasury would establish credits
from time to time, against which representatives of the
borrowing nations would be, permitted to draw, as
money was required to meet payments. The uses for
the funds were to be approved by the Secretary of the
Treasury, and the borrowers were requested to furnish
statements showing for what purpose disbursements
were made. Attention may be called to the fact that, as
a result of America becoming the banker for her associates, it was no longer necessary for the latter to obtain loans in the open market. Moreover, loans which
had previously been granted by American bankers
were paid off out of proceeds of moneys borrowed
from the Government.

In February, 1918, the American Relief Administration was authorized to furnish supplies on a credit
basis to the stricken nations of Europe. In March, the
Secretary of the Treasury was authorized by the terms
of the Victory Loan Act to make advances, in addition
to those authorized in the several Liberty Loan Acts,
"for the purpose only of providing for purchases of
any property owned directly or indirectly by the United
States, not needed by the United States, or of any
wheat the price of which has been or may be guaranteed by the United States." No advances were made
under this authority, but in the appropriation acts of
1918, authorization was granted for the sale of property acquired during the war under such terms as were
deemed expedient.

Less than 24 hours after the bills authorizing loans to the Allies had become law, and three days after the British Commission had arrived in the United States, Great Britain obtained a credit for $200,000,000. By the end of the year, advances made to different countries reached a total of $3,656,129,000, equivalent to well over $10,000 a minute.

In 1918, prior to the Armistice, American advances aggregated $3,640,000,000. From December 1, 1918 to the signing of the peace treaty, June 28, 1919, $1,798,675,000 additional was advanced. After that, there were some further small advances, totalling $371,568,000.

Sums represented by the above advances were obtained from the sale to the American public of United States Government securities. These were readily absorbed by investors, institutions and individuals alike, because of the great patriotic feeling which had taken hold of the nation. It was, or should have been, realized that America had become involved in Europe's affairs, that Europe's war was America's war, that Germany was not the enemy of Great Britain and France, and Italy, Russia, Rumania, and Serbia, Montenegro and Portugal, and countless other states, but had become America's enemy. No sacrifice was too great to achieve the aims which the United States and her Allies had set out to accomplish—the crushing of a common foe.

In an official bulletin issued towards the end of 1917 by the United States Treasury Department, a number of reasons were given for the raising of funds to make possible the rendering of financial assistance to the Allies. Chief among these reasons were the following:

1. Loans are essential to America's protection.

2. America's economic protection and welfare demand that she should sell much of her production to the Allies, because output is greatly in excess of domestic consumption.

3. The commercial welfare of the Allies demands that their export trade be maintained in a suitable measure.

4. It is sound economic policy on the part of the United States to assist the Allies in maintaining their industrial life and commercial welfare.

5. Most of the money is spent in the United States for war materials and foodstuffs.

6. Purchases by Allies are supervised and made with the advice and assistance of the War Industries Board.

7. Loans enable the Allies to do the fighting which otherwise the American Army would have to do at much expense, not only of men but of money—money which would not be returned, and lives that never could be restored.

8. America is not only performing a duty in lending her Allies part of her great wealth, but also to her sailors and soldiers, in making the Allies powerful and effective "thus lessening work and danger and suffering for our own men in bringing the war to an earlier close."

When the Armistice was signed, American loans to her Allies amounted to somewhat more than seven billion dollars. While hostilities had come to an end officially, Europe was confronted with a serious problem. America's Allies, as well as her erstwhile enemies, were starving. Not only were the Central Powers in urgent need of foodstuffs, but Belgium, France, Italy, and even England, were forced for a time to continue food rationing and, for a long time, food control.

America, on the other hand, remained the land of plenty. Enormous supplies of food, which had been produced under the stimulus of high prices, and had been stored in warehouses for the use of the armies and nationals of America's Allies, were suddenly deprived of a market. Wartime prices still prevailed. Loans had stopped. Europe could no longer buy. Herbert Hoover, at that time head of the United States Food Administration, communicated with President Wilson, calling attention to the precarious situation which would develop unless ways and means were found at once to dispose of the country's huge stocks. Mr. Hoover referred especially to "the most acute situation . . . in pork products which are perishable and must be exported."

"We have in January (1919)," Mr. Hoover pointed out, "a surplus of about 400,000,000 pounds, and the French, Italian and Belgian relief and other customary orders when restored will cover 60 per cent of this . . . If there should be no remedy to this situation, we shall have a debacle in the American markets, and with the advances of several hundred million dollars now outstanding from the banks to the pork industry, we shall not only be precipitated into a financial crisis, but shall betray the American farmer who has engaged himself to these ends. The surplus is so large that there can be no absorption of it in the United States, and being perishable, it will go to waste."

Mr. Hoover's analysis of conditions was impressive. Arrangements were made to feed Europe, at the same time helping America. The Allies were enabled to continue to purchase American products at war prices, but were allowed to re-sell to neutral and former enemy countries, the proceeds to apply to further purchases in the United States. In this way, American loans to foreign governments were continued by the

United States until late in 1920. It may perhaps be
mentioned in passing that, in many instances, purchases made by the Allies in the United States were
resold, not for cash, but on credits with respect to
payment on which difficulties are being experienced at
present.

The total advanced during the first two years after
the war aggregated, exclusive of interest, slightly
more than $2,000,000,000, of which about half went
to clear up war accounts, the remainder being spent
for food and other supplies.

Loans made after the Armistice were severely criti-
cized in certain quarters. However, no less a person-
age than William Gibbs McAdoo, in his capacity as
Secretary of the Treasury, answered these critics in
his annual report laid before Congress, by pointing out
that "until certain of the allied countries can resume
their normal activities, the United States should be
prepared to sell them on credit, even after the declaration of peace, foodstuffs, raw materials, and manufactured products of which they may be in need."

The desire of the United States to maintain her
prestige during the peace treaty negotiations, and to
prevent a lapse of the defeated nations into a state of
revolution and anarchy, because of lack of food,
prompted the Government to go ahead and make the
necessary further advances. There was also another
reason: The Food Administration was loaded up with
supplies of meat and cereals for which it was essential
to find a market outside of the United States, in order
to prevent the necessity of throwing upon the home
market huge quantities of food, with a consequent
crisis in the markets for such products. This was in

line with the policy of scrapping thousands of automobiles and motor trucks owned by the Government, in order not to bring the automobile industry into ruin.

Advances to the Allied and Associated Powers, as well as credits and loans to former enemy and neutral countries which came into being as a result of the Allied victory over the Central European nations, aggregated more than ten thousand million dollars, exclusive of interest. Of this sum, about nine billion dollars represented obligations acquired under the so-called Liberty Bond Acts, which authorized the extension of credits to the Allies up to ten billions. Obligations acquired from sales of surplus war material under the Act of July 9, 1918, totalled somewhat less than $575,-000,000, of which France accounted for $407,341,145, or slightly more than 70 per cent of the total. Obligations acquired by the American Relief Administration on account of relief, by Act of February 25, 1919, amounted to $84,093,964, while bonds held by the United States Grain Corporation on account of sales of flour, under Act of March 30, 1920, aggregated $56,858,368.

What became of all these billions loaned to the Allied Powers? Do they represent funds taken out of the pockets of American taxpayers and transferred into those of the Europeans? Excluding expenditure made in the United States by neutrals and former enemy nations immediately after the war, the amount which America's Allies spent within the United States against credits advanced them, aggregated—according to Harvey E. Fisk, well-known American economist— $11,867,943,947, compared with advances of $9,466,-273,000, a difference of almost 2½ billion dollars which may be assumed to have been provided by other resources of the purchasing governments.

In other words, for every dollar advanced, America's Allies spent $1.25 in the United States. According to Albert Rathbone, Assistant Secretary of the United States Treasury, in charge of foreign loans and American financial adviser at the Paris Conference, the total expenditure of the Allies in the United States amounted to $4,275,000,000 over and above advances, equivalent to $1.45 for every dollar advanced.

The obligations of foreign governments were in the form of short term or demand certificates of indebtedness. Interest was first placed at 3 per cent per annum, and shortly thereafter increased. The advance in the rate was purely academic, because payment—except in isolated instances—was not made either at a lower or at a higher rate.

When the process of rebuilding Europe began, America was the only source where supplies could be obtained for the reconstruction of the Old Continent. Since Europe had ceased to be the political ally of the United States, loans and advances could no longer be obtained from the United States Government, but had to be secured through private channels—that is, through the flotation and sale of European securities in the American market to American investors.

It was, however, apparent that Europe, as constituted at the time, would not be able to meet payments on such obligations, as well as on political loans, that is, such obligations as were contracted during and after the war. For this reason, it was deemed necessary to arrange for an adjustment of political debts, thereby facilitating the rehabilitation of a war-torn Continent, by means of privately-arranged loans and credits. To accomplish such adjustment, there was created the World War Foreign Debt Commission, in accordance with an Act of Congress dated February 9, 1922, and entitled "An Act to Create a Commission Authorized under Certain Conditions to Refund or Convert Obligations of Foreign Governments Held by the United States of America and for Other Purposes." The Act specifically provides for the conversion or the funding of all foreign obligations received or held by the United States, including obligations owned by the United States Grain Corporation, the War Department, the Navy Department, or the American Relief Administration.

In speaking of the origin of these various obligations, the United States Secretary of the Treasury made the following pertinent statement: "It should be said that the obligations of foreign governments . . . had their origin almost entirely in purchases made in the United States, and the advances by the United States Government were for the purpose of covering payments for these purchases by the Allies."

The position of the Debt Commission was that the advances made to America's Allies were loans to be repaid, and that each debt was to be funded on the basis of the capacity to pay off the particular debtor. To this policy, the United States seems to have adhered ever since. A series of conferences commenced with the various debtor nations. Settlements were reached, providing for the resumption of payments on a basis determined by the so-called capacity of the respective European countries.

The principal amount of obligations funded in accordance with the terms set forth by the Debt Funding Commission aggregated somewhat less than ten billion dollars. If funded interest is added, the total is brought up to slightly more than 11½ billions. The value of the debt on the basis of a 3 per cent interest rate was, at the time of funding, $9,175,655,000, equivalent to slightly less than 94 per cent of the original principal. In other words, on the basis of the agreements reached with America's debtors, the United States would receive, assuming an annual interest rate of 3 per cent, 94 cents for every dollar advanced.

Details are presented hereunder (in million dollars):

	Funded Principal	Funded Interest	Total Funded Debt	Value at 3 Per Cent
Belgium.	377.0	40.8	417.8	302.2
Czechoslovakia. . .	91.9	23.1	115.0	125.0
Estonia.	12.1	1.8	13.9	14.8
Finland.	8.3	.7	9.0	9.6
France.	3,340.5	684.5	4,025.0	2,734.3
Great Britain.	4,074.8	525.2	4,600.0	4,922.7
Hungary.	1.7	.3	2.0	2.1
Italy.	1,647.9	394.1	2,042.0	782.3
Latvia.	5.1	.6	5.7	6.2
Lithuania.	5.0	1.0	6.0	6.5
Poland.	159.7	18.9	178.6	191.3
Rumania.	36.1	8.5	44.6	48.4
Yugoslavia.	51.0	11.8	62.8	30.3
Total.	9,811.1	1,711.3	11,522.4	9,175.7

Despite the much-proclaimed leniency in dealing with the obligations of America's European Allies, and those of other Continental nations, the present value of the debt, computed on a 3 per cent basis, is in all except four instances very substantially above the original principal.

It is worth calling attention to the fact that when the war debts were originally contracted, interest was placed at 3 per cent per annum, to conform to the rate paid by the United States Government on its short term certificates of indebtedness issued under authority of the Act of April 24, 1917, in anticipation of receipts from the sale of the bonds of the First Liberty Loan.

If a rate lower than 3 per cent is employed in computing the capital value of intergovernmental debts, which would seem proper in view of prevailing low money rates at which the United States can secure financial accommodations, the value on the basis of such rates would, in every case, be very materially in excess of the amounts actually advanced to the various European debtors. It is, therefore, difficult to reconcile the claims of some of America's outspoken opponents to a revision of debts, that the United States has already cancelled a substantial part of such indebtedness. The argument that America's debt has increased spectacularly, standing today at more than $22,000,-000,000, which does not permit of further "downward" adjustments, is not quite tenable. While it is true that the nation's debt has risen very considerably, the same is true of the national wealth, which has increased to well over $300,000,000,000, compared with about $187,000,000,000 prior to the war.

Those who are unalterably opposed to a re-consideration of the war debts, in spite of the many changes which have occurred in the economic and financial structure of nations since the debt funding agreements went into effect, seem to overlook one cardinal point. Reference is made to the fact that payments to the United States by the various debtor countries over a period of more than two generations, as stipulated in the respective debt agreements, are substantially in excess of the principal amount of such debts.

The subjoined table presents statistics relative to the amount originally advanced, and the sums ultimately to be received by the United States from her former allies:

	Original Principal	Amount to be Received	Amount Received for $1 of Advance
Belgium......	$ 377,029,570	$ 727,830,500	$1.93
Czechoslovakia	91,879,671	312,811,434	3.48
Estonia.......	12,066,222	33,331,140	2.78
Finland.......	8,281,926	21,695,055	2.71
France.......	3,340,516,044	6,847,674,104	2.05
Great Britain .	4,074,818,358	11,105,965,000	2.71
Hungary......	1,685,836	4,693,240	2.76
Italy.........	1,647,869,198	2,407,677,500	1.46
Latvia........	5,132,287	13,958,635	2.79
Lithuania.....	4,981,628	14,531,940	2.91
Poland.......	159,666,972	435,687,550	2.72
Rumania.....	36,128,495	122,506,260	3.40
Yugoslavia....	51,037,886	95,177,635	1.87
Total......	$9,811,094,093	$22,143,539,993	$2.26

One of the first nations to fund its debt to the United States was Great Britain. The terms of the settlement provided for the issuance of securities dated December 15, 1922 and maturing December 15, 1984, with interest payable semi-annually, June and December 15, at the rate of 3 per cent per annum from December 15, 1922 to December 15, 1932, and thereafter at the rate of 3½ per cent until maturity.

The terms of the agreement provide that Great Britain may, at its option, make payment in any bonds of the United States Government issued or to be issued since April 6, 1917, to be taken at par and accrued interest to the date of payment upon not less than thirty days' advance notice indicating the minimum amount which it is contemplated to pay at the next due date.

Great Britain has also the option, upon not less than ninety days' advance notice, "to postpone any payment of principal falling due not more than two years distant from due date, on condition that if Great Britain shall at any time exercise this option as to any payment of principal, the payment falling due in the next succeeding year cannot be postponed to any date more than one year distant from the date when it becomes due, unless and until the payment previously postponed shall actually have been made and the payment falling due in the second succeeding year cannot be postponed at all unless and until payment of principal due two years previous thereto shall actually have been made."

The above provisions relative to the payment of debts, and the nature of such payment, are applicable also to other foreign governments. With respect to the amounts ultimately to be discharged by America's debtors, it is interesting to observe from figures presented in the accompanying table that the sums scheduled to be received by the United States are, in every instance, larger than the amount originally advanced.

Great Britain, for example, is scheduled to pay a total of well over 11 billion dollars on an original advance of slightly more than 4 billion dollars, or at the rate of $2.71 for every dollar advanced by the United States to her former principal ally.

In the case of Italy, which obtained the most advantageous settlement, the total to be repaid by the Kingdom amounts to $2,407,677,500, compared with advances originally made to Italy of $1,647,869,198 —or at the rate of $1.46 for every dollar advanced.

The Kingdom of Yugoslavia ranks second from the standpoint of advantageous treatment in connection with the settlement of its debt to the United States. The basis on which the Kingdom's obligations were adjusted is equivalent to $1.87 for every dollar advanced.

The Kingdom of Belgium, which is generally believed to have received more favorable treatment than was accorded other debtors, is scheduled to repay $1.93 for every dollar received from the United States. France, with respect to which nation the United States was particularly anxious to show magnanimity, is scheduled to repay $2.05 for every dollar loaned her. Finland, which was the second of America's debtors to fund the debts, is scheduled to repay $2.71 for every dollar advanced, or equal to the treatment accorded Great Britain.

Poland ranks next with $2.72; followed by Hungary with $2.76; Estonia with $2.78; Latvia with $2.79; and Lithuania with $2.91. Rumania and Czechoslovakia are scheduled to pay very substantially more than any of the other countries, the former agreeing to repay $3.40 for every dollar which was advanced by the United States, while Czechoslovakia is scheduled to pay a total of $312,811,434, as compared with an original principal amount received of $91,879,671 —or equivalent to $3.48 for every dollar of advances.

The aggregate amount which is scheduled to be received by the United States as a result of the debt funding agreements which have been reached with America's debtor countries, is $22,143,539,993, compared with an original principal amount advanced to America's Allies and other European nations of $9,-811,094,093—equivalent to $2.26 for every dollar advanced.

It is difficult to understand how payment on the above basis can be construed as constituting a very drastic scaling down of intergovernmental obligations. While cancellation ought not to be advocated on the ground that elimination of war debts would constitute a mere transfer of the burden to the American people, it would nonetheless appear good policy to give thought to the advantages which are likely to accrue from a re-consideration of the war debts in the light of developments within the past ten years, rather than insist upon debtors carrying out the provisions of an agreement which may have seemed fair and equitable a decade ago, but which, in view of changes, has become impossible or, at least, very difficult of fulfillment.

CHAPTER VI

EXPERIENCE OF CREDITOR NATIONS

THROUGHOUT the greater part of the first generation of the 20th century, significant changes have taken place in regard to the attitude of creditor nations towards contractual obligations. The experience of the London market adequately illustrates this observation. Fifty years ago, about 54 per cent of the entire amount of foreign government obligations listed in London were in default, or about $1,660,000,000 out of a total of $3,070,000,000.[1] At the beginning of 1927, the percentage was only 24 per cent, or $1,742,-804,000 out of a total of $7,211,108,900, of which the amount of defaulted Russian bonds listed in London accounted for nearly 20 per cent.

France has for years taken an active interest in loans to foreign borrowers. It has been maintained, and rightly so, that a loan underwritten in France on behalf of a foreign country is looked upon as a political rather than an economic transaction. In consequence, default does not as a rule arouse the French ire quite so much as does a default on the part of a foreign borrower in Great Britain. The compensation for a French loan to a neighboring country need not, therefore, come in the form of interest and sinking fund payments, but in the form of political advantages

[1] *Foreign Policy Association, Information Service,* Vol. IV, No. 11, p. 242.

which accrue to the French nation. France's loans to Russia are a clear instance, and despite the huge losses experienced by French holders of Russian bonds, to certain Frenchmen these losses are apparent rather than actual, because it was these very loans which have saved France. The default on the major portion of foreign bonds held by Frenchmen is of a so-called technical nature and refers largely to the payment in paper francs when the contract calls directly or by inference for payment in gold.

The United States, the youngest and least experienced among creditor nations, has succeeded in establishing for herself a new record in regard to foreign bonds in default. The total affected exceeds all previous records established anywhere. The American investor who was persuaded to believe implicitly what salesmen of foreign bonds conveyed to him, now finds himself abandoned and left to nurse as best he can these miserable financial post-bellum babies which have gone on losing weight with each successive year until they have reached levels which constitute dim rachitic skeletons of what were once rosy roundnesses.

"Equity," says Hugo Grotius, eminent Dutch statesman and publicist, "which is required, and humanity which is praised, towards individuals, are more requisite and praise-worthy towards nations, inasmuch as injury or kindness is greater with the number."

Various methods have been used from time to time by creditor powers for enforcing payment on contractual debts. Intervention, advocated by some, is rejected by others on the ground that intervention for the collection of debts and the preservation of order should be regarded as unlawful.

The attitude of the British is contained in an address by Lord Palmerston (in his Speech on the Spanish Debt Question and his Circular to the British Diplomatic Representatives in 1848). Says Lord Palmerston: "It has hitherto been thought by the successive Governments of Great Britain undesirable that British subjects should invest their capital in loans to foreign governments instead of employing it on profitable undertaking at home, and with a view to discouraging hazardous loans to foreign governments who may either be unable or unwilling to pay the stipulated interest thereupon, the British Government has hitherto thought it the best policy to abstain from taking up as international questions the complaints made by British subjects against Foreign Governments which have failed to make good their engagements in regard to such pecuniary transactions. For the British Government has considered that the losses of imprudent men who have placed mistaken confidence in the good faith of foreign governments would prove a salutary warning to others, and would prevent any other foreign loans being raised in Great Britain, except by Governments of known good faith and ascertained solvency."

Nonetheless, the venerable Lord, on another occasion, is somewhat more explicit when he points out that "If the question is to be considered simply in its bearing on international right, there can be no doubt whatever of the perfect right which the Government of every nation possesses to take up as a matter of diplomatic negotiation any well-founded complaint which any of its subjects may prefer against the Government of another country."

Palmerston's doctrine was applied successfully in the cases of Mexico (1861), Tunis (1868), Turkey (1881), Egypt (1880), Serbia (1904), Greece (1897), and Venezuela (1902).

On the occasion of the joint intervention against Venezuela by Great Britain, Germany and Italy, in 1902, Dr. Luis Drago, Argentine Minister of Foreign Affairs, in a note addressed to the Argentine Minister at Washington, advanced the proposal, designed to constitute a corollary to the Monroe Doctrine, that "the public debt of an American State cannot occasion armed intervention, nor even the actual occupation of the territory of American nations by a European Power."[2]

The proposal at once aroused the greatest interest. Briefly, the policy was based on the ground that the public bonds of a nation are, by legislative act, an act of sovereignty; that being payable to bearer, they pass from hand to hand, from national to national, by mere delivery; that the price paid takes into account the value of the security, intrinsically and as an investment and, therefore, the credit of the issuing government; and that the issuing State is the sole judge of its ability to pay. The investor, therefore, buys with full notice and assumption of the risks and has weighed the possibilities of large profits against the danger of loss. Hence, Dr. Drago concluded, it is unfair to make the non-payment of a public bond, *not due to fraud or bad faith*, the reason for armed intervention.

The agitation for the introduction of this principle into international law persuaded Mr. Root to instruct the delegates to the Third American Conference at

---

[2] *Encyclopedia of Latin America*, p. 69.

Rio de Janeiro in 1906 to consider the subject, and to recommend that it be referred to the Hague Conference in 1907. There, the United States delegation brought it forward in a somewhat revised form providing that the use of force for the collection of contract debts is not permissible until after the justice and the amount of the debt, as well as the time and manner of payment, shall have been determined by arbitration. This proposal, which is known as the Porter proposition (having been sponsored by General Horace Porter) and as finally adopted in the Convention, by a vote of 39 in favor and 5 abstentions, reads as follows:

The Contracting Powers agree not to have recourse to armed force for the recovery of contract debts claimed from the government of one country by the government of another country as being due to its nationals.

This understanding is, however, not applicable when the debtor state refuses or neglects to reply to an offer of arbitration, or, after accepting the offer, prevents any *compromise* from being agreed on or, after the arbitration, fails to submit to the award.

The first international financial contract containing clauses providing for possible arbitration by the League of Nations was a $50,000,000 loan between Baring of London, and Czechoslovakia. This agreement provided that in the event the Government of Czechoslovakia did not fulfill the immediate obligations, and the Government and Baring Brothers, Ltd. were unable to arrive at an arrangement mutually satisfactory, the Council of the League of Nations shall be empowered to make the best arrangements for the protection of the bondholders, provided that the previous consent of the majority of the value of bondholders at a meeting provided in the general bond shall be obtained before any arrangement is accepted, or the intervention of the Council of the League of Nations is invited.

Force, or, in other words, war, has never been of any use in enforcing payment of obligations. Thomas W. Lamont of the firm of J. P. Morgan & Company, speaking before the Academy of Political Science on November 14, 1924, very aptly explained the latest attempt along these lines when he said:

It was early in 1923 that France and Belgium undertook in effect, by force, through occupation of the Ruhr, to obtain reparation payments from Germany on a large scale. Whatever may have been the moral effect of this course upon Germany, so far as collecting the debt itself force measures could be of little use. In the case of international debts that is always true. . . . The American and British bankers opposed any settlement that would cause investors in the German loan to rely upon force to secure its payment, because the bankers realized that force was never of much use in the case of international debts.

An arrangement similar to that between Czecho-Slovakia and Baring was made by an American banking house in the case of a $6,000,000 loan to the Republic of El Salvador. The loan contract provides that "any disagreement, question or difference of any nature whatever regarding the interpretation or performance of . . . contract shall be referred to the Chief Justice of the Supreme Court of the United States of America for decision, and his decision shall be final and binding. The Loan Contract is to be interpreted according to the laws of the State of New York."

The above safeguard did not prevent the issue from passing into default, by virtue of a decree by Salvador, calling for a moratorium on the entire external debt. But American investors are not to be neglected. There is a Protective Committee whose destinies are guided by man who was prominently identified with the origination and distribution of the Salvador bonds.

While there exist no legal means of compelling a nation to pay its debts, there are strong forces which cause its government to regard the maintenance of its credit in the markets of the world as of the highest importance. Chief among these is public opinion. A nation, like a private corporation, wants the good will of its customers and neighbors, and goes a long way to secure and retain it. Public opinion demands the fulfillment of promises made, especially in regard to the payment of money. A very good reason for this is that if a nation does not pay its debts, it finds difficulty in borrowing money again when it wants it, or, in other words, a desire for further loans generally acts as an inducement to fulfill outstanding obligations.

The policy of using their influence to prevent subscriptions by advertising the fact that they were in default, and otherwise doing what they could to see that people did not again loan them money, was pursued by the Council of Foreign Bondholders with regard to Peru in 1879, North Carolina and Mississippi in 1910, and Louisiana in 1913. It is also understood that the Chinese Consortium intended to put this plan into effect. Evidently, the New York Stock Exchange also had something of this nature in mind when in the Fall of 1924 it made a ruling that all foreign governments who might wish to place their bonds on America's principal market should state, among other items of information, their past debt record with respect to (a) defaults, (b) scaling down interest payments, and (c) suspending interest payments. In this connection, it is also interesting to note the remarks of Calvin Coolidge, who presumably had in mind the war debts of the Allies to the United States, when he stated in his annual message to the 1924 Congress "unless money that is borrowed is repaid, credit cannot again be secured in time of necessity."

The French Government, in the case of *Les Chemins de Fer du Sud de l'Espagne*, which had suspended payment of interest in April, 1898 on its bonds, which were largely held by French investors, while still declaring dividends to the amount of two million pesetas a year on its stock, which was held by a few Spanish people, decided, in order to protect the savings of its people that, in case the Spanish Government did not take any action toward this fraudulent practice of the railway company, or the company did not resume paying interest regularly on its contractual obligations, no new Spanish securities of any description would be granted the listing privilege of the Bourse.[3]

This plan was also put into effect by the Amsterdam Stock Exchange at the beginning of 1925, when it refused to quote Portuguese bonds, because the Portuguese Government refused to pay interest on loans in Dutch currency which, bondholders claimed, was expressly stipulated in the terms of the loans.[4]

In the case of taking legal proceedings against a foreign corporation or an individual, even though

---

[3] *L'Economiste Français*, August 13, 1910, p. 235.
[4] New York *Sun*, January 20, 1924.

action is taken collectively through a Protective Committee, or individually, the fact that parties of two different nationalities are usually involved makes the settling of disputes extremely difficult.

From a legal point of view, the countries of the western world may be roughly divided into two groups, namely, those which possess and those which do not possess codes, such as the Commerce, Civil and Criminal Codes.[5]

In the United States a system of law prevails which is largely transplanted from England. The "common law" which is recognized in that country has also become the basis of the American law system. The common law originated in custom—in what has grown to be considered as right and proper. Most of this common law is evidenced in decisions rendered in specific cases and collected in "reports." These precedents are, as a rule, followed in subsequent cases. In addition to this body of law there are certain statutes, state and federal, and the state or federal constitution, all of which together form the American body of law.

In contrast to this, the law of the countries of Continental Europe and of the majority of South and Central American States is based upon the Roman law and is laid down in codes. Usually the principal codes are the civil, the criminal, and the commerce code. They are supplemented in many cases by special laws regulating ocean shipping, bankruptcy, and bills of exchange. England, the United States and the Scandinavian countries are at present the only important commercial nations which do not possess a commerce

[5] See *Commerce Reports*, March 23, 1925, p. 677, "Companies under Different Systems of Law."

code. In countries where a commerce code is found, the corporation is usually regulated by this code, though sometimes additional laws have been passed to bring the legal treatment of the corporation more in conformity with modern practice.

In undertaking legal proceedings, one of the first essentials is a knowledge of foreign laws and the method of interpretation. By the reorganization of the Bureau of Foreign and Domestic Commerce, there has been created in that Bureau a Legal Division which is prepared to give advice concerning the best methods of pressing claims against foreign corporations or individuals. In case the Bureau deems the matter of sufficient importance, it will also communicate with the Consular Agent or other government representative abroad, with a view of ascertaining the circumstances surrounding any particular case and, if necessary, request the government's representative to do what he can to adjust matters.

The growth of international trade and finance since the World War has set lawyers thinking about the need of an international code of ethics for the protection of the public in all countries, and for the prevention of friction between nations because of commercial and legal disputes. Recognizing this need, the Ohio State Bar Association has recently appointed a committee on "International Bar Association" with authority to make a thorough study of the situation and recommend remedial action. The growing importance of international law has been recognized for some time past by such organizations as the Bureau of Comparative Law of the American Bar Association, the American Society of International Law, the International

Law Association, and those behind the recently established American Foreign Law Association, which was organized to cooperate with the Comparative Law Bureau of the American Bar Association to secure uniformity in the interpretation of laws all over the world.

This new committee on "International Bar Association" intended to seek the cooperation of all these organizations and as many of the State Bar Associations as would join.[6] It was the belief of those in back of this movement that the "International Bar Association" would not only regulate lawyers operating in foreign countries, but would also act as a clearing house where one could obtain full information regarding the record and financial stability of promotors of enterprises from other countries. This lack of complete information no doubt enables blue-sky promotors and international crooks to desert their home field and graze in ease in pastures where they are not known, and to which their "front" and fraudulent credentials gain them an entrance.

A statement given out by the Committee of the Ohio State Bar Association says in part as follows:

Our work may take years before we are ready to make final recommendations, which in some cases may involve change of laws in some countries. Among the matters which will be considered by the committee are the following:

. . . How far a system of international practice can be used to settle disputes which might otherwise become "incidents" between nations.

. . . Aiding in the compilation of the laws of the various nations to the end that the good points of each may be studied

---

[6] New York *Times*, March 29, 1925, Section 9, p. 18.

carefully for adoption elsewhere, as a means to elimination of international friction.

. . . Consideration of bringing to speedy trial international crooks and fugitives from justice.

. . . There would gradually come to be an international confidence in the law as a means of settling disputes—a means which would entail full publicity, in itself a powerful factor for good. Through the close association which an international bar would afford, the attitudes of the various courts throughout the world would tend to be unified to a large extent, and this alone is very desirable. It might even be possible in time that a case which fell within an international consciousness of right and wrong might be tried in the country where it arose, by members of the international bar from both countries involved, with judgment rendered after consideration of the laws of both nations.

The international bar would include a committee on the exchange of ideas between the various bars. This committee would consider the various laws governing certain identical cases, and would be able to recommend changes necessary to make the laws more uniform, thus tending to prevent friction between nations. . . .

In several of the European countries, bondholders of foreign governments or corporations may avail themselves of the services of permanent councils and committees, whose activities are entirely devoted to the protection of the interests of the holders of foreign government bonds. These organizations have come to wield a very potent influence in the adjustment of international financial difficulties.[7]

---

[7] See Chap. VIII for salient features of these organizations.

CHAPTER VII

PROTECTIVE MEASURES

FOLLOWING default by the Egyptian Government on its contractual obligations, the creditor nations, comprising chiefly Great Britain and France, deposed the Khedive and instituted the Anglo-French dual financial control, Major Baring and M. de Blignieres being appointed Controllers-General. This took place in 1879 or one year after the firm of Rothschild had offered to investors in England and France $42,500,000 of Egyptian State Domain 5 per cent Mortgage bonds at 73 per cent. The bonds were to be secured on the Khedivial family property transferred to the State and were to be administered by three Commissioners appointed by the British, French and Egyptian Governments. In 1880, a Law of Liquidation was promulgated in pursuance of the general recommendations of an International Commission of Liquidation, which was appointed in consequence of the Controllers-General reporting that Egypt could not meet her engagements in full. In 1904 an agreement was reached between Great Britain and France, Egypt's principal creditors, providing for important modifications in the country's financial system, which were embodied in a Khedivial Decree promulgated in November, 1904 and stipulating, *inter alia,* that a Commission and a *Caisse de la Dette* be maintained until the entire amortization of the nation's external loans should be effected, and that the *Caisse* be provided with a fixed Reserve Fund of £E1,800,000; a Permanent Balance of £E500,000; and with a sum of £750,000 to facilitate the regular service of the Debt. Egypt has since met her obligations promptly. Difficulties arose in 1924, when the Government denied its liability in respect of Turkish loans secured on the Egyptian tribute, which under the Treaty of Lausanne of 1923 became part of the Service of the Egyptian Public Debt.[1] Payments were suspended in July, 1924. Legal action was taken on behalf of the bondholders in April, 1925 and judgment was rendered in their favor on all points, an appeal of the Government against this judgment being dismissed in April, 1926, after which full payments were resumed.

In 1898, an International Financial Commission was created for the purpose of administering the then existing external debt of the Greek Government and of collecting the revenues pledged as security for the various loans. The Commission was appointed through the intervention of the six great powers after the war between Greece and Turkey in 1897-1898. Certain revenues are specifically assigned to the Commission, which applies them to the payment of interest and sinking fund on the bonds. Actual collection of these revenues and the administration of the assigned monopolies are effected through the *Société de Régie des Revenus affectés au Service de la Dette Publique,* a Greek company under the control of the International Financial Commission. After payment of interest and sinking fund of the Greek loans under its control, the

---

[1] Fifty-Fourth Annual Report of the Council of the Corporation of Foreign Bondholders, pp. 191-196.

Commission hands over to the Greek Government for
its general purposes the balance of such revenue collections for each year.

Thanks to the promulgation of the great Wilsonian
principles, including, *inter alia,* the self-determination
of nations, Austria became a free republic. Defeated
and dismembered, the Dual Monarchy was reduced to
a mere shadow of its former grandeur. When almost
on the verge of complete collapse, the League of Nations arranged for the sale of bonds on behalf of the
dying republic. The loan amounted to $126,000,000
and was secured by a lien on revenues which were to
be turned into an account controlled by a Commis-
sioner-General, whose first duty was to see that sufficient sums were retained for the service of the loan,
before releasing any sums for the uses of the Austrian
Government.

Germany was given an Agent General, Hungary
and Bulgaria and Poland Commissioners-General, to
look after the interest of bondholders whom enterprising bankers had succeeded in persuading that they
were performing the functions of good Americans
when they subscribed to bonds sold on behalf of Central European and Balkan Kingdoms.

Similar policies were adopted by American bankers
with respect to Bolivia which was to enjoy the benefits
of a Permanent Fiscal Commission appointed by the
president of the Republic, in the following manner: Two
of the three Commissioners were to be appointed by the
President upon the recommendation of the bankers. Of
these two, one was to be Chairman and Chief Executive of the Commission. In spite of these precautionary

measures, however, Bolivia suspended payments and has again been in financial difficulties, faithful to the course of her economic history.

The interference by the United States Department of State and the manner in which it is effected, is not original. By virtue of the Regulation of January 18, 1915, it was necessary to secure sanction of the British Treasury for the issue of any prospectus. Upon being consulted the Treasury would, provided it would sanction the loan in question, advise the applicant as follows: "The Treasury has been consulted under the notification dated 18th January, 1915, and raises no objection to this issue. It must be distinctly understood that in considering whether they have or have not any objections to new issues, the Treasury does not take any responsibility for the financial soundness of any schemes, or for the correctness of any of the statements made or opinions expressed with regard to them."

The ruling of 1915 affected but flotations of foreign loans in the London market. It was largely in the nature of an emergency measure rendered necessary by the war. Definite approval is known, however, to have been given by the Treasury in one important instance, which has caused as much difficulty as did the interference of the United States Department of State. The circular descriptive of the French National 5 per cent Rentes of 1916 which were sold to British investors contains the statement: "The Governor and Company of the Bank of England, with the consent and approval of His Majesty's Government, are authorized by the Government of the French Republic to receive applications for this issue." Inasmuch as bonds were scheduled to be paid in French francs, the marked decline in the value of the French currency reduced to about one-fifth the income on, as well as the principal of, the investment made by all the British patriots who were enlisted in the cause of liberty and democracy. The margin of honor in favor of France over Czarist Russia is only 20 per cent. Attempts on the part of the British to collect in full proved futile. In vain does Horace B. Samuel,[2] British economist, undertake to bring home to the French the significance of the situation. The French remain ′adamant. Their Gallic equanimity cannot be upset by the mere reasoning of an Anglo-Saxon. To the legalistic French mind there can be no question as to the nature of payment. The bonds call for francs, and not for gold francs. It is of interest to study Article 2 of the French Monetary Law of June 25, 1928, which provides, *inter alia,* that the franc, the monetary unit, should consist of 65.5 milligrams of gold, .900 fine, and that this definition should not be applicable to international payments which prior to the promulgation of the 1928 law could validly be stipulated in gold francs.

In a speech delivered in the French Senate, the *Rapporteur-Général* made the following pertinent remarks: "The drafting adopted in Article 2 has as its object to avoid foreign states or individuals benefiting by the stabilization to the benefit of French holders of obligations stipulated in gold, and consequently the new law does not touch international contracts prior to its promulgation which have been stipulated in gold,

---

[2] Samuel, Horace B. "The French Default—An Analysis of the Problems Involved in the Debt Repudiation of the French Republic," London, 1930.

that is to say, in francs as defined by the Germinal Law."

By virtue of this law, France insisted upon payment on the basis of 100 cents on the dollar from Costa Rica and Rio Grande do Norte, from Tucuman and Santa Fé, Mendoza and San Juan, while France herself complacently offered to her creditors 20 cents on the dollar.

The British critic suggests that it might have been much more dignified to reduce the value of the currency, as did the Romans two thousand years earlier, and some of the daring medieval princes! He calls it legal evaporization of external obligations, and likens France's attitude to that adopted by the Republic of Haiti. The latter had contracted, in 1897, a debt of $183,000 from an American firm, having given for it a bond to that amount. When payment appeared inconvenient, as payments ordinarily do, the Haitians introduced a bill providing for the conversion of their debt at a rate equivalent to one-third the original value. It was only after the United States intervened, that the bill was dropped. Of course, intervention in the case of Haiti was a relatively simple matter.

It is difficult to agree with our British colleague. France never obligated herself to pay in anything but francs, regardless of their value in terms of pounds. What does Mr. Samuel say in regard to Great Britain's refusal to meet the interest on bonds sold to the American investor in accordance with the provisions of the loan agreement? While the contract calls for payment in gold or the equivalent, England, creditor nation *par excellence,* calmly discharges her commitments in depreciated dollars. France on the other hand, is meeting her gold debt in gold, or at par of exchange. This refers to the Republic's commercial obligations and not to the so-called political debts which are discussed elsewhere in this study.

CHAPTER VIII

PROTECTIVE MEASURES[1] (*Continued*)

THE Corporation of Foreign Bondholders of Great Britain, was founded in 1868, incorporated in 1873 under License from the Board of Trade, and reconstituted in 1898 by Special Act of Parliament. Under that Act the Council of the Corporation consists of twenty-one members, of whom six are nominated by the British Bankers' Association, six by the London Chamber of Commerce, and nine are co-opted by the Council as a whole—that is, by the votes of both the representative and the co-opted members. A majority of the members of the Council are thus appointed by independent outside bodies.

The principal object of the Corporation is the protection of the interests of the holders of foreign securities. In addition to this, however, it keeps elaborate records regarding the economic and financial condition of the various States with whose debts it is called upon to deal, and these records are readily placed at the disposal of investors or other interested parties. The Annual Reports of the Council contain a large amount of valuable information and are circulated all over the world.

---

[1] The information regarding the organizations in various European countries for the protection of foreign bondholders is obtained from the report prepared by H. Merle Cochran, U. S. Consul at Basle, Switzerland, published as Special Circular No. 359 by the Bureau of Foreign and Domestic Commerce, August 5, 1931.

The Council may, and in some cases does, act on its own initiative. For instance, it appoints the British representatives on the Councils of the Repartitioned Public Debt of the Former Ottoman Empire and of the *Caisse Commune* of the Austrian and Hungarian pre-war Public debts, and it has frequently intervened on behalf of individuals whose rights have been prejudiced by the action of foreign governments.

As a general rule, however, the Council acts through various bondholders' committees associated with it under the rules and regulations of the corporation. In the case of the default of a foreign State, or in other circumstances where the rights of bondholders are interfered with, the practice of the Council is, on their intervention being solicited by a requisition from those interested, to convene a public meeting of bondholders, and to suggest that a committee, to take charge of the particular interests affected, should be appointed either by the meeting or by the Council on its nomination, the former course being usually adopted.

The president and vice president of the Council are *ex officio* members of all committees, and, if deemed desirable, the Council appoints one or two of its other members to serve thereon in order that the Council and the committees may be kept in touch. These committees carry on the negotiations for a settlement, and advise the Council as to whether proposals made by a foreign State shall or shall not be recommended for acceptance by the general body of the creditors. The Council, of course, reserves entire freedom of action to itself, but happily no case involving any material difference of opinion has yet arisen, and the history of the past fifty-seven years shows that the relations between the Council and the various bondholders' committees have been of a thoroughly harmonious and cordial character.

The Council provides the committees with houseroom and supplies them with skilled assistance: It places at their disposal the benefit of long experience in dealing with defaulting States and, in addition to this, advances such sums of money as it may consider desirable in order to defray the necessary expenses connected with the negotiations.

In many cases these negotiations are spread over many years, and the expenses involved are often very heavy, especially in instances like that of Virginia, where costly and complicated legal proceedings were undertaken on behalf of the bondholders against the State, and case after case was carried up to the Supreme Court of the United States. Apart from the outlays involved in such negotiations and litigation, the ordinary expenditure of the Corporation averages about £12,000 a year. In accordance with the provisions of the Act of Parliament, the president receives £1,000, the vice president £500, and the other members of the Council £100 each annually based on their attendance at meetings of the Council.

The members of the bondholders' committees affiliated with the Council act gratuitously, but on the other hand they incur no pecuniary responsibility and, if a settlement is arrived at, the Council is authorized to pay the members of the committee concerned in such settlement a moderate fee for each attendance. No such fees are, however, paid to the president or vice president of the Council, and as regards other members of the Council who serve on the bondholders' committees, the amount received by them on this account is quite insignificant.

The invested funds of the Corporation amount to about £200,000, and yield a revenue of about £9,000 a year. Any surplus remaining, after defraying expenses, becomes part of the general fund of the corporation, which is held by the Council as trustees for the benefit of British investors, and neither the president nor the members of the Council have any personal interest in it beyond the sums fixed for their remuneration by Act of Parliament, as mentioned above.

It has always been the hope of the Council that the income derived from the invested funds of the Corporation would some day be sufficient to cover all expenses, so that they would not have to make any charge whatever for their services. In most cases, however, the expenses have been borne by the Governments concerned, and no charge has fallen on the bondholders.

When it is borne in mind that the corporation has been concerned in the settlement of debts aggregating over £1,000,000,000, it is evident that even had the whole of the charges fallen on the bondholders, the percentage of cost on this amount would have been exceedingly light in view of the labor expended and the results achieved.

Resolutions expressing cordial appreciation of the services of the Council, and thanking them for their support and assistance, have been passed at public meetings of the holders of the debts of many of the countries with whom arrangements have been effected.

The *Association Nationale des Porteurs Français*

de Valeurs Mobilières (National Association of French Holders of Securities) is the principal non-governmental agency in protecting the rights of French holders of foreign securities. This association was founded in 1898, under the patronage of the Stock Brokers' Syndicate of Paris. It was recognized as of public utility by a decree dated September 24, 1919. Its board of directors includes such personages as the honorary general secretary of the Stock Brokers' Association of Paris, the under-governor of the *Credit Foncier de France*, the director-general of the Bank of Algeria, a professor of the Faculty of Law of Paris, a prominent government engineer, and the honorary inspector-general of finances. The Association Nationale is made up of groups of French holders of private French securities or of foreign securities, whether governmental or private. It does not represent the holders of rentes and other securities issued by the French State. It negotiates in the name of its members up to the point where the affair becomes one of diplomatic or government interest. It brings suits in the name of its members. When diplomatic action is taken, it serves in a consultant capacity, aiding with documentary and legal counsel. This organization controls the bulk of the interests of French holders of foreign securities. In recent years a number of other associations have sprung up in France, having for their avowed purpose the protection of the holders of some specific bonds or the bonds issued from particular areas. Many of these have, however, disappeared, some of them following disclosures of irregularities on the part of their organizers.

The German protective organization is known as

the *Staendige Kommission zur Waehrung der Interessen Deutscher Besitzer Auslaendischer Wertpapiere* (Permanent Commission for the Protection of the Interests of German Holders of Foreign Securities). The regulations of the organization were approved by the board of directors of the Central Association of German Banks and Bankers on February 24, 1927. An understanding of the working of this association can best be gained from the rules themselves, and the following is a translation of them:

1. With the cooperation of the Central Association of German Banks and Bankers, the Chamber of Industry and Commerce at Berlin for the Berlin Exchange, the Chamber of Industry and Commerce at Frankfort-on-the-Main for the Frankfort Exchange, the Committee of the Securities Exchange at Hamburg for the Hamburg Exchange, there is herewith organized a Permanent Commission for the Protection of the Interests of German Holders of Foreign Securities.

2. The founding associations are of the opinion that the protection of the interests of German holders of foreign securities against the issuing parties is primarily the task of the German banks and banking firms which participated in the emission. They consider for this reason the activities of the Commission chiefly as supplementary, that is to say, in the following sense:

(a) In cases where protection is necessary for foreign securities placed in Germany which have been issued or introduced by a bank or banking concern belonging to the Central Association of German Banks and Bankers, the protection of the interests of the owners of the securities against the issuing party is left as a matter of principle to the issuing or introducing firm, providing the latter is agreeable. The Commission will come to an understanding in such cases with the firm in question concerning eventual wishes which would be in the general interest of the banks, of the exchange traffic and of the owners of the securities, as well as with regard to measures which are to serve for the enlightenment of the owners of the securities and of the German banks and bankers with respect to the legal and actual conditions of the emissions. The Commission is to be authorized to empower the introducing firm, when negotiating with loan debtors, to act in its name; it has furthermore the right, with the consent of the issuing firm, to participate directly in such negotiations.

(b) So far as in cases sub (a), with the cooperation or acknowledgment of the issuing house, associations for the protection of the owners of certain securities are already formed, the Commission is ready to recognize the competency of these associations and will work with them by adopting the principles mentioned in sub (a).

(c) So far as in cases sub (a) the formation of special associations for protection is considered for the future, it is desired that these be organized, as far as possible with the cooperation of the Commission and the issuing firm. The Commission reserves the right to examine and to publish openly the result of its examination of the right and qualifications of protective associations otherwise organized.

(d) In cases where there is a necessity for protection, but there is no party willing or suitable to take over the protection, the Commission itself will take over the suitable measures for the protection of German owners, that is, in all cases by the establishment and direction of a special protective association. Securities which are not quoted officially on any German exchange will only be protected if, in the opinion of the Commission, it is to the interest of German economy to provide such protection.

3. The founding corporations agree that the emissions mentioned in the Enclosure I refer to Case No. 2a, and those designated in Enclosure II refer to No. 2b.

4. The Chambers of Industry and Commerce in Berlin and Frankfort-on-the-Main and the Committee of the Security

Exchange in Hamburg are to appoint two representatives each to the Commission. Moreover, the founding corporations agree that the composition of the Commission be the same as that of the committee established by the Central Association of German Banks and Bankers according to the decision of December 16, 1926, and that those parties authorized at the time to introduce motions shall retain the same rights in the present Commission. The Commission has the right to be enlarged by co-option.

5. The Commission appoints sub-committees for separate countries, when necessary for various emissions of one and the same country, without being limited to its own members. In these subcommittees the participating issuing houses are to be represented adequately.

6. For the work of the Commission, and particularly for the decisions according to No. 5 for the formation of subcommittees, a manager is to be appointed. Up to the time of the appointment of such a manager the Central Association of German Banks and Bankers is willing to take over the management temporarily.

7. Insofar as the Commission is faced with special tasks in connection with the protection of certain emissions, it is entitled to levy fees from the interested party. Apart from this, the expenses incurred by its activities will be covered by contributions from the founding corporations and the professional associations entitled to submit motions.

8. The transformation of this Commission into an association with its own legal rights is reserved; for this purpose, however, the consent of each of the founding corporations is necessary.

The enclosures to the rules consisted of three lists, I, II a and II b. The first designated the securities which should be protected by the issuing houses; the second named the bonds which would be looked after by the Association for the Protection of the Interests of German Owners of Loans of the former Austro-Hungarian Monarchy; and the third enumerated securities which would be protected indirectly through the Association mentioned in II a. The German Association maintains a deadly silence in regard to the virtual repudiation of German commitments towards nationals of other countries.

The Swiss Bankers Association, representing 250 institutions, was found in 1912. It has a special department designed to protect the rights of Swiss holders of foreign bonds. This organization, known as the *Spezial-Organisazion zur Vertretung der schweizerischen Finanzinteressen im Ausland* (Special Organization for the Defense of Swiss Financial Interests Abroad), has been found of extreme value in coordinating Swiss efforts with those of other countries in looking after the interests of its investors, particularly since Switzerland has, to a large degree, cooperated in international financing in which the syndicates included banks situated in countries other than Switzerland. Close cooperation with the other protective associations is, therefore, essential from the Swiss point of view. The Association now has seven protective committees, namely, those looking after Swiss interests in (1) The Balkans, (2) Germany, (3) France, (4) Italy, (5) Mexico, (6) the succession states of former Austria-Hungary, and (7) South America. These committees are made up of high officials of Swiss banks belonging to the Bankers Association.

In Antwerp is situated the headquarters of the *Association Belge pour la Défense des Détenteurs de Fonds Publics* (The Belgian Association for the Protection of Holders of Public Securities). This organization corresponds closely with those of other European countries, and has committees looking after interests in various areas. It cooperates very closely with the French Association and issues circulars to its members repeating many of the announcements gotten out from Paris. It is interesting to note that the Statutes of this Association expressly prohibit it from participating in Belgian politics. This organization is thorough in its study of legal phases of foreign loan questions. It includes among its executives representatives of the Antwerp Chamber of Commerce and of the *Chambre Syndicale et Arbitrale des Changes et des Fonds Publics.*

In the Netherlands the Association of Security Dealers at Amsterdam is the organization which corresponds to those of the other nations hereinabove described. This Association has 817 members as of January 1, 1930. Within the organization there is a committee for litigation, which deals with the difficulties connected with service on foreign bonds.

The French, Swiss, German, Belgian, and Dutch associations issue special circulars upon their activities whenever some accomplishment is effected, or whenever they deem it advisable to bring certain conditions to the cognizance of their members. The frequent announcements of the British Association receive wide publicity. The French Association issues a small annual report; the Belgian, Dutch, and Swiss rather comprehensive annual reports; and the British a very comprehensive report. The German Association does not issue an annual report.

In the United States, the Investment Bankers Association organized in 1919 the Committee of Foreign

Securities, presumably to protect American holders of foreign issues. The manner in which this Committee has afforded relief is current history.

The attitude on the part of the United States towards foreign loans is contained in a statement made by Henry L. Stimson, Secretary of State during the Hoover administration under date of January 7, 1932. The statement is presented hereunder in full:

The Department of State has not passed on the security or the merits of foreign loans. The sole aim of the department has been in the interest of the citizens of the United States in connection with its foreign relations.

These ideas have been repeatedly communicated to the public and the public has been made to understand that the department's action carried no implication as to government approval of loans. In fact, it may be said that no foreign loan has ever been made which purported to have the approval of the American Government as to the intrinsic value of the loan.

The arrangement in accordance with which banks or other institutions publicly offering foreign securities for sale inform the American Government of contemplated issues in advance of sale arose after the war, when the American capital market assumed leading importance as a source of financial aid and reconstruction.

President Harding early in his administration expressed informally to American bankers the desire of the government to be informed. In order to clarify the government's purposes and to establish uniformity of procedure, the Department of State on March 3, 1922, issued the public announcement attached requesting that communications regarding loans which the bankers proposed to issue, should be in writing and addressed to the Secretary of State.

The procedure of consultation between various interested branches of the government has varied slightly from time to time, as well as the range of lending activity of which the department has wished to take notice, and the phrases employed in replying to the bankers. But the principles expounded in this first public notice have remained fully in force and continue to represent accurately the basis, the purposes and the limitations of department practice.

On the whole the department does not ask that it be notified of purchases of foreign securities without intention of public sale, nor of issues of stock or listing of stock of foreign enterprises on American Stock Exchanges. Similarly, security issues of American enterprises, the proceeds of which are employed to acquire or operate properties abroad have generally not been referred to it for notice.

The practice of notifying the department of contemplated issues of securities for foreign private industrial enterprises has on the whole been less strictly observed and construed than that of notification of government security issues.

The practice was first established with the idea of safeguarding essential American interests that might be affected by the process of foreign investment; it has been maintained as an informal, comparatively light and flexible check against the possibility that contemplated loan issues might run counter to some governmental policy or aim.

At every opportunity the department has made clear to the bankers and interested public that this practice of advanced notification to the department and the absence of objection and comment by the department must in no way be considered or portrayed as approval of the loan.

The department has never assumed responsibility for the wisdom or worth of the loans of which it was informed. Its responses avoid all judgment of the matters of business risk involved, and in no way represent measurement of the merit of any foreign loan as a business proposition either for the bankers or investors.

In various instances the department, without assuming authority or taking responsibility, has pointed out to banking groups features of contemplated loan arrangements which seemed obscure or unsound, or has called their attention to some feature of the financial or economic position of the borrowing country or enterprise that might be overlooked; but all this was done merely as information and without assumption of responsibility.

This attitude has perhaps been best stated in the report of the Secretary of the Treasury of 1926:

"The question of the soundness of a particular loan is not one upon which the Federal Government should pass, but it is the banker floating the loan in this country who must decide this question in the first instance, and it is the investor using his savings to acquire the security who must finally decide whether or not the risk is to be accepted."

Furthermore, the department has guarded against the possible employment by banking houses of the exchange of communications between them and the department in such a way as to assist in the sale of securities. It instructed all institutions that announcements offering foreign loans for sale should not state that they are contingent upon an expression from the Department of State regarding them and that prospectuses and contracts should contain no reference to the attitude of the department.

Furthermore, as was stated in the report made by the Secretary of State in response to Senate Resolution No. 293 (see Senate Document No. 187, Seventy-first Congress, second session), the Department of State has often been the spokesman of considerations advanced by other executive departments of this government. For example, the Department of State carried out the policy recommended by the World War Foreign Debt Commission of objections to loans to nations which had not funded their national indebtedness to the United States.

In ordinary practice the form of words employed by the Department of State in acknowledging the advance notice of contemplated loan issues has been, with immaterial variation, as follows:

"In the light of the information before it, the Department of State offers no objection to the flotation of this issue in the American market."

Or, in the very infrequent instances where some reason led the department to the contrary judgment, the department, usually after explaining the reason therefor, employed in general merely the negative of this form:

"You will, therefore, appreciate that this department is not in a position to indicate that it perceives no objection to the financing to which you refer."

This form of reply was, after a first brief period, regularly supplemented by the further paragraph:

"You, of course, appreciate that, as pointed out in the department's announcement of March 3, 1922, the Department of State does not pass upon the merits of foreign loans as business propositions nor assume any responsibility in connection with such transactions, also that no reference to the attitude of this government should be made in any prospectus or otherwise."

Beginning August, 1929, it was decided to expedite the procedure of consultation with other departments of this government, and to simplify the forms used. Replies to bankers' letters were reduced merely to a brief paragraph of acknowledgment, followed by the sentence:

"In reply, you are informed that the department is not interested in the proposed financing."

In the case of Germany, where the German financial authorities endeavored to guard and control borrowing by public authorities and set up for this purpose an advisory board which, however, under the German Constitution could not be given mandatory powers, the department took cognizance of this situation and also of certain other special considerations, and its replies to the bankers called attention to various special features of the German situation.

The replies, therefore, took on a somewhat more extended form, preserving, however, the notice to the effect that the department did not pass upon the merits of loans as business propositions nor assume any responsibility in connection with them.

A somewhat similar policy was observed with respect to Austrian loans for a limited time.

At a conference held last Summer between the President, certain members of the Cabinet and a number of American investment bankers, the interest of the government in the public flotation of issues of foreign bonds in the American market was informally discussed, and the desire of the government to be duly and adequately informed regarding such transactions before their consummation, so that it might express itself regarding them if that should be requested or seem desirable, was fully explained. Subsequently, the President was informed by the bankers that they and their associates were in harmony with the government's wishes and would act accordingly.

The desirability of such cooperation, however, does not seem sufficiently well understood in banking and investment circles.

The flotation of foreign bond issues in the American market is assuming an increasing importance and on account of the bearing of such operations upon the proper conduct of affairs it is hoped that American concerns that contemplate making foreign loans will inform the Department of State in due time of the essential facts and of subsequent developments of importance. Responsible American bankers will be competent to determine what information they should furnish and when it should be supplied.

American concerns that wish to ascertain the attitude of the department regarding any projected loan should request the Secretary of State in writing for an expression of the department's views. The department will then give the matter consideration and, in the light of the information in its possession, endeavor to say whether objection to the loan in question does or does not exist, but it should be carefully noted that the absence of a statement from the department, even though the department may have been fully informed, does not indicate either acquiescence or objection. The department will reply as promptly as possible to such inquiries.

The Department of State cannot, of course, require American bankers to consult it. It will not pass upon the merits of foreign loans as business propositions, nor assume any responsibility whatever in connection with loan transactions. Offers for foreign loans should not, therefore, state or imply that they are contingent upon an expression from the Department of State regarding them, nor should any prospectus or contract refer to the attitude of this government.

The department believes that in view of the possible national interests involved it should have the opportunity of saying to the underwriters concerned, should it appear advisable to do so, that there is or is not objection to any particular issue.

Prior to the putting into force of the Dawes Plan in October, 1924, and the issue of the Dawes loan, there were no flotations in the American market of German loans payable in dollars, and in regard to the few public offerings of mark securities of which the department was notified by American investment houses the department merely reserved its complete liberty of action in any contingency that might arise.

The American slice of the Dawes loan, issued in October, 1924, was the first German dollar loan distributed in this country. The department in reply to the bankers' notification of this issue merely employed the common "no objection" form given above.

With the first subsequent German dollar loans, in December, 1924, the department began to call attention to various special considerations which it believed should be taken into account in arranging German financing. The earliest form used to convey these observations (as taken from a letter written in regard to a proposed issue for the State of Bremen) was as follows:

"In connection with this financing, the department has already invited your attention to the provisions of Article 248 of the Treaty of Versailles under which the cost of reparations and other costs arising under that treaty and all agreements supplementary thereto are constituted a first charge upon all the assets and revenues of the German Empire and its constituent States, subject to such exceptions as the Reparations Commission may approve.

"The department has also referred you to the provisions of a decree passed by the German Government on Nov. 1, 1924, providing that authority must be obtained from the Federal Minister of Finance for the flotation of foreign loans.

"The possible bearing of the Dawes Plan upon the future service of German loans floated in foreign markets has also been brought to your attention.

"Subject to these considerations, and in the light of the information at hand, I take pleasure in informing you that this department offers no objection to the financing in question."

In February, 1925, as exemplified in the letter written as regards the first issue of Saxon public works bonds, the form was reduced as follows:

"The department assumes that appropriate examination has been made in connection with the proposed loan of the provisions of Article 248 of the Treaty of Versailles, and of the possible effect of the Dawes Plan upon the transaction.

"Subject to the foregoing considerations, I beg to inform you that, in the light of the information before it, the Department of State offers no objection to the flotation of this issue in the American market."

During this period (October, 1924-August, 1925), in regard to the flotation of loans by private German enterprises, the department used merely the "no objection" formula in common use.

Beginning Aug. 11, 1925 (in the case of a proposed issue from the city of Munich) the department developed the following form, which, with variants, it continued until October, 1925, to send to bankers considering the issue of all German loans:

"It is presumed that in considering the disposal of these securities to your American clients you have made sufficient investigation into the purposes to which the money proceeds will be devoted to assure yourselves that the loan will increase the productivity of Germany in an amount at least sufficient to furnish, directly or indirectly, the exchange necessary for the service of the loan and to facilitate payments under the Dawes Plan. It is also presumed that, in connection with the proposed loan, you have considered the provisions of the Dawes Plan relating to the control of the transfer of German payments made pursuant to that plan.

"The Department of State does not wish to express any view at this time as to the interpretation and application of these provisions or as to their effects if any upon the service and repayment of loans such as that in question, and the department, of course, reserves full liberty to take such action if any in the matter in the future as may be appropriate. The department feels, however, that it should call these matters to your attention."

Beginning in October, 1925, a still more extensive form of reply was developed, which ran as follows (as exemplified by the city of Frankfort loan):

"Since the flotation of the German external loan provided for by the Dawes Plan, offerings of German loans in the American market have aggregated, according to the information before this department, more than $15,000,000, and it appears that a considerable volume of additional German financing is now in contemplation. In addition to the public offerings referred to above, the department is informed that a large amount of private bank and commercial credits has been extended to German interests during the past year.

"In these circumstances the department believes that American bankers should examine with particular care all German financing that is brought to their attention, with a view to ascertaining whether the loan proceeds are to be used for productive and self-supporting objects that will improve, directly or indirectly, the economic condition of Germany and tend to aid that country in meeting its financial obligations at home and abroad.

"In this connection I feel that I should inform you that the department is advised that the German federal authorities themselves are not disposed to view with favor the indiscriminate placing of German loans in the American market, particularly when the borrowers are German municipalities and the purposes are not productive.

"Moreover, it cannot be said at this time that serious complications in connection with interest and amortization payments by German borrowers may not arise from possible future action by the agent general and the transfer committee.

"While the Department of State does not wish to be understood as passing upon the interpretation or application of the provisions of the Dawes Plan, or upon their effect, if any, upon loans such as the one now under consideration by you, it desires to point out that there is no objection to the loan in question.

In the case of proposed issues of loans for constituent States of the German Reich, the department added in the above form letter a paragraph regarding Article 248, similar to the one in use in the earlier periods. This added paragraph ultimately read, with minor variants adapted to the particular case, as follows:

"A further point which the department feels should be considered by you in connection with the proposed loan is the provision of Article 248 of the Treaty of Versailles under which 'a first charge upon all the assets and revenues of the German empire and its constituent States' is created in favor of reparation and other treaty payments, subject 'to such exceptions as the Reparation Commission may approve.' "

This letter with the omission of the penultimate paragraph was stabilized Nov. 21, 1925, and continued in use with changes only in the introductory paragraph and in the reference to the indications of the attitude of the Agent General for Reparation Payments, until July, 1929, after the report of the Young committee.[2]

When the number of foreign defaulted bonds held by American investors reached a figure appreciably in excess of the amount of foreign bonds in default held in other countries, steps were taken to remedy the situation. This was done through the creation of the

---

[2] The two most important of varying forms in referring to the attitude of the Agent General for Reparations Payments were as follows:

"(1) Used in the earlier period beginning in December, 1925:

" 'Moreover, it cannot be said at this time that serious complications in connection with interest and amortization payments by German borrowers may not arise from possible future action by the agent general and the transfer committee. In this connection your attention is called to a public statement by Mr. Gilbert on Nov. 11, 1925, to the effect that the transfer committee is not in a position to give assurances concerning the payment of interest or amortization on the German loans floated abroad. While the Department of State does not wish to be understood as passing upon the interpretation or application of the provisions of the Dawes Plan, or upon their effect, if any, upon loans such as the one now under consideration by your firm, it believes that in the interest of yourselves and of your prospective clients you should give careful consideration to this question.'

"(2) Beginning in January, 1928, the following was substituted for the second sentence in the preceding form:

" 'In this connection your attention is called to the statement in the report of the Agent General for Reparations Payments on Dec. 10, 1927, that with the one exception of the German External Loan, 1924, the transfer committee and the Agent General for Reparation Payments have always stated in answer to inquiries that they were not in a position to give any assurance whatever as to the service of loans of the German Reich, the States or the communes, or of German companies or other undertakings that might be floated abroad.' "

enactment of the Corporation of Foreign Bondholders Act, approved by the President of the United States on May 27, 1933, as a part of the Securities Act of 1933. The provisions pertaining to the Corporation are presented hereunder:

Sec. 201. For the purpose of protecting, conserving, and advancing the interests of the holders of foreign securities in default, there is hereby created a body corporate with the name "Corporation of Foreign Security Holders" (herein called the "Corporation"). The principal office of the Corporation shall be located in the District of Columbia, but there may be established agencies or branch offices in any city or cities of the United States under rules and regulations prescribed by the board of directors.

Sec. 202. The control and management of the Corporation shall be vested in a board of six directors, who shall be appointed and hold office in the following manner: as soon as practicable after the date this Act takes effect the Federal Trade Commission (hereinafter in this title called "Commission") shall appoint six directors, and shall designate a chairman and a vice chairman from among their number. After the directors designated as chairman and vice chairman cease to be directors, their successors as chairman and vice chairman shall be elected by the board of directors itself. Of the directors first appointed, two shall continue in office for a term of two years, two for a term of four years, and two for a term of six years, from the date this Act takes effect, the term of each to be designated by the Commission at the time of appointment. Their successors shall be appointed by the Commission, each for a term of six years from the date of the expiration of the term for which his predecessor was appointed, except that any person appointed to fill a vacancy occurring prior to the expiration of the term for which his predecessor was appointed shall be appointed only for the unexpired term of such predecessor. No person shall be eligible to serve as a director who within the five years preceding has had any interest, direct or indirect, in any corporation, company, partnership, bank or association which has sold, or offered for sale any foreign securities. The office of a director shall be vacated if the board of directors shall at a meeting specially convened for that purpose by resolution passed by a majority of at least two-thirds of the board of directors, remove such member from office, provided that the member whom it is proposed to remove shall have seven days' notice sent to him of such meeting and that he may be heard.

Sec. 203. The Corporation shall have power to adopt, alter, and use a corporate seal; to make contracts; to lease such real estate as may be necessary for the transaction of its business; to sue and be sued, to complain and to defend, in any court of competent jurisdiction, State or Federal; to require from trustees, financial agents, or dealers in foreign securities information relative to the original or present holders of foreign securities and such other information as may be required and to issue subpenas therefor; to take over the functions of any fiscal and paying agents of any foreign securities in default; to borrow money for the purposes of this title, and to pledge as collateral for such loans any securities deposited with the corporation pursuant to this title; by and with the consent and approval of the Commission to select, employ, and fix the compensation of officers, directors, members of committees, employees, attorneys, and agents of the Corporation, without regard to the provisions of other laws applicable to the employment and compensation of officers or employees of the United States; to define their authority and duties, require bonds of them and fix the penalties thereof, and to dismiss at pleasure such officers, employees, attorneys, and agents; and to prescribe, amend, and repeal, by its board of directors, bylaws, rules, and regulations governing the manner in which its general business may be conducted and the powers granted to it by law may be exercised and enjoyed, together with provisions for such committees and the functions thereof as the board of directors may deem necessary for facilitating its business under this title. The board of directors of the Corporation shall determine and prescribe the manner in which its obligations shall be incurred and its expenses allowed and paid.

Sec. 204. The board of directors may—

(1) Convene meetings of holders of foreign securities.

(2) Invite the deposit and undertake the custody of foreign securities which have defaulted in the payment either of principal or interest, and issue receipts or certificates in the place of securities so deposited.

(3) Appoint committees from the directors of the Corporation and/or all other persons to represent holders of any class or classes of foreign securities which have defaulted in the payment either of principal or interest and determine and regulate the functions of such committees. The chairman and vice chairman of the board of directors shall be ex officio chairman and vice chairman of each committee.

(4) Negotiate and carry out, or assist in negotiating and carrying out, arrangements for the resumption of payments due or in arrears in respect of any foreign securities in default or for rearranging the terms on which such securities may in future be held or for converting and exchanging the same for new securities or for any other object in relation thereto; and under this paragraph any plan or agreement made with respect to such securities shall be binding upon depositors, providing that the consent of holders resident in the United States of 60 per centum of the securities deposited with the Corporation shall be obtained.

(5) Undertake, superintend, or take part in the collection and application of funds derived from foreign securities which come into the possession of or under the control or management of the Corporation.

(6) Collect, preserve, publish, circulate, and render available in readily accessible form, when deemed essential or necessary,

documents, statistics, reports, and information of all kinds in respect of foreign securities, including particularly records of foreign external securities in default and records of the progress made toward the payment of past-due obligations.

(7) Take such steps as it may deem expedient with the view of securing the adoption of clear and simple forms of foreign securities and just and sound principles in the conditions and terms thereof.

(8) Generally, act in the name and on behalf of the holders of foreign securities the care or representation of whose interests may be entrusted to the Corporation; conserve and protect the rights and interests of holders of foreign securities issued, sold, or owned in the United States; adopt measures for the protection, vindication, and preservation or reservation of the rights and interests of holders of foreign securities either on any default in or on breach or contemplated breach of the conditions on which such foreign securities may have been issued, or otherwise; obtain for such holders such legal and other assistance and advice as the board of directors may deem expedient; and do all such other things as are incident or conducive to the attainment of the above objects.

Sec. 205. The board of directors shall cause accounts to be kept of all matters relating to or connected with the transactions and business of the Corporation, and cause a general account and balance sheet of the Corporation to be made out in each year, and cause all accounts to be audited by one or more auditors who shall examine the same and report thereon to the board of directors.

Sec. 206. The Corporation shall make, print, and make public an annual report of its operations during each year, send a copy thereof, together with a copy of the account and balance sheet and auditor's report, to the Commission and to both Houses of Congress, and provide one copy of such report but not more than one on the application of any person and on receipt of a sum not exceeding $1: *Provided,* That the board of directors in its discretion may distribute copies gratuitously.

Sec. 207. The Corporation may in its discretion levy charges, assessed on a pro rata basis, on the holders of foreign securities deposited with it: *Provided,* That any charge levied at the time of depositing securities with the Corporation shall not exceed one-fifth of 1 per centum of the face value of such securities: *Provided further,* That any additional charges shall bear a close relationship to the cost of operations and negotiations including those enumerated in sections 203 and 204 and shall not exceed 1 per centum of the face value of such securities.

Sec. 208. The Corporation may receive subscriptions from any person, foundation with a public purpose, or agency of the United States Government, and such subscriptions may, in the discretion of the board of directors, be treated as loans repayable when and as the board of directors shall determine.

Sec. 209. The Reconstruction Finance Corporation is hereby authorized to loan out of its funds not to exceed $75,000 for the use of the Corporation.

Sec. 210. Notwithstanding the foregoing provisions of this title, it shall be unlawful for, and nothing in this title shall be taken or construed as permitting or authorizing, the Corporation in this title created, or any committee of said Corporation, or any person or persons acting for or representing or purporting to represent it—

a) to claim or assert or pretend to be acting for or to represent the Department of State or the United States Government;

b) to make any statements or representations of any kind to any foreign government or its officials or the officials of any political subdivision of any foreign government that said Corporation or any committee thereof or any individual or individuals connected therewith were speaking or acting for the said Department of State or the United States Government; or

c) to do any act directly or indirectly which would interfere with or obstruct or hinder or which might be calculated to obstruct, hinder or interfere with the policy or policies of the said Department of State or the Government of the United States or any pending or contemplated diplomatic negotiations, arrangements, business or exchanges between the Government of the United States, or said Department of State and any foreign government.

CHAPTER IX

SUMMARY

IN THE remainder of this volume, it is proposed to show, in tabular form, the extent of the defaults. It is, one is tempted to say, the temperature chart depicting the degree of fever of nations. The amount involved is staggering. It is bound to grow rather than diminish.

We stop this recital with misgiving, for our prophetic soul tells us what will happen in the future. Adjustments will be made. Debts will be scaled down and nations will start anew. The investor will receive sufficiently satisfactory explanations as to how it is to his advantage to accept new promises in place of old ones which were repeatedly broken. All will at last be forgotten. New foreign loans will once again be offered, and bought as eagerly as ever. New methods will be employed by originators and distributors of loans. Prospectuses will be made more roseate and impressive than ever. They will give more unreliable information. And the process known for more than two thousand years will be continued. Defaults will not be eliminated. Investors will once again be found gazing sadly and drearily upon foreign promises to pay.

Nevertheless, there is some hope in the future. The most proximate cause, as we have seen, has always been unwise, uninformed lending. The most effective remedy for this is the wider and more reliable dissemination of information concerning the floated loans. "Sunlight," says Supreme Court Justice Louis D. Brandeis, "is said to be the best of disinfectants." Under date of February 2, 1925, the New York Stock Exchange Committee on Stock Lists, prompted, it seems, by the desire to afford protection to purchasers of foreign bonds listed on the Exchange, issued certain regulations (in the preparation of which the writer was called upon to assist) in connection with proposed listings. The announcement referred to, follows:

COMMITTEE ON STOCK LIST
NEW YORK STOCK EXCHANGE

February 2, 1925.

FOREIGN GOVERNMENT BONDS

Data required in addition to Regular Requirements in connection with proposed Listings

1. (a) Statement of debt, internal and external, and currency in which it is to be paid; statement of external debt to be computed in dollars.
   (b) Contingent and actual liabilities, and priority.
   (c) Revenue or assets pledged, if any, under present and other loans, and nature of administration.
   (d) Summary of such revenue receipts and income from such assets for preceding five years, stated in dollars, if available.
   (e) Status of the law under which said revenue or assets are pledged.
2. Past debt record with respect to:
   (a) Defaults;
   (b) Scaling down interest payments;
   (c) Suspending sinking fund payments.
3. Where listed.
4. Currency in which interest and principal are to be paid.
5. Tax liability and exemption.

6. Statement of governmental income and expenditure for whatever account in the preceding five years.
7. Statement of the sums required, in dollars, to meet foreign interest charges in each of the five preceding years.
8. Statement in terms of weight and dollars (converted) of merchandise imports and exports in each of the preceding five years.
9. Statement of covenants, if any, with respect to payment of principal and interest of bonds dependent upon state of Peace or War and nationality of holder.

Fundamentally, there is nothing wrong with the above, but in many cases the information furnished was not what one might call accurate. The writer has always held that bankers, when issuing securities, should make public all particulars relative to new flotations, including the commissions or profits they are receiving. That is to say, let every circular, prospectus or advertisement pertaining to a foreign bond show clearly what the underwriters received and what the bonds netted the borrowing government. Let the underwriters also state the amount that is immediately turned over to the borrower or if certain sums are retained by the bankers, the nature of these balances, and the employment thereof should be clearly stated. The law should not undertake to fix bankers' profits, nor should it seek to prevent investors from acquiring securities of dubious quality. But there should be full disclosures to the investor. These will tend not only to put investors on their guard, but will also lead to an automatic adjustment of bankers' compensation to what is fair and reasonable. The Securities Act of 1933, referred to earlier, may possibly take care of the above.

GOVERNMENT, STATE AND CITY BONDS IN DEFAULT (DIRECT AND CONTINGENT)

Issue	Amount Issued	Amount Outstanding	Interest in Arrears
ARGENTINA			
Buenos Aires (Province) 7½s, 1925–47	$ 14,472,000	$ 11,534,100	$ 865,055
Buenos Aires (Province) 7s, 1926–52	10,600,000	9,195,300	643,670
Buenos Aires (Province) 6s, 1928–61	41,101,000	38,878,000	2,332,680
Buenos Aires (Province) 6½s, 1930–61	11,675,000	10,904,500	708,790
Cordoba (City) 7s, 1927–57	4,669,500	4,254,500	446,745
Cordoba (City) 7s, 1927–37	2,547,000	1,477,000	103,390
Corrientes (Province) 6s, 1910–25	1,984,125	496,525	402,185
Mendoza (Province) 7½s, 1926–51	6,500,000	5,533,500	415,010
Santa Fe (Province) 5s, 1910–60	9,576,000	8,018,100	801,810
Santa Fe (Province) 7s, 1924–42	10,188,000	7,472,500	784,610
Rosario (City) 4s, 1907	10,000,000	9,975,875	598,550
Santa Fe (City) 6s, 1889	1,500,000	1,455,000	130,950
Santa Fe (City) 7s, 1927–45	2,122,500	1,752,000	183,960
Tucuman (City) 7s, 1928–51	3,396,000	2,917,000	306,285
Total	$130,331,125	$113,863,900	$8,723,690
AUSTRIA			
Upper Austria 7s, 1925–45	$ 5,000,000	$ 3,963,000	$ 416,115
Upper Austria 6½s, 1927–57	7,500,000	7,032,500	685,670
Lower Austria 7½s, 1925–50	2,000,000	1,767,500	198,845
Lower Austrian Hydro-El. 6½s, 1924–44	3,000,000	2,215,500	216,010
Styria 7s, 1926–46	5,000,000	3,459,900	363,290
Graz 8s, 1924–54	2,500,000	2,341,400	280,970
Tyrol Hydro-Electric 7s, 1927–52	3,000,000	2,668,000	93,380
Tyrol Hydro-Electric 7½s, 1925–55	3,000,000	2,753,000	103,235

Vienna 6s, 1927–52	2,449,350	27,215,000	30,000,000
Total	$4,806,865	$53,415,800	$61,000,000
BOLIVIA			
Bolivia 6s, 1917–40	$ 233,280	$ 1,296,000	$ 2,400,000
Bolivia 8s, 1922–47	3,045,935	22,072,000	29,000,000
Bolivia 7s, 1927–58	1,403,220	13,364,000	14,000,000
Bolivia 7s, 1928–69	4,764,900	22,690,000	23,000,000
Bolivia 7s, 1930–50	202,285	1,926,525	2,000,000
Total	$9,649,620	$61,348,525	$70,400,000
BRAZIL			
A—Sterling Debt			
4½s of 1883	£ 202,500	£ 2,250,000	£ 4,599,600
4½s of 1888	243,335	3,605,000	6,297,300
4s of 1889	996,000	16,600,000	19,837,000
5s of 1895	492,000	6,560,000	7,422,000
4s of 1900	809,320	10,116,500	16,619,320
5s of 1903–05	538,125	7,175,000	8,500,000
5s of 1908	73,000	730,000	4,000,000
4s of 1910	569,700	9,495,000	10,000,000
4s of 1911 (Port of Rio)	204,900	3,415,000	4,500,000
4s of 1911 (Ceará Rwy.)	187,480	2,343,500	2,400,000
5s of 1913	795,035	10,600,500	11,000,000
6½s of 1927	816,560	8,375,000	8,750,000
Total	£ 5,927,955	£ 81,265,500	£103,925,220
Idem, in dollars	$29,639,775	$406,327,500	$519,626,100

GOVERNMENT, STATE AND CITY BONDS IN DEFAULT (DIRECT AND CONTINGENT) (*Continued*)

Issue	Amount Issued	Amount Outstanding	Interest in Arrears
BRAZIL (*Continued*)			
B—*Franc Debt*			
5s of 1908–09	Fcs. 100,000,000	Fcs. 97,250,000	Fcs. 9,725,000
5s of 1909	40,000,000	39,450,000	3,945,000
4s of 1910	100,000,000	96,720,000	7,737,600
5s of 1910 (Curralinho-Diamantina Ry.)	14,850,500	14,638,000	1,463,800
4s of 1911	60,000,000	59,220,000	4,737,600
5s of 1916 (Goyaz Ry.)	25,000,000	24,350,000	2,435,000
Total	Fcs. 339,850,500	Fcs. 531,628,000	Fcs. 30,044,000
Idem, in dollars	$ 67,970,000	$ 66,325,600	$ 6,008,800
C—*Dollar Debt*			
8s of 1921	$ 50,000,000	$ 31,352,000	$ 5,016,320
7s of 1922	25,000,000	17,503,000	2,450,420
6½s of 1926	60,000,000	56,108,000	7,294,040
6½s of 1927	41,500,000	39,709,000	5,162,170
Total	$176,500,000	$144,672,000	$19,922,950
Alagoas 5s, 1906–58	1,500,000	1,500,000	450,000
Alagoas 5s, 1909–58	1,000,000	1,000,000	300,000
Amazonas 5s, 1906–57	16,800,000	16,047,300	13,239,020
Amazonas Funding 5s, 1915–25	4,100,000	4,011,820	3,309,750
Manaos (City) 5½s, 1906–36	1,750,000	1,349,000	1,261,315
Bahia 5s, 1888–1939	1,600,000	1,302,900	130,290
Bahia 5s, 1904/05–55	5,311,800	4,874,600	487,460

Bahia 5s, 1910-60	9,000,000	8,335,800	833,580
Bahia 5s, 1913-63	5,000,000	4,879,900	487,990
Bahia Funding 5s, 1915	3,936,650	3,221,400	322,140
Bahia 6s, 1918-33	1,775,000	489,785	48,980
Bahia 7s, 1930-33	1,474,500	981,675	98,165
Bahia Funding 5s, 1928-33	1,692,500	1,678,600	167,860
Bahia (City of) 5s, 1905-40	5,000,000	4,304,000	3,228,000
Bahia (City of) 5s, 1912/13-63	8,000,000	7,981,500	5,986,125
Bahia (City of) 6s, 1914	7,605,000	7,605,000	8,213,400
Bahia (City of) 5s, 1916-46	4,200,000	4,200,000	3,360,000
Ceará 5s, 1910-48	3,000,000	2,480,000	1,264,255
Ceará 8s, 1922-47	2,000,000	1,980,000	475,200
Espírito Santo 5s, 1908-48	6,000,000	550,100	55,010
Espírito Santo 5s, 1919-73	199,600	199,600	19,960
Maranhão 5s, 1910-42	3,600,000	3,372,500	337,250
Maranhão 7s, 1928-58	1,750,000	1,682,000	235,480
Minas Geraes 5s, 1907-47	5,000,000	623,300	62,330
Minas Geraes 4½s, 1910-73	24,000,000	4,280,000	385,200
Minas Geraes 4½s, 1911-74	10,000,000	1,937,600	174,385
Minas Geraes 5½s, 1916-40	4,195,800	1,347,700	148,245
Minas Geraes 6½s, 1928-58	8,500,000	8,132,000	1,003,815
Minas Geraes 6½s, 1928-58	8,750,000	8,425,500	1,095,315
Minas Geraes 6½s, 1929-59	8,000,000	7,812,000	1,015,560
Bella Horizonte 6s, 1905-33	1,125,000	199,600	23,950
Pará 5s, 1901-51	7,250,000	6,348,900	2,857,000
Pará 5s, 1907-45	3,250,000	2,844,800	1,778,000
Pará 5s, 1915-56	5,350,000	5,183,400	3,239,625
Pará (Port of) 5½s, 1906-10	18,000,000	15,706,400	10,600,000
Pará (Port of) 5s, 1911-13	22,263,600	20,043,500	10,963,810
Pará (City of) Improvements Co., Ltd. 5s, 1915	2,000,000	2,000,000	1,300,000

GOVERNMENT, STATE AND CITY BONDS IN DEFAULT (DIRECT AND CONTINGENT) (*Continued*)

Issue	Amount Issued	Amount Outstanding	Interest in Arrears
BRAZIL (*Continued*)			
Belém 5s, 1905–55	$ 5,000,000	$ 4,605,200	$ 2,993,380
Belém 5s, 1906–58	3,000,000	2,852,000	1,853,800
Belém 5s, 1912	3,000,000	2,954,300	1,920,295
Belém 6s, 1919–29	1,363,300	1,363,300	1,063,475
Belém Funding 5s, 1915	4,425,000	4,057,400	2,637,310
Paraná 5s, 1905–55	4,000,000	1,200,000	120,000
Paraná 5s, 1913–73	7,070,000	3,888,500	388,850
Paraná Funding 6s, 1916–41	1,332,695	784,560	94,145
Paraná 7s, 1928–58	4,860,000	4,642,000	649,880
Paraná 7s, 1928–58	5,000,000	4,757,500	666,050
Pernambuco 5s, 1904/05–42	5,000,000	2,568,200	256,820
Pernambuco 5s, 1909–47	7,500,000	5,277,000	659,625
Pernambuco 7s, 1927–47	6,000,000	5,233,000	915,775
Pernambuco (City) 5s, 1910–60	2,000,000	1,361,400	136,140
Rio de Janeiro 5½s, 1927–49	9,632,500	8,571,300	1,178,555
Rio de Janeiro 7s, 1927–64	10,500,000	9,455,000	1,985,550
Rio de Janeiro 6½s, 1929–59	6,000,000	5,961,000	580,975
Nictheroy 7s, 1928–68	4,000,000	3,914,500	685,035
Rio de Janeiro (City) 5s, 1904–54	20,000,000	17,178,400	2,146,750
Rio de Janeiro (City) 4½s, 1912–51	12,500,000	8,867,100	997,550
Rio de Janeiro (City) 8s, 1921–46	12,000,000	8,055,000	1,933,200
Rio de Janeiro (City) 6½s, 1928–53	30,000,000	29,492,000	4,495,555
Rio de Janeiro (City) 6s, 1928–33	1,770,000	1,770,000	265,500
Rio Grande do Norte 5s, 1910–48	1,750,000	1,335,000	166,875
Rio Grande do Sul 8s, 1921–46	10,000,000	5,900,500	1,416,120
Rio Grande do Sul 7s, 1926–66	10,000,000	9,746,000	1,705,750

Rio Grande do Sul 7s, 1927–67	4,000,000	3,912,500	684,685
Rio Grande do Sul 6s, 1928–68	23,000,000	23,000,000	3,450,000
Pelotas 5s, 1911–61	3,000,000	2,154,200	269,275
Porto Alegre 5s, 1909–44	3,000,000	1,530,000	191,250
Porto Alegre 8s, 1921–61	3,500,000	3,320,000	664,000
Porto Alegre 7½s, 1926–66	4,000,000	3,890,000	583,500
Santa Catharina 5s, 1909–35	1,250,000	341,130	511,695
Santa Catharina 8s, 1922–47	5,000,000	4,704,800	1,557,285
São Paulo 5s, 1904–34	5,000,000	839,200	83,920
São Paulo 5s, 1905–44	19,000,000	10,899,845	817,485
São Paulo 5s, 1907–57	10,080,000	8,016,000	601,200
São Paulo 8s, 1921–36	27,236,000	16,925,200	2,708,030
São Paulo 8s, 1925–50	15,000,000	14,719,000	1,884,030
São Paulo 7½s, 1926–56	50,000,000	45,574,500	5,127,130
São Paulo 7s, 1926–56	20,000,000	18,427,000	2,044,400
São Paulo Mtge. Bank 6s, 1927/28	18,750,000	16,641,000	1,996,920
São Paulo 6s, 1928–68	15,000,000	14,698,000	1,763,760
São Paulo 6s, 1928–68	17,500,000	17,148,000	2,058,760
São Paulo (City) 6s, 1908–43	3,750,000	2,001,550	1,801,395
São Paulo (City) 8s, 1922–52	4,000,000	3,156,500	631,300
São Paulo (City) 6½s, 1927–57	5,900,000	5,602,000	910,325
Santos 7s, 1927–57	11,300,000	10,914,600	1,910,055
Total	$1,445,045,045	$1,169,433,065	$198,693,350

BULGARIA

Bulgaria 7s, 1927–67	$16,500,000	$15,683,000	$1,097,810
Bulgaria 7½s, 1928–68	27,200,000	26,883,500	2,016,250
Bulgaria 6s, 1892	24,992,500	720,415	43,225
Bulgaria 5s, 1902	21,200,000	15,874,815	793,750
Bulgaria 5s, 1904	20,000,000	15,769,630	789,475

GOVERNMENT, STATE AND CITY BONDS IN DEFAULT (DIRECT AND CONTINGENT) (*Continued*)

Issue	Amount Issued	Amount Outstanding	Interest in Arrears
BULGARIA (*Continued*)			
Bulgaria 4½s, 1907.............	$ 29,000,000	$ 25,329,255	$ 1,139,815
Bulgaria 4½s, 1909.............	20,000,000	3,197,500	143,885
Bulgaria 6½s, 1923 (Mixed Arbitration Courts)..	1,943,410	1,943,410	126,320
Bulgaria 7s, 1923 (Declosiere Loan)...	630,445	630,445	44,125
Bulgaria 5s, 1930 (Italian Issue)...	94,295	94,295	4,715
Bulgaria 5s, 1930 (Rumanian Issue)...	340,735	340,735	17,035
Sofia 4½s, 1910–59.............	3,000,000	2,438,100	165,000
Total.............	$164,901,385	$108,905,100	$6,381,405
CANADA (*See Notes*)			
CHILE			
Antofagasta 5s, 1913.............	$ 1,000,000	$ 394,000	$ 39,400
Chile 4½s, 1885.............	4,044,500	191,000	17,190
Chile 4½s, 1886.............	30,050,000	5,319,500	478,755
Chile 4½s, 1887.............	5,801,000	730,500	65,745
Chile 4½s, 1889–1941.............	7,731,950	3,134,160	282,075
Chile 5s, 1892.............	9,000,000	3,310,000	331,000
Chile 4½s, 1893.............	3,150,000	1,060,500	95,440
Chile 4½s, 1895.............	10,000,000	4,155,000	360,925
Chile 5s, 1896.............	20,000,000	8,868,500	886,850
Chile 4½s, 1899 (Coquimbo Ry.).............	1,300,400	542,800	48,850
Chile 5s, 1905 (Internal Gold Loan).............	2,372,500	1,132,500	113,250
Chile 5s, 1905.............	6,750,000	3,427,000	342,700
Chile 5s, 1909.............	15,000,000	11,154,500	1,115,450
Chile 5s, 1910.............	13,000,000	7,079,400	707,940

Chile 5s, 1911	49,525,000	28,739,800	2,873,980
Chile 4½s, 1911	1,375,000	505,800	45,020
Chile 7½s, 1922	8,287,500	7,567,000	1,135,050
Chile 7s, 1922-42 (Internal Loan)	18,000,000	15,089,000	2,112,460
Chile 8s, 1924-26 (Internal Loan)	456,000	223,500	35,760
Chile 6s, 1928 (Railway Refunding)	45,912,000	44,152,000	5,298,240
Chile 6s, 1929-61 (Swiss Issue)	5,000,000	4,895,200	587,425
Chile 6s, 1930-62 (Swiss Issue)	12,000,000	11,814,000	1,417,280
Chile 6s, 1930-63	25,000,000	24,745,000	2,969,400
Chile 8s, 1922-50 (Internal Loan)	1,200,000	1,139,400	182,300
Chile 6s, 1926 (Sterling Issue)	14,045,000	13,608,500	1,633,020
Chile 6s, 1926-60	42,500,000	40,116,000	4,813,920
Chile 6s, 1927-61	27,500,000	25,935,000	3,112,200
Chile 6s, 1928-61	10,000,000	9,735,000	1,168,200
Chile 6s, 1928-61	16,000,000	15,577,000	1,869,240
Chile 6s, 1929-62 (Sterling Issue)	10,000,000	9,791,000	1,174,920
Chile 6s, 1929-62	10,000,000	9,790,000	948,000
Chile 6¼s, 1931	8,000,000	8,000,000	1,080,000
Chile 7s, 1929-60 (Consol. Munics.)	15,000,000	14,684,000	2,055,760
Concepcion 5¼s, 1928	750,000	722,000	79,420
Mortgage Bank External 5s, 1911-12	10,260,000	5,391,000	539,100
Mortgage Bank 6½s, 1925-57	20,000,000	18,612,000	2,419,560
Mortgage Bank 6¾s, 1926-61	20,000,000	13,365,000	1,804,275
Mortgage Bank 6s, 1926-31	10,000,000	10,000,000	1,200,000
Mortgage Bank 6s, 1928-61	20,000,000	19,353,000	2,322,360
Mortgage Bank 6s, 1929-62	20,000,000	19,582,000	2,349,840
Santiago 7s, 1928-49	4,000,000	3,600,000	504,000
Santiago 6s, 1929-62 (Swiss Issue)	5,000,000	4,923,000	590,760
Santiago 7s, 1930-61	2,200,000	2,175,500	304,570
South Longitudinal Ry. 5s, 1912-13-14	19,286,950	8,626,500	862,650

GOVERNMENT, STATE AND CITY BONDS IN DEFAULT (DIRECT AND CONTINGENT) (Continued)

Issue	Amount Issued	Amount Outstanding	Interest in Arrears
CHILE (Continued)			
Transandine Ry. 8s, 1922–52	$ 4,125,000	$ 3,609,950	$ 577,590
Transandine Ry. 7½s, 1923–53	2,710,000	2,472,080	370,810
Valparaiso 5½s, 1912	1,250,000	609,000	66,990
Valparaiso 6s, 1915–39	480,000	229,000	27,480
Valparaiso-Viña del Mar (Avenida España) 8s, 1920–22	720,000	698,500	11,175
Viña del Mar 5s, 1913	1,000,000	485,700	48,570
Total	$590,782,800	$451,060,790	$53,476,895
CHINA			
Austrian Loan 8s, 1912/15	$ 6,165,000	$ 6,165,000	$ 8,381,400
Austrian Loan 6s, 1914	23,750,000	23,750,000	24,225,000
Canton Kowloon Ry. 5s, 1907–37	7,500,000	5,552,500	1,539,750
China Internal issues (various)	....	27,550,000	27,550,000
China Treasury Notes 6s, 1919–21	5,500,000	5,500,000	4,950,000
Federal Wireless 8s, 1921–31	2,083,750	2,083,750	1,483,400
Federal Wireless Supplemental 8s, 1921–41	6,500,000	6,500,000	6,240,000
French 5s, 1914–64	20,000,000	20,000,000	11,000,000
Honan Ry. 5s, 1905–35	4,000,000	2,478,500	969,440
Hukuang Ry. 5s, 1911–51	30,000,000	28,184,300	6,341,470
Improvement Development of Tel. 9s, 1920–33	7,500,000	7,500,000	8,100,000
Lung-Tsing-U-Hai Ry. 5s, 1913–57	20,000,000	20,000,000	7,000,000
Lung-Tsing-U-Hai Ry. 8s, 1922–33	10,240,000	10,240,000	5,713,400

Lung-Tsing-U-Hai Ry. 8s, 1923–33	27,588,600	27,588,600	2,091,415
Lung-Tsing-U-Hai Ry. 8s, 1925–35	4,250,000	4,250,000	2,880,000
Marconi Wireless Advance 8s, 1918–22	1,000,000	1,000,000	880,000
Marconi Wireless 8s, 1918–28	3,000,000	3,000,000	1,980,000
Mitsui Wireless Agreement 8s, 1919	2,681,335	2,681,335	1,769,015
National Wireless Telegraph 8s, 1919	500,000	500,000	480,000
Nishihara Loans:			
Bank of Communications 7½s, 1918	10,000,000	10,000,000	5,250,000
Mine and Forestry 7½s, 1918–28	15,000,000	15,000,000	7,875,000
Miscellaneous issues	25,000,000	25,000,000	11,250,000
War Participation 7s, 1918	10,000,000	10,000,000	4,900,000
Pacific Development Loan 6s, 1916	5,500,000	5,500,000	5,940,000
Pekin-Hankow Ry. 5s, 1911–36	5,000,000	2,690,000	1,444,000
Pekin-Mukden Ry. 6s, 1914–34	1,875,000	1,875,000	690,000
Refunding 8s, 1922–28	19,804,350	19,804,350	12,668,695
Seven Per Cent Loan of 1917/18–20/21	15,000,000	15,000,000	12,600,000
Shanghai-Taku Cable 5s, 1900–30	1,050,000	1,050,000	630,000
Telegraph 8s, 1918–23	10,000,000	10,000,000	9,600,000
Telegraph Charges Advance 5s, 1911–30	2,500,000	2,500,000	1,500,000
Taku-Chefoo Cable 5s, 1900–30	240,000	240,000	144,000
Telephone Extension 8s, 1918–21	5,000,000	5,000,000	4,800,000
Tientsin-Pukow Ry. 5s, 1908–38	25,000,000	18,075,750	6,325,110
Tientsin-Pukow Ry. Supplementary Loan 5s, 1910–40	15,000,000	7,652,640	2,981,060
Treasury Notes 6s, 1916–19	5,500,000	5,500,000	4,620,000
Treasury Notes 6s, 1919–21	5,500,000	5,500,000	3,960,000
Vickers Treasury 8s, 1919–29	9,016,000	9,016,000	7,934,080
Total	$368,244,035	$346,377,725	$228,686,235

GOVERNMENT, STATE AND CITY BONDS IN DEFAULT (DIRECT AND CONTINGENT) (*Continued*)

Issue	Amount Issued	Amount Outstanding	Interest in Arrears
COLOMBIA			
Colombia 5s, 1906 (Bogota-Sabana Ry.)......	$ 1,500,000	$ 438,700	$ 7,310
Colombia 6s, 1911-41..............	1,500,000	612,800	12,255
Colombia 6s, 1913-47........	7,336,840	4,043,850	80,875
Colombia 5s, 1916-83 (Central Ry.)....	400,000	236,750	3,950
Colombia 6s, 1920-54 (North Central Ry.).....	2,142,900	1,685,700	33,715
Colombia 6s, 1927-61............	25,000,000	23,171,500	463,430
Colombia 6s, 1928-61............	35,000,000	32,691,500	653,830
Agricultural Mortgage Bank 7s, 1926-46.	3,000,000	1,983,000	92,540
Agricultural Mortgage Bank 7s, 1927-47.	3,000,000	2,627,000	122,595
Agricultural Mortgage Bank 6s, 1927-47.	5,000,000	3,634,000	72,680
Agricultural Mortgage Bank 6s, 1928-48.	5,000,000	3,960,000	158,400
Agricultural Mortgage Bank 6½s 1929-59 (Sterling Issue)........	6,000,000	5,783,500	125,340
Antioquia Gold 8s, 1926-46.	857,970	837,040	133,925
Antioquia 7s, 1925-45 Ser. A.	6,000,000	5,088,100	712,335
Antioquia 7s, 1925-45 Ser. B	6,000,000	5,042,600	705,965
Antioquia 7s, 1925-45 Ser. C.	2,500,000	2,100,800	294,110
Antioquia 7s, 1925-45 Ser. D.	5,500,000	4,940,500	691,670
Antioquia 7s, 1927-57 1st Ser.	4,000,000	3,716,000	530,240
Antioquia 7s, 1927-57 2nd Ser.	4,000,000	3,670,000	513,800
Antioquia 7s, 1927-57 3rd Ser.	4,350,000	4,121,000	576,940
Barranquilla 8s, 1925-49.	2,500,000	1,780,400	213,650
Bogota 8s, 1924-45......	6,000,000	4,749,000	759,840
Bogota 6½s, 1927-47......	2,700,000	2,257,500	293,475
Caldas 7½s, 1926-46......	10,000,000	8,591,000	966,485
Cauca Valley 7½s, 1926-46.	4,000,000	3,408,500	383,455

Cauca Valley 7s, 1928–48	4,500,000	3,865,000	541,100
Cali 7s, 1927–47	2,885,000	2,408,000	337,120
Cundinamarca 6½s, 1928–59	12,000,000	11,537,000	1,272,300
Medellin 7s, 1926–51	3,000,000	2,644,000	434,675
Medellin 6½s, 1928–54	9,000,000	8,378,000	1,285,185
Santander 7s, 1928–48, Ser. A	2,000,000	1,791,000	200,590
Tolima 7s, 1927–47	2,500,000	2,112,000	238,650
Total	$189,172,710	$163,905,740	$12,912,430
COSTA RICA			
Costa Rica 5s, 1911–58	$8,847,300	$7,364,000	$184,100
Costa Rica 5s, 1911–46 (French issue)	7,000,000	958,700	71,900
Costa Rica 6s, 1912–42 (Mortgage Issue)	943,600	423,800	12,715
Costa Rica 7s, 1926–51	8,000,000	7,198,000	590,235
Costa Rica 7½s, 1927–49 (Pacific Railway)	1,800,000	1,746,000	197,925
Costa Rica (Government Credit)	1,000,000	1,000,000	60,000
Total	$27,590,900	$18,690,500	$1,116,875
ECUADOR			
Ecuador 4s, 1904 (Condores)	$389,500	$356,500	$213,900
Ecuador 4s, 1908 (Salt Loan)	1,075,500	459,900	73,590
Ecuador 6s, 1909–46 (Port of Bahia de Caraquez)	700,000	700,000	860,000
Ecuador 6s, 1911–58 (Central Railway)	1,000,000	637,500	798,250
Ecuador 6s, 1916–50 (Central Railway)	212,500	212,500	216,750
Ecuador 8s, 1953	1,986,900	1,986,900	476,855
Ecuador Railway 5s, 1909–73	1,400,000	1,400,000	1,360,000
Ecuador Mortgage Bank 7s, 1949	1,000,000	1,000,000	210,000
Guayaquil & Quito 5s, 1899–1932	12,282,000	10,722,000	10,185,900
Total	$20,046,400	$17,475,300	$14,395,245

GOVERNMENT, STATE AND CITY BONDS IN DEFAULT (DIRECT AND CONTINGENT) (*Continued*)

GERMANY

Issue	Amount Issued	Amount Outstanding	Interest in Arrears
German 6s, 1930–80 (Match Loan)	$50,000,000	$50,000,000	$ 1,500,000
Anhalt 7s, 1926–46	2,000,000	1,400,000	49,000
Bavaria 6½s, 1925–45	25,000,000	18,732,000	608,790
Bremen 7s, 1925–35	15,000,000	10,727,000	375,445
Hamburg 6s, 1923–73 (British Issue)	4,539,780	3,817,020	114,510
Hamburg 6s, 1926–46	10,000,000	10,000,000	300,000
Hamburg 6s, 1926–51 (British Issue)	10,000,000	10,000,000	300,000
Oldenburg 7s, 1925–45	3,000,000	2,364,000	82,740
Prussia 6s, 1927–52	30,000,000	26,918,000	807,540
Prussia 6½s, 1926–51	20,000,000	19,743,000	641,645
Saxony 6s, 1927–52 (British Issue)	3,750,000	3,432,800	102,985
Westphalia 7s, 1926–51 (British Issue)	4,175,000	3,756,500	131,475
Wurttemberg 6½s, 1931–56 (Swiss Issue)	5,000,000	5,000,000	162,500
Wurttemberg Consol. Municipal 7s, 1925–45	8,400,000	5,880,000	205,800
Hanover 6s, 1927–57 (Hartz Water Works)	1,000,000	982,500	29,475
Hanover 6½s, 1929–49 (Hartz Water Works)	4,000,000	3,930,500	127,740
Baden Consol. Municipal 7s, 1926–51	4,500,000	3,691,500	129,200
Bavarian Palatinate Consol. Cities 7s, 1926–45	3,800,000	3,134,500	109,705
Berlin 6s, 1928–58	15,000,000	14,066,000	421,980
Berlin 6½s, 1925–50	15,000,000	11,355,000	369,035
Berlin 6s, 1927–57 (British Issue)	17,500,000	16,601,000	498,030
Cologne 6½s, 1925–50	10,000,000	7,983,000	259,445
Cologne 6s, 1928–53 (British Issue)	5,750,000	5,325,500	159,765
Dresden 7s, 1925–45	5,000,000	3,420,500	119,715
Dresden 5½s, 1927–52 (British Issue)	3,000,000	2,672,500	73,495
Duesseldorf 7s, 1925–45	1,750,000	1,137,500	39,810

Duisburg 7s, 1925–45	3,000,000	1,950,000	68,250
Frankfurt-on-Main 6½s, 1928–53	6,250,000	5,837,000	189,700
Frankfurt-on-Main 7s, 1925–45	4,000,000	2,600,000	91,000
Hanover (City) 7s, 1929–39	3,500,000	3,374,000	118,090
Heidelberg 7½s, 1925–50	1,500,000	1,287,000	48,260
Leipzig 7s, 1926–47	5,000,000	4,121,000	144,235
Munich 7s, 1925–45	8,700,000	5,655,000	197,925
Munich 6s, 1928–53 (British Issue)	8,125,000	8,125,000	243,750
Nuremberg 6s, 1927–52	5,000,000	4,082,000	122,460
Central Bank 6s, 1927–52	5,000,000	4,243,000	127,290
Central Bank 6s, 1927–51	10,000,000	6,025,000	180,750
Consol. Agricultural Bank 6½s, 1958	25,000,000	20,378,500	652,305
Building & Land Bank 6½s, 1928–48	5,250,000	4,981,000	161,880
Consolidated Municipal 6s, 1928–47	17,500,000	15,233,000	456,990
Consolidated Municipal 7s, 1926–47	23,000,000	18,985,000	664,475
Consolidated Municipal 5s, 1926–36 (Swiss Issue)	7,332,800	4,880,000	122,000
Municipal State Bank of Hesse 7s, 1925–45	3,000,000	2,340,000	82,900
Nassau Land Bank 6½s, 1928–38	3,000,000	3,000,000	97,500
Provincial Bank of Westphalia 6s, 1928–33	3,000,000	3,000,000	90,000
Saxon State Mortgage 6s, 1927–47	2,000,000	1,704,000	51,120
Saxon State Mortgage 6½s, 1926–46	4,000,000	3,346,000	109,845
Saxon State Mortgage 7s, 1925–45	5,000,000	4,046,000	141,610
Protestant Church 7s, 1926–46	2,500,000	2,145,500	75,090
Roman Catholic Church in Bavaria 6½s, 1926–46	5,000,000	3,997,000	126,975
Roman Catholic Church Welfare 7s, 1926–46	6,000,000	5,048,500	176,695
Berlin Electric Elevated 6½s, 1926–56	15,000,000	13,125,000	426,560
Consol. Hydro-Electric of Upper Wurttemberg 7s, 1926–56	4,000,000	3,671,000	128,485
Dortmund Municipal Utilities 6½s, 1928–48	3,000,000	2,663,000	86,545
East Prussian Power 6s, 1928–53	3,500,000	3,349,000	100,470
Electric Power 6½s, 1925–50	7,500,000	6,937,500	225,470

GOVERNMENT, STATE AND CITY BONDS IN DEFAULT (DIRECT AND CONTINGENT) (Continued)

Issue	Amount Issued	Amount Outstanding	Interest in Arrears
GERMANY (*Continued*)			
Electric Power 6½s, 1928–53	$ 5,000,000	$ 5,000,000	$ 162,500
German-Atlantic Cable 7s, 1925–45	4,000,000	3,236,500	113,275
Hamburg American Line 6½s, 1925–40	6,500,000	4,000,000	130,000
North German Lloyd 6s, 1927–47	20,000,000	17,682,000	530,460
Prussian Electric 6s, 1929–54	4,000,000	3,825,000	114,750
Rhine-Main-Danube 7s, 1925–50	6,000,000	4,889,000	171,115
Saxon Public Works 6s, 1932–37	6,485,000	5,867,000	176,010
Saxon Public Works 6½s, 1926–51	15,000,000	12,752,000	414,440
Saxon Public Works 7s, 1925–45	15,000,000	15,000,000	525,000
United Industrial 6s, 1925–45	6,000,000	4,950,000	148,500
United Industrial 6½s, 1926–41	6,000,000	5,490,000	178,425
Unterelbe Power 6s, 1928–53	5,000,000	4,700,000	141,000
Vesten Electric 7s, 1927–47	1,750,000	1,506,500	52,725
Westphalia United 6s, 1928–53	20,000,000	19,357,000	580,710
Total	$603,157,580	$524,364,320	$16,667,360
GREECE			
Greek 7s, 1924–64	$61,000,000	$57,105,000	$5,998,250
Greek 8s, 1925–35 (Ry. Loan)	5,867,400	5,786,300	694,355
Greek 8s, 1925–52 (Athens Water Works)	11,000,000	9,688,000	1,162,560
Greek 8½s, 1926–54 (Match Loan)	5,000,000	4,714,420	801,450
Greek 6s, 1928–68	37,354,800	36,369,900	3,273,290
Greek 6s, 1928–68	43,000,000	42,574,400	3,831,695
Greek 6s, 1930–54 (Kreuger and Toll Issue)	5,000,000	5,000,000	450,000
Total	$168,222,200	$161,238,020	$16,011,600

GUATEMALA

Guatemala 8s, 1924–34 (Los Altos Ry.)............	$4,950,000	$1,836,000	$73,440
Guatemala 8s, 1927–48................	2,515,000	2,214,000	88,560
Guatemala 7s, 1930–40 (Match Loan)........	2,500,000	2,474,110	86,595
International Rys. of Central America (Zacapa-Salvador Extension).............	169,500	169,500	169,500
Los Altos Maintenance Contract............	196,800	196,800	196,800
Total............	$10,331,300	$6,890,410	$614,895

HUNGARY

Hungarian Land Reform 5½s, 1929–79 (Match Loan)............	$36,000,000	$35,773,130	$2,951,285
Hungarian Consolidated Municipal 7½s, 1925–45.	10,000,000	8,048,000	603,400
Hungarian Consolidated Municipal 7s, 1926–46..	6,000,000	5,219,145	548,010
Hungarian Counties 7½s, 1926–46 (British Issue).	6,250,000	5,071,500	380,330
Hungarian Counties 6s, 1926–46 (British Issue)..	5,000,000	4,208,500	252,510
Budapest 6s, 1927–62............	20,000,000	18,890,000	2,266,800
Debreczin 7s, 1928–63............	3,400,000	3,309,000	347,445
Total............	$86,650,000	$80,519,275	$7,349,780

JUGOSLAVIA

Serbian 4s, 1895–1967............	$71,058,400	$62,212,000	$3,732,720
Serbian 4s, 1895–1967 (British Issue)............	5,000,000	4,590,000	275,400
Serbian 5s, 1902–52............	12,000,000	8,187,600	614,070
Serbian 4½s, 1906–56............	19,000,000	13,421,000	905,915
Serbian 4½s, 1909–59............	30,000,000	24,784,000	1,672,920
Serbian 5s, 1913–63............	50,000,000	42,757,000	3,206,775
Serb, Croats & Slovene, 8s, 1922–62............	15,250,000	14,875,000	1,785,000
Serb, Croats & Slovene, 7s, 1927–62............	30,000,000	28,729,000	3,016,545

Government, State and City Bonds in Default (Direct and Contingent) (*Continued*)

Issue	Amount Issued	Amount Outstanding	Interest in Arrears
Jugoslavia (*Continued*)			
Serb, Croats & Slovene, 6½s, 1928–58 (Match Issue)	$ 22,000,000	$ 22,000,000	$ 2,062,500
Serb, Croats & Slovene, 7s, 1931–71 (French Issue)	41,000,000	41,000,000	4,305,000
Montenegro 5s, 1909–45	1,250,000	967,500	193,500
State Mortgage Bank 4½s, 1910–60	6,000,000	438,205	29,580
State Mortgage Bank 4½s, 1911–61	6,000,000	457,865	30,905
State Mortgage Bank 7s, 1924–36	3,000,000	2,065,000	216,825
State Mortgage Bank 7s, 1927–39	2,000,000	1,532,500	160,910
State Mortgage Bank 7s, 1927–57	12,000,000	10,987,500	1,153,685
Total	$325,558,400	$279,004,170	$23,362,250
Latvia			
Riga (City of) 4½s, 1941	$6,513,500	$6,409,000	$5,479,810
Wolmar Railway 4½s, 1910	899,400	893,800	482,940
Total	$7,412,900	$7,302,800	$5,962,750
Mexico			
Aguascalientes 5s, 1910	$ 650,000	$ 650,000	$ 650,000
Chihuahua 5s, 1900	300,000	299,040	284,055
Coahuila 6s, 1900	752,000	752,000	857,290
Cordoba 6s	500,000	413,300	471,145
Durango 5s, 1907/10	1,700,000	1,700,000	1,617,000
Interoceanic Ry. 4s, 1950	5,750,000	5,750,000	4,370,000
Interoceanic Ry. 4½s, 1950	6,500,000	6,500,000	5,557,500
Jalisco 6s, 1898/1900	2,500,000	2,500,000	2,850,000

Jalisco Silver 6s	500,000	418,600	477,180
Mexican 5s, 1899–1945	113,500,000	49,786,300	47,296,980
Mexican 4s, 1904	40,000,000	37,037,500	28,128,150
Mexican 4s, 1910	56,055,000	50,688,125	39,971,900
Mexican 6s, 1913	30,000,000	30,000,000	34,200,000
Mexican 6s, 1913, Ser. "B"	59,707,500	59,707,500	71,649,000
Mexican 6s, 1913, Ser. "C"	15,125,000	15,125,000	18,150,000
Mexico (City of) 5s, 1899	12,000,000	6,927,500	6,581,100
Mexican Central Ry. 5s, 1901	6,597,000	1,374,000	1,167,900
Mexican Central Ry. Equip. 5s	2,342,000	792,000	752,400
Mexican Eastern Ry. 5s, 1984	2,000,000	2,000,000	1,900,000
Mexican Internal 3s, 1886	24,238,500	21,191,975	11,231,740
Mexican Internal 5s, 1894	48,307,550	46,450,000	44,127,500
Mexican Int'l RR 4½s, 1897	6,000,000	6,000,000	4,059,000
Mexican Int'l RR 4s, 1897	4,499,000	4,499,000	3,419,220
Mexican Irrigation 4½s, 1908	25,000,000	21,877,100	20,034,835
Mexican National Packing 1st Mtge. 6s, 1913	3,000,000	3,000,000	3,420,000
Mexican National Packing 2nd Mtge. 6s, 1913	1,500,000	1,500,000	1,890,000
Mexican Southern Ry. 4s, 1908	861,315	861,315	654,500
Morelos 6s	100,000	90,700	102,400
National Railways 4s, 1907	78,613,115	50,738,575	38,493,200
National Railways Prior Lien 4½s, 1907	84,786,115	84,786,115	64,873,500
National Railways 6s, 1913–14	5,529,130	5,529,130	6,303,145
National Railways 6s, 1913–14	26,730,000	26,730,000	30,472,100
National RR Co. 4½s, 1902	23,000,000	23,000,000	18,495,200
National RR Co. 4s, 1902	27,289,000	24,740,000	17,103,200
Oaxaca 5s	900,000	900,000	855,000
Pan American RR 5s, 1903	2,400,000	2,003,000	1,702,550
Pan American RR 5s, 1903	6,597,000	1,374,000	1,167,900
Parral 6s	150,000	149,520	170,440

GOVERNMENT, STATE AND CITY BONDS IN DEFAULT (DIRECT AND CONTINGENT) (*Continued*)

Issue	Amount Issued	Amount Outstanding	Interest in Arrears
MEXICO (*Continued*)			
Saltillo 6s	$ 250,000	$ 234,300	$ 267,065
Saragossa 5s	1,750,000	1,744,400	1,657,190
San Luis Potosi 6s, 1889	1,000,000	936,500	1,067,630
Tehuantepec Nat'l Ry. 5s, 1902–04–05	10,000,000	9,776,500	6,354,700
Tehuantepec Nat'l Ry. 4½s, 1905	2,000,000	1,927,700	1,648,145
Texas Mexican Ry. 7s, 1910	960,000	960,000	1,276,900
Texas Mexican Ry. 6s	1,380,000	1,380,000	1,573,100
Vera Cruz & Pacific RR 4½s, 1904	7,000,000	7,000,000	5,355,000
Total	$750,319,225	$621,800,695	$554,706,760
PANAMA			
Panama 5s, 1928–63	$12,000,000	$11,356,000	$283,900
Banco Nacional 6½s, 1926–46	1,000,000	697,500	45,335
Banco Nacional 6½s, 1927–47	1,000,000	750,000	73,125
Banco Nacional 6½s, 1928–48	1,000,000	800,000	78,000
Banco Nacional 6½s, 1929–49	1,000,000	850,000	55,250
Panama (City) 6½s, 1927–52	500,000	459,000	14,915
Total	$16,500,000	$14,912,500	$550,525
PERU			
Peru 7½s, 1922–48 (Guano Loan)	$ 6,250,000	$ 5,228,000	$ 588,150
Peru 8s, 1922–44 (Internal Loan)	1,400,000	1,216,600	291,985
Peru 7s, 1927–59	15,000,000	14,357,500	2,512,560
Peru 6s, 1927–60	50,000,000	48,383,000	8,708,940
Peru 6s, 1928–61	25,000,000	24,469,500	4,404,510

Peru 6s, 1928-61 (British Issue)	10,000,000	9,791,000	1,762,380
Peru 8s, 1929 (Internal Loan)	4,200,000	4,200,000	1,176,000
Callao 7½s, 1927-44	1,500,000	1,189,000	222,935
Lima 5s, 1911-65	3,000,000	2,419,500	302,435
Lima 6½s, 1928-58	3,000,000	2,887,000	469,135
Total	$119,350,000	$114,141,100	$20,439,030
RUMANIA			
Rumania 4½s, 1913-53	49,500,000	$ 42,790,570	$ 962,785
Rumania 4s, 1922-68	131,680,150	131,680,150	2,633,605
Rumania 4s, 1922-42	12,500,000	7,773,200	155,465
Rumania 7s, 1929-59	101,000,000	90,500,000	......
Rumania 7½s, 1931-71	53,000,000	52,500,000	1,706,250
Total	$347,680,150	$325,243,920	$5,458,105
RUSSIA			
Pre-war debt	$ 5,250,000,000	$ 4,623,849,300	$ 3,050,000,000
External war loans	75,000,000	75,000,000	50,125,000
Advances from Allies	3,854,644,750	3,854,644,750	2,500,000,000
Internal war loans	8,500,000,000	8,500,000,000	5,335,000,000
Total	$17,679,644,750	$17,053,494,050	$10,940,125,000
SALVADOR			
Salvador 8s, 1923-48	$ 6,000,000	$ 3,798,000	$ 455,760
Salvador 6s, 1923-57 (British Issue)	5,250,000	4,369,150	393,225
Salvador 7s, 1923-57	10,500,000	9,033,100	948,475
Total	$21,750,000	$17,200,250	$1,797,460

GOVERNMENT, STATE AND CITY BONDS IN DEFAULT (DIRECT AND CONTINGENT) (*Continued*)

Issue	Amount Issued	Amount Outstanding	Interest in Arrears
TURKEY			
Lottery 3s, 1870–72	$	$ 25,806,950	$ 1,548,400
Osmanieh 4s, 1890	......	3,960,785	316,800
Tobacco Priority 4s, 1893	......	1,087,630	86,800
Oriental Railway 4s, 1894	......	4,357,260	348,600
Turkey 5s, 1896	......	6,349,900	635,000
Customs Lien 4s, 1902	......	22,026,500	1,762,120
Unified 4s, 1903	......	90,833,950	7,266,700
Fisheries 4s, 1913	......	6,056,650	484,500
Bagdad Ry. 4s, 1904, Ser. I	......	6,362,950	509,000
Turkey 4s, 1904	......	7,197,500	575,900
Turkey 4s, 1904/05	......	13,814,300	1,105,100
Tedjhizat-Askerie 4s, 1905	......	6,352,100	508,100
Bagdad Ry. 4s, 1908, Ser. II	......	12,837,500	1,027,000
Bagdad Ry. 4s, 1908, Ser. III	......	14,148,500	1,131,900
Ottoman Bank 4s, 1908	......	12,572,300	1,005,800
Imperial Ottoman 4s, 1909	......	18,370,100	1,469,600
Soma Panderma 4s, 1910	......	4,673,200	373,800
Hodeaidah-Sanaa Ry. 4s, 1909	......	2,597,600	227,800
Customs Lien 4s, 1911	......	16,984,350	1,359,700
Treasury 5s, 1911	......	2,549,350	203,900
Koniah Irrigation Loan	......	2,762,450	221,000
Docks, Arsenal and Naval Constr. Loan	......	4,392,700	351,400
Turkey 5s, 1914	......	74,052,675	7,405,200
Turkey 6½s, 1930–55 (Match Loan)	10,000,000	10,000,000	1,300,000
Total	$424,500,000	$370,147,200	$31,224,120

UNITED STATES

Alabama Ry. Loans	$	$ 4,700,000	$ 15,745,000
Arkansas Ry. Loans	......	7,900,000	22,515,000
Florida Bank and Ry. Loans	......	7,900,000	28,380,000
Georgia Ry. Loans	......	14,152,000	40,797,200
Louisiana Ry. and Settlement Loans	......	22,000,000	39,820,000
Mississippi Bank Loans	......	7,000,000	37,120,000
North Carolina Ry. and Tax Loans	......	13,886,030	40,428,605
South Carolina	......	7,500,000	25,005,000
Total	$85,038,030	$85,038,030	$249,810,805

URUGUAY

Uruguay 3½s, 1891–96	$102,500,000	$ 64,082,275	$1,121,440
Uruguay 5s, 1896	8,335,000	8,221,000	205,525
Uruguay 5s, 1905	34,564,180	19,905,900	497,645
Uruguay 5s, 1909–45	6,372,960	4,113,505	102,835
Uruguay 5s, 1914–51	5,500,000	4,290,700	107,265
Uruguay 5s, 1915	1,505,000	1,281,000	32,025
Uruguay 5s, 1919 (British Issue)	2,500,000	882,085	22,050
Uruguay 5s, 1919	3,025,000	2,360,000	59,000
Uruguay 8s, 1921–46	7,500,000	6,861,000	274,440
Uruguay 6s, 1926–60	30,000,000	27,694,500	830,835
Uruguay 6s, 1930–64	17,581,000	17,144,500	514,335
Montevideo 6s (now 5s) 1889	6,882,975	3,247,890	389,745
Montevideo 7s, 1922–52	6,000,000	5,604,000	784,560
Montevideo 6s, 1926–59	5,171,000	4,852,000	582,240
Total	$237,437,115	$170,540,355	$5,523,940

GOVERNMENT, STATE AND CITY BONDS IN DEFAULT (DIRECT AND CONTINGENT) (Continued)

RECAPITULATION

Country	Original Amount	Amount Outstanding	Interest in Default*
Argentina	$ 130,331,125	$ 113,863,900	$ 8,723,690
Austria	61,000,000	53,415,800	4,806,865
Bolivia	70,400,000	61,348,525	9,649,620
Brazil	1,445,045,045	1,169,433,065	198,693,350
Bulgaria	164,901,385	108,905,100	6,381,405
Canada	**	**	**
Chile	590,782,800	451,060,790	53,476,895
China	368,244,035	346,377,725	228,686,235
Colombia	189,172,710	163,905,740	12,912,430
Costa Rica	27,590,900	18,690,500	1,116,875
Ecuador	20,046,400	17,475,300	14,395,245
Germany	603,157,580	524,364,320	16,667,360
Greece	168,222,200	161,238,020	16,011,600

Guatemala	10,331,300	6,890,410	614,895
Hungary	86,650,000	80,519,275	7,349,780
Jugoslavia	325,558,400	279,004,170	23,362,250
Latvia	7,412,900	7,302,800	5,962,750
Mexico	750,319,225	621,800,695	554,706,760
Panama	16,500,000	14,912,500	550,525
Peru	119,350,000	114,141,100	20,439,030
Rumania	347,680,150	325,243,920	5,458,105
Russia	17,679,644,750	17,053,494,050	10,940,125,000
Salvador	21,750,000	17,200,250	1,797,460
Turkey	424,500,000	370,147,200	31,224,120
United States	85,038,030	83,038,030	249,810,805
Uruguay	237,437,115	170,540,355	5,523,940
Total	$23,951,066,050	$22,334,313,540	$12,418,446,990

* As of December 31, 1933.
** See text.

Notes on Defaulted Loans

ARGENTINA

As a part of the New Year's greetings to its foreign creditors, the *Province of Buenos Aires*, on January 30, 1933, announced that legislation had been enacted providing for temporary and partial relief of the difficulty of continuing full service on external debt. The offer to American holders of provincial dollar bonds includes the following features:

1. During a three years' period from January 1, 1933 to December 31, 1935, sinking funds on all internal and external loans will be suspended, except on the 6½ per cent Consolidation Loan of 97 million pesos, of which 45 millions have been issued in satisfaction of urgent short term liabilities of internal creditors.

2. During the above period, the Government will make available an amount in paper pesos equal at par of exchange to interest charge on dollar bonds. Such pesos will be converted into dollars as and when exchange is available, and remitted for application toward payment of interest to bondholders assenting to the plan.

3. Any balance of interest due will be resumed after December 31, 1935, and sums due annually thereafter for amortization will be devoted, in first instance, to retirement of arrear certificates. Owing to special (sic) circumstances, full interest payment on loans floated and held in Europe will continue to be paid.

The defaults of the *City of Cordoba* embrace two loans sold exclusively to American investors. They include a 7 per cent issue offered originally in 1927 to the amount of $4,669,500, and secured by a first charge on revenues from stockyards and slaughter

houses, the vehicle tax, and certain payments to the
City from income of the electric tramways. Proceeds
were said to have been applied to redemption of certain existing municipal loans, to street widening, and
the construction of public works. How much was used
for each of these projects, the prospectus descriptive
of the loan does not state. While opponents to foreign
loans see in this a very serious omission on the part of
the banker, those familiar with foreign government
borrowing do not incline to attach much significance
to it. Irrespective of how funds are used by the borrower, his bonds constitute, in the final analysis,
merely a promise to pay, and the quality of the loan is
as dependable as the promise.

The other loan was sold in the same year to the
amount of $2,547,000. In connection with the flota-
tion, it was stated that a part of the loan would be
offered in Argentina, by the Buenos Aires firm of
Ernesto Tornquist & Co. Bonds were secured by a
first charge on taxes on real estate benefited by improvements financed with the proceeds of the loan.
Maturity was scheduled for 1937, while the above
issue was to mature in 1957. The chances are that
neither date will be adhered to. The bankers identified
with the short term loan, that is, the 7 per cent issue of
1927-1937, were not the same who floated the 20-year
issue.

Such is the reward for the eagerness with which
Americans absorbed practically all post war loans of
the Province.

The only external loan contracted by the *Province
of Corrientes* comprises a 6 per cent issue, to the

amount of £396,825, in 1910, at 98 in London, by Erlangers, to the extent of £196,825, and in Paris by the *Banque Argentine et Française* with respect to the remaining £200,000. Bonds were authorized for the purpose of extending the Corrientes Railway and of organizing agricultural colonies. They are secured by a first mortgage on the Railway, the proceeds from the sale of public lands, and 0.1 per cent of the *contribucion territorial*. They were defaulted in August, 1916, with respect to interest, sinking fund payments having ceased in 1915. No payments have been made since August, 1921, when the February, 1919 interest was disbursed.

In February, 1928, the Supreme Court at Buenos Aires ordered the Provincial Government to pay bondholders £404,627 for interest and sinking fund in arrears, and it was later announced that the Province had deposited £7,208 to apply on this payment.

The temporary adjustment of the debt of the *Province of Mendoza* provides as follows: Coupons appertaining to bonds deposited under plan and maturing from June 1, 1933 to December 1, 1937, inclusive, will be paid at a reduced rate of interest of 4 per cent per annum. Semi-annual sinking fund payments from December 2, 1932 to December 1, 1937, inclusive, will be suspended, but commencing June 1, 1934, the Province agrees to make payments which will be applied to purchase or redemption of bonds. The plan provides also for waiver during the period December 2, 1932 to December 1, 1937 of security fund provided for under the loan contract. The offer to bondholders is not conditional upon acceptance of any specified percentage of bonds, and acceptance by any bondholder will make the plan operative as to his assenting bonds. In connection with the default by the *Province of Santa Fé*, it is of more than academic interest to recall the circumstances under which the Province obtained its first financial accommodations in the United States. In a letter to bondholders, attention is directed to the fact that "the Province will not do anything for the relief of bondholders until the latter are actively represented by a committee" and that "it might be necessary to assess bondholders for any pro rata share of any expenses incurred by a committee."

Defaulted loans of the Province comprise the 5 per cent issue of 1910, issued in France to the amount of Fcs. 47,880,000. Payments were to be made in Paris in francs, or in Argentina in the currency equivalent to the gold peso values named on bonds and coupons, namely, Fcs. 500 equal 100 pesos (gold). The issue is secured by the income from the operation of the Port of Santa Fé; on the harbor property; the revenues from the duty on quebracho; and 10 per cent of the proceeds of the *contribucion directa*. Coupons are to be accepted in payment of taxes.

America's first contact with the Province took place in 1924, when $10,188,000 was sold in the United States. Bonds were secured by a pledge of the entire revenues of Santa Fé from the tax on alcoholic beverages and the tax on tobacco, to be deposited each week as collect in the *Banco de la Nacion Argentina* to the order of the Administrative Directorate of the Loan, until the sum necessary to cover semi-annual requirements has been accumulated. Although the loan was authorized in 1922, a public offering was not made until June, 1925. Americans were adequately rewarded for their patience: Their investment, costing 96 cents on the dollar, has shrunk to less than one-sixth the original price, in spite of the "productive" character of the loan, proceeds having been employed in the construction of roads, bridges, a cold storage plant, schools, and in the payment of floating indebtedness. A tabulation of Santa Fé defaults might also comprise 6 per cent Treasury "Gold" Notes, outstanding at $5,000,000, and technically referred to as a short term issue. The American bank holding these Notes, while receiving interest on them, has however discovered that a Santa Fé short term issue is an obligation which exists only in the imagination of the most confirmed optimists.

The record of political subdivisions in the Province of Santa Fé is equally unimpressive. Bonds of the *City of Rosario*, the second largest city in Argentina, and of the City of Santa Fé, capital of the Province, are in complete default, although guaranteed by the Province. *Quis custodiet custodios ipsos?* The Rosario bonds were sold in London in 1907, to the amount of £1,995,175. Half of the issue was an obligation of the Province, the City being responsible for the other half, although the Province guaranteed the entire amount. Until 1919, the Province met its share in Treasury Bills which were handed to the City, the latter discounting them in Buenos Aires, and remitting the full service to the Fiscal Agents in cash. In 1919, the City was unable to discount these bills, and interest due in May was paid in September. Regular payments commenced in May, 1923. In November, 1931, the Province took care of service charges. In the following year, default was complete.

The fiscal record of the City of *Santa Fé* is somewhat more complex. In 1889, it borrowed £257,900 in London at 6 per cent. In 1904, payments were suspended. In the following year, £42,100 were issued to take care of back interest on the 1889 loan. Interest from 1905 on was to be paid at the rate of 4 per cent, and from 1915 at 6 per cent, the City agreeing to deposit daily 10 per cent of its total tax receipts until the full service of the loan is covered. In the event of default on two consecutive coupons, the old rights of bondholders are to revive. Not only has there been no revival of old rights, but bondholders seem to have lost all rights. Default on the loan is complete.

The City's dollar debt is represented by a 7 per cent loan sold in 1927 to the amount of $2,122,500. Bonds are secured by a first lien on the gross receipts of the municipal Electric Light and Power Company, and by a lien on certain markets, slaughter houses, and other works acquired or constructed with the proceeds of the loan. Although the City agreed to maintain rates for light and power so that pledged revenues will each year produce an amount equal to at least one and one-half times annual service requirements, the default on bonds is complete.

Up to the time of borrowing in the United States in 1928, the City of *Tucuman*, capital of the Province of that name, had a perfect fiscal record. It had not borrowed abroad before. The 1928 loan contracted to the amount of $3,396,000 at 7 per cent was secured by a first pledge on the taxes on Market Provisions, Letting of Shops, and on Vehicles, and if these became insufficient, by pledge on certain paving instalments and of any public buildings constructed with the proceeds of the loan. Other purposes included paving, redemption and consolidation of floating debts.

AUSTRIA

American investors enjoy the dubious distinction of owning all bonds of Austria's political subdivisions which are in default. The loans of the Republic which have been placed with American, as well as European, investors are being taken care of.

Defaulted bonds comprise two loans of the *Province of Upper Austria*, sold in 1925 and 1927, to the amount of $5,000,000 and $7,500,000, respectively. The 1925 issue bears interest at 7 per cent, and is secured by a first charge on the revenues derived from the real estate tax and such part of the Province's proportionate share of federal taxes as will, when added to the real estate tax, amount to three times interest and sinking fund requirements; a first closed mortgage on real estate owned by the Province, valued at the date of the loan at $13,000,000; and a pledge of the Province's entire stock buildings in certain hydro-electric and industrial companies operating in the Province, and estimated at $1,500,000. In addition, bonds were an obligation of the Provincial Mortgage Bank, secured by first mortgages on farm property specifically pledged, covering the full amount of the funds of the loan, received by the Bank. Proceeds were to be used for hydro-electric and coal mining development, for loans to the Provincial Mortgage Bank to be re-loaned on first mortgages for the development of agriculture, and for "other productive purposes." The expenditure of the proceeds was to be supervised by a representative of the bankers who must countersign all withdrawals.

What has become of all the protection and safeguards? Apparently nothing. Bondholders have been waiting for an answer, but in vain. They are informed that interest on their bonds is being deposited in schillings in Austrian banks, for transfer abroad as and when conditions allow. Needless to add, the contract calls for payment in U. S. gold dollars.

The 1927 loan bears interest at the rate of 6½ per cent, and is secured by a first lien on revenues derived from the gross sales of electric current; on revenues received from municipalities; and on "certain other provincial income, estimated to aggregate at least $1,200,000 a year." Proceeds were used for loans to the Communal and Mortgage banks, for payment of floating debt, and for "other purposes."

The *Province of Lower Austria* is also represented by two bond issues sold in 1924 and early in 1926, to the amount of $3,000,000 and $2,000,000, respectively. Both issues are in default, except for the reported deposit of native currency to the account of American creditors.

The 1924 loan, bearing interest at 6½ per cent, is an obligation of the Lower Austrian Hydro-Electric Power Company, organized in 1922 under the auspices of and controlled by the City of Vienna and the Province of Lower Austria. Bonds are secured by a closed first mortage on the entire property, and guaranteed unconditionally by the Province of Lower Austria by endorsement on each bond.

The 1925 issue has a 7½ per cent coupon, and is secured by pledge of revenues from the Provincial Real Estate Tax, and a mortgage on real estate owned by the Province, and valued at $2,000,000. The Province agreed that if in any year the Real Estate Tax should yield less than four times the interest and sinking fund requirements, seven other taxes would be pledged which, in 1924, yielded $3,844,000. One has good reasons for speculating whether the default would have been less complete, if the security had been inferior.

The *Province of Styria 7* per cent loan was contracted in 1926 to the amount of $5,000,000. The security was more than adequate. It consisted of a first charge on income from real estate taxes; a first charge on the share of the Province in Federal taxes; and a first lien on real estate, shares and securities owned by the Province, having an aggregate estimated value of more than $10,000,000. The Province also agreed that unless pledged revenues will yield at least four times annual interest and sinking fund requirements, other revenues will be pledged to produce such an amount. The naive creditor inquires whether the pledged collateral may not be disposed of to satisfy his claims. Those identified with the sale of bonds have nothing to say.

American investors were privileged to acquire, in 1925, $2,500,000 of 8 per cent bonds of the *City of Graz*, capital of the Province of Styria. The loan is se-

cured by a closed first mortgage, registered in favor
of the Trustee (the Chase National Bank of New
York), on the electric, gas and water enterprises
owned by the City, and on over one hundred munici-
pally-owned apartment houses and other revenue-producing buildings and real estate; and by a first charge
on special municipal revenues from direct taxation.
Pledged income was to be credited to a Special Account, out of which there was to be paid monthly to
the *Wiener Bankverein* in Graz one-twelfth of the annual interest and sinking fund requirements, and
thirty days preceding each interest date accumulated
funds were to be deposited in New York to meet the
service of the loan. The Graz bonds represent a perfect
case of non-compliance with provisions in the debt
contract.

The defaulted bonds of the *Province of Tyrol* comprise two issues, bearing interest at 7½ and 7 per cent,
and floated in 1925 and 1927, respectively. The 1925
loan was sold to the amount of $3,000,000, is secured
by a closed first mortgage on the property of the
Tyrol Hydro-Electric Power Company, and by a first
mortgage on the electric and gas plants of the City of
Innsbruck, capital of the Province. The Province and
the City guarantee the bonds jointly and severally by
endorsement. By virtue of an agreement with the *Bayernwerk A. G.* (owned by the State of Bavaria), the
company supplies power to the German concern, the
income therefrom amounting to $530,000 annually.
As a result of this contract, the service on the Tyrol
bonds could be maintained longer than on all other
Austrian provincial issues. Default became complete

when Germany suspended payment on all external commitments.

The 7 per cent loan of 1927 is secured by a first charge on proceeds from all sales to the Bayernwerk A. G.; a closed first mortgage on the transformer station at Innsbruck; and a second mortgage on the property of the Tyrol Hydro-Electric Power Company, subject to the loan of 1925.

The *City of Vienna* is in default with respect to a 6 per cent loan sold in the United States in 1927 to the amount of $30,000,000. Bonds do not enjoy the benefit of specific security, but the default is just as complete as if all the assets of Vienna had been pledged.

BOLIVIA

Of the total population of *Bolivia*, placed at more than 3,000,000, about one-seventh is white, one-quarter mixed, and the remainder chiefly Indian. The country is in a comparatively primitive stage of economic development. The purchasing power of the people is extremely restricted, for the Indian and mestizo, who comprise the great bulk of the population, have small earning capacity. It has been authoritatively stated that even during prosperous times, not over 10,000 families have incomes exceeding $1,800 a year, and that less than 100 families have incomes exceeding $15,000 a year.

Notwithstanding the above, loans aggregating close to $70,000,000 were advanced to Bolivia. A fact which proved of material aid in the sale of Bolivian loans to the investor was the statement pertaining to the low per capita debt of the nation. How dependable such statistical presentation is, was discussed above. How dependable it has turned out to be, can be told by the present holders of Bolivian bonds.

The Bolivian 6 per cent loan of 1917 was sold in New York and Philadelphia by a syndicate headed by Chandler & Co., and in Chicago by Counselman & Co., at 97½ and interest. Bonds were to be used exclusively for construction and equipment of an electric railroad from La Paz to Youngas. The contract appears to have provided for the purchase of materials either in Bolivia or the United States. The loan was secured by:

1. A first mortgage on the electric railway line from La Paz to Coripata on which the Government had expended $500,000 prior to the flotation of the 6 per cent loan;

2. A first lien on the general revenue of the Department of La Paz, and upon the reimbursements of the supplemental tax collected upon cocoa leaves;

3. A first mortgage on the railway line between the Tarejra Station on the Arica-La Paz Railway and the City of Corocero;

4. A first lien upon the revenues of the Republic derived from railway concessions in force at the time of the flotation of the loan;

5. A first lien upon the revenues from the tax on foreign merchandise imported into the Department of La Paz;

6. A subsidiary lien on the general revenues of the Republic, subject only to such other liens as existed at the time of the issue of the bonds.

The Bolivian Government agreed to deposit semi-annually $96,000 to cover interest and amortization. The latter was to be effected by drawings of bonds by lot at par and interest. Default occurred April 1, 1931.

The Bolivian 8 per cent loan of 1922 was authorized to the amount of $33,000,000, of which $19,000,000 was issued for refunding purposes and for railroad and highway construction, and $7,000,000 for exchange for a like amount of Railroad bonds. The remaining $7,000,000 was reserved for issue "under careful restrictions" to provide for the completion of the Atocha-Villazon Railroad and the Potosi-Sucre Railroad. The bonds were secured by:

1. A first lien on all export and import duties, surcharge on import duties and taxes on mining claims, alcohol monopoly, 90 per cent of the tobacco monopoly, corporations other than mining and banking, interest on mortgage bonds, net income of banks, and net profit of mining companies;

2. A first mortgage on the Atocha-Villazon and the Potosi-Sucre Railroads, together with a pledge of the net income of the roads;

3. A first lien on the Government's continuing controlling stock interest in the *Banco de la Nacion Boliviana* and the dividends declared upon such stock.[1]

The loan contract also provided for the introduction of additional taxes and revenues to be pledged as security for the loan if the proceeds derived from the above should fall below one and one-half times annual service requirements.

During the life of the loan, the pledged revenues and taxes were to be supervised by a Permanent Fiscal Commission to be appointed by the President of Bolivia, but of the three members two were to be appointed upon the nomination of the bankers, and of these two, one would be the Chairman and Chief Executive of the Commission.

---

[1] It would be of interest to learn what has become of this collateral and whether the bondholders might not call upon the Trustee to dispose of it for the benefit of holders of the above loan.

On May 1, 1931, $22 was paid on coupons. No payment has been made since.

The 7 per cent loan of 1927 was authorized for the purpose of constructing a railroad from Cochabamba to Santa Cruz, of continuing the construction of the Potosi-Sucre railway, and for "other purposes." Bonds were secured by pledge of certain revenues, the Government agreeing that the proceeds of such revenues available for the service of the loan shall be maintained at not less than one and one-half times the amount required for such service. Among the revenues hypothecated are those derived from the royalties of the Government from the exploitation of oil lands in the Department of Chuquisaca. Bonds were offered in New York to the amount of $14,000,000, but it was stated than an appreciable amount had been withdrawn for sale in Amsterdam. Bonds defaulted on January 1, 1931.

The 7 per cent loan of 1928 was issued for the purpose of redeeming the 6 per cent loan of 1920, the Potosi-Sucre 8 per cent loan of 1924, the Quillacollo-Arana Railroad loan, and of repaying certain debts to the national banks and of amounts due under the Vickers contract. The balance was to be invested in railroads, highway construction, and for "other purposes."

The security is similar to that enjoyed by the 7s of 1927. Default on this issue occurred on March 1, 1931.

In regard to the default of the Bolivian obligations held almost exclusively by United States investors, an announcement was made in February, 1931 that a final settlement of the Bolivian debt problem would be postponed until after the provisional Military Government goes out of office and the new administration comes in

on March 10, 1931. Bondholders are still awaiting a settlement.

The Bolivian 7s of 1930 refer to the Match Monopoly Loan issued to the *Union Allumettière*, Belgian subsidiary of the Swedish Match Company. Interest up to and including the May, 1932 coupon is understood to have been paid by the Company. The loan was issued in consideration of receiving for 20 years the sole right to manufacture, import and sell matches in Bolivia, the Company agreeing to pay the Government 750,000 bolivianos annually, or about $250,000 at par of exchange.

BRAZIL

In connection with the partial default of the *Brazilian* Government, the following statement was issued by its New York representative:

In view of the impossibility of acquiring foreign exchange for the transfer of funds to the markets where the coupons of the external debt are payable, the *Brazilian Federal Government*, after placing before their bankers all the facts regarding the position of the country, are reluctantly obliged to authorize them to communicate to the holders of Brazilian bonds that they are only in a position to pay in full in cash, on the dates stipulated in the contracts, the interest and sinking fund on the 5 per cent funding loan of 1898 and on the 5 per cent funding loan of 1914. Service in full of Brazil 1922 7½ per cent coffee security bonds issued in London and New York, is already provided for and payments will also be made in cash.[2]

---

[2] Reference to this issue is not quite clear. As of December 31, 1923, it was officially reported that the entire stock of coffee hypothecated as security for the loan had been sold and the proceeds turned over to the London bankers (Baring Brothers; N. M. Rothschild and Sons; and J. Henry Schroeder & Co.), with whom they had been on deposit until October 1, 1932 when bonds were paid off.

The interest on all other loans, will be paid on their respective due dates during a period of three years in special scrip,
bearing interest at 5 per cent per annum and divided into two
series; the first series, redeemable in 20 years, will be in respect
of the bonds issued against the following loans: Brazil 1903
5 per cent sterling bonds; Brazil 1909 5 per cent French
franc bonds; Brazil 1921 8 per cent gold dollar bonds; Brazil
1922 7 per cent gold dollars bonds; Brazil 1926 6½ per cent
gold dollar bonds; Brazil 1927 6½ per cent sterling and gold
dollar bonds.

The second series, redeemable in 40 years, will be in respect
of all other existing Brazilian Federal Government foreign
loans.

The Brazilian Federal Government undertakes to review the
situation at the end of the first and second years with a view to
extending cash payments should circumstances permit. The
sums in milreis at the rate of exchange last fixed for stabilization, namely, 6 pence, corresponding to the interest not being
remitted, will be deposited in an approved bank in the city of
Rio de Janeiro and applied in the purchase of bills of exchange,
provided that the market can supply them. Such remittances
would be sent to the Government's bankers and applied to the
redemption of the new scrip, either by purchase if below par
or by means of drawing if at par. The scrip of the series
redeemable in 20 years will be dealt with first. Should the
market not supply the necessary foreign exchange, the Government will acquire bonds of the internal debt, which will be held
in trust until such time as exchange can be obtained.

The Brazilian Federal Government will pay the interest and
the sinking fund on the new scrip in cash on their due dates.
The sums in milreis earmarked for the payment of the suspended sinking fund, which are being deposited and which
will continue to be deposited also at exchange of 6 pence, will
be destroyed as soon as possible, and deflation will continue so
long as market conditions permit. The Brazilian Federal Gov-

ernment have authorized their bankers to take the necessary steps for the execution of this program.

The Brazilian issues affected include loans sold to and held by British, American, and French investors. Converting the sterling debt as well as the franc debt at par of exchange, we find that over a period of 50 years, Brazil has borrowed in the British market about $500,000,000, of which about $110,000,000 has been repaid, or 22 per cent of the original amount.

Brazil's loans in Paris, covering a period of only eight years, total at par of exchange $65,000,000, of which more than $60,000,000 is still outstanding.

The country's experience with American bankers covers a period of only about six years, in which loans were obtained aggregating $176,500,000, or at the rate of about $30,000,000 a year, as compared with an annual borrowing rate of only $10,000,000 in Great Britain, and about $8,000,00 in France.

Alagoas, one of the smaller States of Brazil, has a population of about 1,200,000. The area is less than 22,600 square miles. Annual income approximates $1,-000,000. Expenditure as a rule exceeds governmental receipts.

In 1909, a syndicate of British and French bankers placed an issue on behalf of the State of Alagoas, aggregating £500,000. Of the total, £200,000 were sold in England at 85, bonds bearing interest at the rate of 5 per cent per annum, and subject to redemption by a cumulative sinking fund of 5½ per cent per annum, calculated to retire the whole issue by July 1, 1958. The bonds were sold for the purpose of consolidating existing state obligations and for the purpose of providing funds for effecting improvements. The loan is specifically secured by a first lien on the export duties, the State of Alagoas undertaking not to contract any other liens which will rank prior to or pari passu with these bonds. The issue has been in complete default since 1929 and no payments appear to have been made on the French portion of the loan since 1921. Sinking fund has been in arrears since 1921.

Embracing an area greater than that of any country in Europe except Russia, *Amazonas* is the largest state in Brazil. The population is less than 450,000, or only 1.62 to the square mile. As the prosperity of the State depends almost entirely upon rubber, the decline in the price of this commodity and competition from plantations in the Far East have greatly reduced its income and rendered difficult, if not impossible, the continuance of payments on its debt.

The 1906 loan was issued to the amount of Fcs. 84,000,000 in Paris, Brussels and Antwerp and was secured by pledge of 1 per cent of revenues from license taxes; 2 per cent of revenues from taxes on rubber; and 3 per cent of revenues from lease or operation of the tramways and electric light facilities of the City of Manaos, capital and chief city of the State. Cash payments were suspended in November, 1915 for a period of 5 years, holders receiving instead 5 per cent Consolidation or Funding bonds equivalent to the amount of interest due them. Payment of cash was not resumed in 1920 and has been in default ever since.

The Funding Loan of 1915 of Fcs. 20,500,000 was for the purpose of taking care of unpaid coupons on the 1906 loan and was to be redeemed in 1925. It appears that payments on the Funding Loan were met until 1918, but none have been made since that date.

The 5½ per cent Loan of the *City of Manaos* for £350,000 was issued in London in 1906, and was secured by a first lien on the revenue derived from the operation of the city-owned market and slaughterhouse. No payments have been made since April, 1918 when the November, 1916 coupon was taken care of. The sinking fund has also been in default since 1917.

The *Manaos Improvements, Limited* has outstanding two bond issues, of which £500,000 are represented by 6 per cent debentures and £37,700 by 6 per cent prior lien registered bonds. In accordance with an agreement made between the company and the State of Amazonas in 1916, the State took over the company's concession and assets in consideration of the payment of 7,500,000 milreis in 5 per cent internal bonds, which were to be redeemed by a sinking fund of 1 per cent per annum commencing in 1921. In addition, the State undertook to make up any deficiency in meeting the interest and sinking fund payments on the outstanding bonds of the company. In spite of these arrangements the debentures have been in default since November, 1913, while the prior lien bonds have been in default since 1921.

Under date of November 4, 1927, a contract was signed with the Brazilian Federal Treasury whereby Brazil would endorse a loan of 40,000 contos to be obtained for the State of Amazon as by the Bank of Brazil, the proceeds to be used to pay off the State's external and internal indebtedness.

Bahia, one of the Atlantic States of Brazil, is the second largest cocoa-producing area in the world, and grows as much tobacco as Cuba. The mineral wealth of Bahia is extensive and includes manganese, dia-

monds, gold, copper, lead, and graphite. Output, however, is restricted except for manganese and diamonds.

The first external loan of the State was contracted
in 1888 and bore interest at the rate of 5 per cent per
annum. The loan was authorized at Fcs. 20,000,000
and issued to the amount of Fcs. 8,000,000 by a syndicate of French banks headed by the *Banque de Paris et
des Pays Bas.* Bonds are secured by a first charge on
the general revenues of the State. Default occurred in
December, 1917. In 1919, an agreement was reached
whereby coupons from December, 1917 to June, 1919
were paid 40 per cent in cash, and the remainder in 6
per cent Treasury Bonds. Coupons due December,
1919 and June, 1920 were likewise dealt with, 50 per
cent in cash and the other half in Treasury Bonds. Payments were suspended entirely in January, 1922 and
in December of the following year an Agreement was
reached between the State and the Ethelburga Syndicate, Ltd. of London and the *Association Nationale des
Porteurs Français de Valeurs Mobilières.* A summary
of the Agreement is presented hereunder:

The Government of Bahia will for a period of four years,
beginning October, 1923, deposit in a bank in Bahia the sum
of 500 contos per month, of which one-fourth shall be allo-
cated for payment of interest on the French loans of 1888
and 1910, and three-fourths for payment of interest on the
British loans of 1904, 1913, 1915 and 1918. These sums are
to be applied to each loan *pro rata* to the nominal amount
outstanding.

Coupons will be paid from time to time as and when the
amount in the hands of the respective bankers is sufficient for
the purpose.

In respect of any matured coupons remaining unpaid on

January 1, 1928, the Government of Bahia will issue to the holders a Funding bond for the amount thereof.

All payments in respect of redemption up to January 1, 1928, will be deferred.

As from January 1, 1928, the Government of Bahia has undertaken to resume on the due dates the normal service of the external loans. The payments of the principal of the Treasury Bonds falling due in 1923, 1924 and 1925 were to be extended for 5 years, interest for such period accruing at the rate provided by the Bonds in question.

According to a supplemental agreement with the Ethelburga Syndicate reached in December, 1927, it was provided that:

a. Matured coupons unpaid on January 1, 1928 are to be exchanged for bonds of a new 5 per cent Funding Loan at par;

b. Payment in cash of all coupons to be resumed after January 1, 1928;

c. Treasury Bills of 1918 to be repaid in cash by drawings at par in 12 semi-annual installments;

d. Sinking fund to be resumed as soon as Treasury Bills have been repaid.

All obligations under the above agreement were duly met and full interest payments in cash resumed as from January 1, 1928. In 1931, the entire indebtedness of the State went into default once again.

The Bahia 5 per cent loan of 1904-05 was sold in London and on the Continent, including Belgium, Holland and Switzerland. Part of the proceeds was used to redeem a portion of the 1888 loan. Interest defaulted in November, 1914, but was paid in May, 1915 with interest at 5 per cent. No payments were made on account of 1916 interest and amortization. In 1916, the Government announced intention to fund the interest and suspend operation of sinking fund for three years. Holders received £120 par value of Funding Bonds for £100 of unpaid coupons. In July, 1918, a similar arrangement was made in regard to coupons for 1918-1920. Payment in 1920 was made, partly in cash and partly in Treasury Bonds.

The 5 per cent loan of 1910 issued at Fcs. 45,000,000 in France was specifically secured by a first lien on railroad revenues and receipts from various export duties, including those from coffee and cocoa, subject to the 1904-05 issue. Default and subsequent adjustment are similar to those relative to other Bahia loans.

The 5 per cent loan of 1913 was sold largely in London, although relatively appreciable amounts were placed in France, Switzerland, Belgium, Holland and Germany. The bonds were secured by a pledge of the tax on industries and professions and the property transfer tax.

In 1915, the State issued through the Ethelburga Syndicate, Ltd. of London a 5 per cent Funding Loan for the purpose of funding the interest for a period of 3 years on Bahia external obligations, pledging as security the internal taxes of the State, known as the *collectorias*. Interest on the funding bonds was paid in cash up to and including July 1, 1924. Payment due January and July, 1925 was made in November, 1927, while subsequent coupons were taken care of by the Funding Loan of 1928.

The Bahia 6 per cent Treasury Bills of 1918-19-20 were issued in part payment of coupons due on the 5 per cent loans of 1905 and 1913 for the years 1918,

1919 and 1920. The original amount was £355,000 of which £127,500 is still outstanding.

The 7 per cent loan is the result of an agreement made with the holders of the City of Bahia 6 per cent loan of 1914, whereby the State agreed to pay £294,-500 in the form of 3-year Notes, the first of which fell due in May, 1930 and was promptly discharged.

The City bonds were created in 1914 in exchange for the assets of the *Bahia Tramway Light and Power Company* and the *Compagnie d'Eclairage de Bahia*, and are secured by a first mortgage on the properties. The first coupon due in 1915 was met partly in cash and partly in promissory notes due in 1916. At maturity, however, these notes were not taken care of and no other payment had been made up to the time of the arrangement referred to above.

The Bahia Funding 5 per cent loan of 1928 was issued in accordance with the arrangement of December, 1927 with the Ethelburga Syndicate. Bonds are secured by a pledge of the territorial tax.

The funded debt for which the *City of Bahia* or *São Salvador* is responsible includes the 5's of 1905; the 5's of 1912-13; and the Consolidation Loan of 1916.

The 1905 issue was placed almost exclusively in France and was secured by a first charge on the revenue from water drainage and markets. Interest due in February, 1915 and subsequent coupons were paid partly in cash and partly in Consolidation bonds. No payment has been made since. Inasmuch as the water and sewage system was taken over by the State of Bahia in 1915, it appears that the State is, in part at least, also liable for this loan.

The 5 per cent loan of 1912-13 was sold in London

to the extent of £500,000, and in Paris to the extent of Fcs. 27,500,000, and is payable at the option of the holder in sterling or francs. Bonds are secured on the house, industry and profession taxes. Default occurred in 1915 and outside of payments made partly in cash and partly in bonds for the period 1915-18, no disbursements were made to bondholders.

The Consolidation Loan bears interest at the rate of 5 per cent per annum and was issued to the amount of £840,000 to fund coupons in default, due February, 1915 to August, 1920. The issue was specifically secured by a first charge on revenues derived from licenses and weights and measures, and a tax of 7 per cent on all existing taxes except house tax and municipal markets tax. It is further secured, subject to the 5 per cent loan of 1912-13 and the Bahia Light and Power Loan, on the house tax and the industries and professions tax. In June, 1918, default occurred and no payment has been made since.

Ceara is one of the smaller northern Atlantic States of Brazil, embracing an area of 40,000 square miles, with an estimated population of over 1,600,000. Its principal product is cotton. A 5 per cent loan contracted in Paris in 1910 was secured by a first charge on export taxes, and proceeds were to be used for the construction of water works and a sewage system in Fortaleza, capital and chief commercial center of the State. The loan is scheduled to be payable in gold. In October, 1925, the State announced that it would redeem in May, 1926 the outstanding balance in French francs, which bondholders regarded as a violation of the original loan contract. The funds for this operation were derived from the sale to American bankers of an

8 per cent loan offered in 1923 to the amount of $2,-000,000. The loan was secured by a charge upon all export duties and taxes of the State, including the industries and professions tax and the sewage and water tax. Of the proceeds, $1,000,000 was to be used for the retirement of the 5 per cent loan and the balance to complete the construction of the sewage and water system at Fortaleza. By September 30, 1928, interest and sinking fund in arrears totalled $278,443, which the State undertook to liquidate by semi-annual installments of $40,000 beginning April 1, 1929, sinking fund to be reduced to $20,000 until arrears are paid off in 1932, when the original amortization of $40,000 per annum was to be restored. Bonds are in complete default.

Maranhão succeeded in obtaining accommodations in the United States in 1923. A loan of $1,500,000 was reported to have been taken privately. The State is understood to have received very little actual cash when the transaction was over. In 1928 a refunding operation was effected through the sale of a loan of $1,750,000, bearing interest at the rate of 7 per cent per annum and maturing in 30 years. Bondholders are apparently optimistic when referring to loans on the basis of the date of repayment. They are gradually discovering that the only date on which they can depend is that of issue.

At any rate, the Maranhão loan is endowed with all the security and safeguards imaginable. Those identified with the issue knew how to secure, theoretically, at least, a foreign loan, especially one of Latin American origin. While bonds are outstanding, an American firm is to administer the properties pledged as security for the bonds and collect all revenues hypothecated therefor. Default commenced in November, 1931 with the suspension of sinking fund. Interest was withheld on May 1, 1932.

In 1910 the State contracted an issue in Paris to the amount of 18,000,000 francs, of which about 16,000,-000 francs remain outstanding. Bonds enjoy the benefit of specific security. It is stated that interest covering 1915 and 1916 was deposited in Brazil but could not be transferred to Paris owing to the war. Payment was made in October, 1916. Sinking fund payment was also postponed until 1928.

Adjoining Bahia on the north and Rio de Janeiro on the south, lies *Espirito Santo*, whose accommodations were taken care of by French bankers. A loan sold in 1908 to the amount of 30,000,000 "gold" francs went into default in 1914 and remained in default until 1927, when the French Bondholders Association offered on behalf of the State to redeem all outstanding bonds (14,696,000 francs) at their face amount and all arrears of interest, payment to be made in French francs only.

In 1919, the State obtained a loan of 23,023,160 francs which was to replace the obligations of the *Banque Hypothécaire et Agricole de l'Etat d'Espirito Santo*, which was acquired by the State. The bonds are specifically secured by a pledge of revenues derived from the property transfer tax and stamp tax; also by a pledge subject to the 5 per cent loan of 1908 of the revenues derived from the export taxes. Default occurred in December, 1931, while the 1908 loan defaulted in April, 1932.

Minas Geraes, fifth largest and one of the richest

States of Brazil, embarked on a borrowing campaign in 1907. Within four years, loans totalling almost $40,-000,000 were contracted in Paris. In 1916, a Consolidation loan was arranged for the purpose of consolidating State obligations, including three coupons of the 6 per cent loan of the City of Bello Horizonte which is guaranteed by the State. The loans were payable in gold francs, and Minas Geraes refused to make payment in gold. Bondholders brought suit against the State. Judgment was rendered against it, but Minas Geraes did not incline to recognize the jurisdiction of the French courts. Despite the checkered career of the State as a borrower, American bankers underwrote an $8,500,000 loan in 1928, bearing interest at the rate of 6½ per cent per annum. A loan of £1,750,000 was underwritten and offered in London. The new loans provided for the liquidation of 312,424,000 francs, of which 234,405,000 francs were paid in 1928, and about 160,000,000 francs for interest on these loans in respect of the period 1926-29. Inasmuch as the French loans which were to be retired with the proceeds from the sale of new bonds bore interest at 4½, 5 and 5½ per cent, one may perhaps question the wisdom on the part of the State to borrow at 6½ per cent.

In 1929, the State obtained additional $8,000,000 in the United States. This time, England did not come along although British bankers may have been instrumental in placing some of the bonds in Europe.

The interest as well as the sinking fund on the above loans were paid in September, 1931, out of a reserve fund. The March, 1932 and subsequent payments were not honored.

The same is true of the 6 per cent issue of the *City of Bello Horizonte*, known also as Minas, capital and principal city of the State. The loan referred to was contracted in 1905 to the amount of £225,000, of which about £95,000 remain outstanding. One half of the loan was placed in Amsterdam, the other half being sold in London. Default occurred in September, 1914, was rectified in January, 1915. The March, 1915 interest was not paid until June of that year. Payments were made promptly beginning September 30, 1918. The March, 1932 and subsequent coupons were not paid.

Para, third largest State, lies directly under the equator. The climate is tropical and rubber represents the chief and practically only product. The Ford interests have undertaken the development of a plantation rubber industry with a concession covering 2,500 square miles. The State has a population of over 1,-400,000, most of it concentrated at widely separated points on the coast and near navigable rivers. The State has been in complete default on its entire indebtedness since 1921, although on the 5 per cent loan of 1901-02 a coupon was paid in January, 1930 on account of July, 1924 interest. Bonds are held in England, Holland, Portugal and Brazil, and are all specifically secured by export taxes, revenues of State railways and water works, alcohol and tobacco taxes, and various other revenues.

Para, capital and chief city of the State and officially known as Belem has also been in default for more than a decade. The population is about 280,000. The city's bonds are held largely in England, France and Brazil.

The bonds of the *Port of Para Company*, a Maine
enterprise, have been in default since 1922 as a result
of non payment of the guarantee by the Brazilian Government. Although incorporated under the laws of the
State of Maine, U. S. A., relatively few of the company's securities are held by American investors. The
bulk of the various issues is held chiefly in England,
Belgium, France, Holland, and Switzerland.

In May, 1931, the *City of Pernambuco*, capital and
principal city in the State of the same name and third
largest city in Brazil, defaulted with respect to interest.
The bonds affected are the 5s of 1910, were sold largely
in England, Belgium, and Germany, and are unconditionally guaranteed by the *State of Pernambuco*, which
defaulted on September 1, 1931 on its 7 per cent Loan
of 1927.

Default also occurred in August, 1931 in the bonds
of Brazil's capital and second largest city, *Rio de
Janeiro*. The bonds were issued to an amount of $30,-
000,000 in the American market, at 97 per cent and
interest.

Other defaults of Rio de Janeiro include two loans
sold in Great Britain, and two more issues placed in
the United States. The latter, particularly the $12,-
000,000 loan of 1921, have been the subject of an investigation by the U. S. Senate. In the course of the
hearings, it was revealed that bonds were purchased
by the underwriters at 89 per cent, giving the City a
total of $10,680,000. Of this amount, $8,900,000 was
to be used in leveling Castle Hill, one of the mountains
around which the City clusters; $1,000,000 was turned
over to the Equitable Trust Company and used in the

purchase of outstanding bonds other than the 1921 loan; $250,000 went into a general fund, out of which $239,518 was used in meeting interest payment due October 1, 1931; and $500,000 was drawn down by the Mayor of Rio de Janeiro. The inquiring senators seemed somewhat exercised because the bankers could not account for the entire amount obtained by the City. Do they realize that the investment quality of the loan is not affected one iota by what the Brazilian municipality chose to do with the money? Americans were advancing funds only because they felt that Rio was a good risk. They obtained a promissory note in return. It might interest inquiring senators to know that the Rio default would have occurred even if the bankers had been able to trace every cent advanced to Brazil's capital.

The default of the State of *Rio Grande do Norte* refers to a 5 per cent loan issued in France in 1910 to the amount of Fcs. 8,750,000, of which Fcs. 7,031,500 remain outstanding. Bonds were specifically secured by a 1 per cent tax on the exportation of salt, a 2 per cent sewer tax and by a lien on the navigation dues. Payments are scheduled to be made on a gold basis, which the State refused to carry out, in spite of a court decision rendered in February, 1930 in favor of the bondholders. At present bonds are in complete default.

Parana, one of the southern Atlantic States of Brazil, emulated the more powerful State of Minas Geraes. With the aid of American bankers, the State was persuaded to liquidate three French "gold" loans bearing interest chiefly at 5 per cent with only a relatively small amount paying 6 per cent, through the sale to American and British investors of 7 per cent loans. The latter were underwritten by Chase Securities and Blair and Company of New York and by Lazard Brothers of London, to the amounts of $4,860,-000 and £1,000,000, respectively. The State failed to remit funds covering the September, 1931 interest and sinking fund. The former was paid out of an existing reserve fund, while amortization was not taken care of. In March, 1932, the default became complete.

On October 20, 1931, the Fiscal Agents of the *State of Rio Grande do Sul* 6 per cent Loan of 1928, announced the receipt of a cable from the Secretary of Finance of the State to the effect that, being unable to purchase dollar exchange, the State cannot remit on October 25 funds to pay the coupon maturing December 1. The cable renews the suggestion that deposit be made in Brazilian currency at 8.5 milreis to the dollar for conversion into dollars as soon as the exchange situation allows. The same is true of other loans sold abroad on behalf of Rio Grande do Sul or the various municipalities in the State for which the latter has assumed responsibilities.

All of the Rio Grande do Sul loans have been sold in the American market. The State is located at the most southern point of Brazil, embraces an area of somewhat more than 91,000 square miles, and has a population of close to 3,000,000 of whom one-third are foreign-born, chiefly Italian and German. In connection with the sale of its bonds, the wealth of the State has been estimated at $976,000,000 as compared with a total indebtedness of about $65,000,000. The latter figure includes also guaranteed loans.

The 8 per cent loan of the State is scheduled to be redeemed by semi-annual drawings by lot at 105 to the extent of one-thirtieth of the amount each, calculated to retire the whole issue by 1946. Bonds are specifically secured by a first lien on all taxes imposed by the State on the transmission of property, on inheritances and legacies, and on the net annual revenues of the port of Porto Alegre. In the event that pledged revenues should prove insufficient, the State agrees to mortgage such additional revenues and taxes as may be necessary. Proceeds from the sale of the loan were to be used for the improvement of transportation facilities of the State through construction in connection with the wharf work of Porto Alegre, channel improvements, the installation of equipment for coal properties, and for the retirement of funded debt. Bonds were offered in the American market at 99½ and interest. Default occurred in April, 1932.

The 7 per cent loan of 1926 was issued to the amount of $10,000,000 for the purpose of retiring floating debt, for capital expenditures for railroads, for inland canals, and other public works. Bonds are specifically secured by a first lien on the consumption tax and transportation tax; by a lien, subject to the 1921 loan, on the property transfer tax and inheritance tax, and on the net revenues of the port of Porto Alegre. Bonds were offered in 1927 at 98 and interest. Interest defaulted in November, 1931.

The 7 per cent loan of 1927 was issued for the construction or acquisition of water works and other revenue-producing properties. Bonds are an obligation of eight municipalities, including Pelotas, Rio Grande, Cachoeira, Bage, São Leopoldo, Sant' Ana do Livramento, Uruguayana, and Caixas. Each municipality is liable in proportion to its share in the proceeds of the loan. In addition, the issue is secured by a first lien on certain taxes levied by the respective communities and is unconditionally guaranteed by the State of Rio Grande do Sul. Bonds were offered in June, 1927 at 97 and interest. Default occurred in December, 1931.

The 6 per cent loan of 1928 was offered in July, 1928 at 94½ and interest and was scheduled to be redeemed by semi-annual drawings by lot at par, commencing December 1, 1932. Proceeds from the sale of bonds, issued to the amount of $23,000,000 of a total authorized issue of $42,000,000, were to be applied to the redemption of the State's 6 per cent loan of 1919, the redemption of certain internal loans, subscription of the State to the capital of the Rural Credit and Mortgage Bank, and to advances to the municipalities of Cruz Alta, Santa Maria, Itaquay and Alegrete for sanitation works. The above loan did not enjoy the benefit of any specific security. Rio Grande do Sul, however, agrees that bonds shall have a prior lien on any of the State's revenues or income which may hereafter be pledged to secure any future loan. Bonds defaulted in December, 1931.

Pelotas, a city with 82,500 inhabitants, is located in the southern part of the State. Its first appearance as a foreign borrower occurred in 1911 when the City obtained a loan in London to the amount of £600,000, to be redeemed by drawings at par or purchase in the open market. Bonds are secured by a lien on the House Tax and are, in addition, guaranteed by the State by endorsement.

The capital and chief city of the State, *Porto Alegre* has a population of 276,000. Three of the City's external loans have been sold in the American market, bearing interest at the rate of 7 to 8 per cent per annum. One loan, a 5 per cent issue, was sold in London and Amsterdam prior to the war to the amount of £600,000 at 93½.

In 1921, the City secured an 8 per cent loan of $3,-500,000, sold to the public at 99. Bonds were scheduled to be redeemed by drawings by lot. Proceeds were to be applied to road construction, sanitation works, street lighting and redemption of funded debt. As security, the City assigned the taxes imposed for the services of water, drainage and light. The State is also liable for the bonds, which it guarantees unconditionally as to both principal and interest.

The 7½ per cent loan of 1926 is redeemable by means of a sinking fund operated by drawings only and is secured by a pledge of certain municipal taxes and surtaxes.

The proceeds from the sale of the 7 per cent loan of 1928 were to be used for sanitation works and construction and paving of streets. The sinking fund is applied to drawings at par or purchase of bonds in the market. The bonds do not enjoy the benefit of any specific security but are unconditionally guaranteed by the State.

The *State of Rio de Janeiro*, which is entirely distinct from the Federal District of the same name, has outstanding three external loans, all sold within a period of five years. The first was a 5½ per cent issue contracted for the purpose of retiring a 5 per cent loan and enabling the State to contract a 7 per cent loan. The issue was offered to the amount of £1,-926,500, in conversion, par for par, of the 5's of 1912. Following the example set by their American cousins, the British bankers stipulated that the sinking fund be applied to half-yearly drawings of bonds by lot.

Of the 7 per cent loan of 1927, authorized to the amount of £2,100,000, only £1,863,500 was issued at 97. The loan was specifically secured by a lien on a new gold tax on the export of sugar and coffee, subject to the 5½ per cent loan of 1927. The December, 1931 coupon was paid. The June, 1932 and subsequent payments have been withheld. In 1929, the State contracted a 6½ per cent loan in the American market, amounting to $6,000,000. Bonds were secured on various taxes and duties and were sold at 91½ and interest. Interest due in January, 1932 was paid in full. The July payment was not made.

The bonds of the *City of Nictheroy*, capital of the State, with a population of about 110,000 were sold in London to the amount of £400,000. Principal and interest are payable in pounds or, at the option of the holders, in U. S. dollars at the fixed rate of $4.86 to the pound. Bonds are secured on twenty different tax revenues of the City and are, in addition, guaranteed by the State of Rio de Janeiro. Despite the apparently adequate protection, default occurred on December 15, 1931. That is to say, the City deposited funds with local banks, but bondholders abroad received nothing.

The *City of Rio de Janeiro* is the capital of the United States of Brazil and the second largest city in South America. Of the five external loans two have been placed in London, the 5 per cent loan of 1904 of £4,000,000, and the 4½ per cent loan of 1912 issued to the amount of £2,500,000 of an authorized amount of £10,000,000. The former is payable in pounds sterling only, while the latter is also payable in Swiss francs and guilders at fixed rates of exchange.

São Paulo, often referred to as the Empire State of Brazil, embraces an area as large as New York and the New England States combined. The population, numbering 6,500,000, is chiefly of Italian, Spanish, German, and Portuguese extraction. The wealth of the State is estimated at $4,000,000,000, whereas the total indebtedness amounts to about $350,000,000. The principal issues in default, the first of which São Paulo is guilty throughout its entire history as a borrower, comprise loans issued for productive purposes and enjoying as a rule the benefit of specific security.

The 5 per cent loan of 1905 was sold abroad, largely in England, France and Germany, for the purpose of purchasing the Sorocabana Railway and of providing funds for extension and improvements. Bonds are secured by a first mortgage on the railway property and the net operating revenues. Payments are scheduled to be made in gold sterling. Bonds were issued originally for £3,800,000. Payments ceased in January, 1932.

A 5 per cent loan contracted in London in 1904 to the amount of £1,000,000 defaulted in April, 1932.

The 5 per cent loan of 1907 was sold almost exclusively in France although large amounts are known to be held in England, Holland and the United States. Bonds are payable in gold francs or the equivalent and are secured, subject to the 5 per cent loan of 1905, by a pledge of net receipts derived from the operation of the Sorocabana-Ituana Railway and extensions. Bonds defaulted in January, 1932.

The São Paulo 6 per cent loan of 1928 was issued in the United States and Great Britain to the extent of $15,000,000 and £3,500,000, respectively. Payments are made either in New York or London at the fixed rate of $4.8665 to the pound. Proceeds of the loan were to be used for additions, betterments and extensions to the water supply and sewage system of the City of São Paulo, and for extension of the Sorocabana Railway from Mayrink to the Port of Santos. Bonds are not specifically secured. Default occurred in January, 1932.

An 8 per cent loan was contracted in 1921 to the amount of $10,000,000, £2,000,000, and 18,000,000 guilders. Bonds are secured by a first charge on the surtax of 5 francs per bag on all coffee exported from the State. Of the surtax, 44 per cent is pledged for the service of the American loan of $10,000,000 and is to be remitted in weekly installments to Speyer and Company. While interest was paid in January, 1932, sinking fund payments were partly in default on that day.

The 7 per cent loans of £7,500,000 and £2,500,000 contracted in 1926 defaulted in March, 1932, although technically, default occurred in January because of the failure on the part of the State to remit funds monthly as provided in the Loan contracts.

Default also took place in respect of the 6 per cent mortgage bonds of the Bank of the State of São Paulo, which are unconditionally guaranteed by the State. Bonds comprise Series A of 1927, issued at £1,250,000 (defaulted expected in May, 1932); Series B of 1928, issued at £1,250,000 (default expected in March, 1932) ; and Series C also of 1928, issued at £1,250,000.

The 8 per cent loan of 1925 was sold to the amount of $15,000,000 for the purpose of improving and making additions to the State-owned Sorocabana Railway. It is somewhat difficult to understand how financiers continued to pour millions of investors' funds into an obviously unprofitable Government venture. The ease with which funds were obtainable at the time is probably responsible for the frequency of borrowing on behalf of the Sorocabana system. Bonds are secured by a first charge on the receipts from the tax on transfer of real property and from the inheritance tax; by a first lien on about 560 miles of road; a second lien on 500 miles, subject to the loan of 1905; and a charge on the net earnings subject to existing charges. The loan contract provides that service requirements should be remitted in weekly installments to the fiscal agents. The State did not remit interest due January 1, 1932. Payment was made out of the Reserve Fund. Sinking fund was partly in default at the beginning of the year. Complete default took place in July, 1932.

The State has also outstanding a 7½ per cent loan of about £9,500,000 of an original issue of £10,000,-000. Bonds were sold for the purpose of regulating and furthering the coffee industry. It is understood that Lazard Frères of New York were advised by the State Department not to sell bonds in the American market, on the grounds, presumably, that the consumer in the United States would be called upon to pay more for coffee than is warranted by the statistical position of the commodity. The American bankers heeded the advice of the United States Department of State.

Bonds were subsequently sold in London by Lazard Brothers. One wonders how the State Department feels on learning that these bonds are being paid promptly, while many a São Paulo loan which had received the Department's sanction, pays no longer.

No default is anticipated in respect of the so-called Coffee Realization Loan of 1930, contracted in New York to the amount of $35,000,000; and in London to the amount of £10,000,000.

While the State of São Paulo, whose past fiscal record may safely be said to have been better than that of any other political entity in all Latin America, is in complete default with respect to practically all its external engagements, creditors may derive some consolation from a decree issued on April 28, 1932, providing for payment of interest in two-year 5 per cent Notes of the State on the Sterling 5 per cent loans of 1904 and 1905, the Gold Franc 5 per cent loan of 1907, the Dollar 8 per cent loan of 1925, and the Dollar and Sterling 6 and 7 per cent loans of 1928 and 1926, respectively.

The above Notes were to be delivered to the Fiscal Agents of the loans in question on the dates when service payments normally fall due, and were scheduled to mature two years from date of issue. They are to be held by the Fiscal Agents until redemption by the State, and are not to be distributed to the bondholders. The State reserved the right to extend the plan for a third year, in which case it must furnish documentary proof for the necessity of such prolongation, and must make monthly deposits of five million milreis (about $600,000 at par of exchange).

As security for the Notes, the State agreed to deposit on the Bank of Brazil, for a period of nine months beginning April 30, 1932, four million milreis monthly, five million for the next following nine months, and six and a half million for the following six months. It is also provided that such deposits can be withdrawn or negotiated only for the purpose of being converted into the foreign currencies needed for the loan service. Proceeds are to be employed for the redemption of Notes, the State having the right to redeem them prior to maturity. Pending conversion into foreign currency, the deposits are to be employed in the country in "securities easily realizable" and subject to prior arrangement with the Fiscal Agents.

The *City of São Paulo* is the third largest city in all South America and the second in Brazil. Population is about 900,000. Funded debt is relatively small, latest figures placing the total at not much in excess of $25,-000,000. Until 1932 the City could boast of a perfect fiscal record.

The 6 per cent loan of 1908 was placed in London to the amount of £750,000 and is secured by a lien on the revenue derived from the tax on trades and professions. Interest defaulted January 1, 1932.

The 6 per cent loan of 1919 was sold in New York and was among the first Latin American loans placed in the American market immediately after the war. Proceeds were used to refund an internal loan and an issue sold in New York in 1916, of which $4,950,000 remained outstanding. The loan is secured by a lien on the transportation tax and the tax on industries and professions. Default took place in May, 1932.

The 6½ per cent loan of 1927 appear to have been sold largely for the purpose of covering budgetary deficits. Nonetheless, American bankers obtained the business only as a result of very keen competition. The loan is secured by a first charge on the Municipal Fees, License and Publicity Taxes, as well as by a lien, subject to existing charges, upon the Industries and Professions, Transportation, Sanitation and Vehicle Taxes. Bonds defaulted in November, 1931, as did also the 8 per cent loan of 1922 which were sold in the United States to the amount of $4,000,000. Proceeds were to be used in the construction and improvement of streets, tunnels and the municipal market. Bonds are secured by a charge on the receipts from the Sanitation and Vehicle Taxes; a charge on the Transportation Tax and the Industries and Professions Taxes, subject to existing liens. According to the loan contract, the City agrees to pay the Fiscal Agent annually (on April 1) $137,931 to be applied during the succeeding 12 months to the purchase of not less than $138,000 par value of bonds. Any unused balance at the end of such period is to be credited to the account of the City. Default occurred in November, 1931.

Santos, the seaport of São Paulo, is the greatest coffee shipping center of the world. It handles about half of Brazil's exports and 30 per cent of her imports. The debt comprises a loan contracted in London in 1927 for the purpose of redeeming existing issues and for "other purposes." Bonds are secured by a general charge on the municipal assets and revenues. Interest defaulted in December, 1931.

BULGARIA

By virtue of an agreement between the *Bulgarian* Government and representatives of its external loans, the service on foreign engagements is being met only partly in cash, the balance being paid in leva into a so-called blocked account, to be invested within the country "in a certain specified manner." With regard to the League of Nations Loans (the Refugee Settlement 7 per cent issue of 1926, and the 7½ per cent Stabilization Loan of 1928), the following arrangements were recommended to bondholders by the League Loans Committee:

Payments covering the period April 15-September 15, 1933 were to be paid in cash by the Bulgarian Government to the extent of 50 per cent, the remainder to be invested in blocked leva. For the following six months (October 15, 1932-April 15, 1933), 40 per cent was to be paid in cash, and the remaining 60 per cent in blocked leva.

CANADA

The situation in some parts of Canada is disheartening. At the beginning of 1933, municipalities in the *Province of Alberta*, in default on certain of their obligations, included Bow Island, Barrhead, Carbon, Kitscoty, Mundare, Magrath, and Calgary. Of school districts, 113 have made partial payment, and 73 have made no payment on their defaulted obligations.

Municipalities in the Province of *British Columbia* in default include, Merritt, North Vancouver, Prince Rupert, Rossland, Burnaby District, and North Vancouver District.

Municipalities in the *Province of Quebec* in default include, St. Joseph d'Alma (town and parish), St. Henri-de-Taillon, Tache, St. Honore, St. Simeon, St. Camille-de-Lellis, Black Lake, Greenfield Park, Amherst, Low, Macamic, Begin, St. Fulgence, Bourget, St. Jerome, Tremblay, Quebec-West, St. Joseph-de-la-Rivière-Bleue, Delisle, and St. Coeur-de-Marie. The following school districts, located in the Province of Quebec, were also reported in default, as of March 1, 1933: Bagotville, Ste. Anne, St. Honore, Chicoutimi, St. Simeon, Escoumains, St. Camille, St. Remi d'Amherts, Tache, St. Coeur-de-Marie, St. Jerome, St. Jean l'Evangéliste, Royal Roussillon, Bourget, Jonquiette, Harvey, and St. Joseph d'Alma. The following municipalities in the *Province of Ontario* have been reported in default with respect to certain of their obligations: Border Cities, Scarboro, Pelee, and Hawkesbury.

CHILE

In connection with the complete collapse, in 1931, of the fiscal structure of the *Republic of Chile*, for years the spoiled darling of the American investing public, the following statement was issued by the Fiscal Agents of the Chilean Government in the United States:

Chile, a country which during 89 years had promptly paid interest and principal on its debts, and as promptly met sinking fund requirements except in wartime in 1880-83, during the past month has deferred payments currently due abroad on public obligations, and her economic difficulties have culminated, as in a number of other South American countries, in an overturn of government. . . .

On July 16th the government . . . made formal announcement that payment of service on foreign obligations could not at present be made in foreign currency, and that the amounts due to be remitted abroad prior to August 1st would be deposited in Chilean currency in the Central Bank of Chile. The desire of the new government to keep faith with its creditors is not in question, and its personnel supplies assurance that its endeavors to solve the country's economic problem will be soundly conceived and able in execution. . . .

Payments due were made during the first half of this year, but available resources for the purchase of foreign exchange were gradually exhausted. The flow of private investment capital into the country has dwindled to nothing, incident to the slowing down of enterprise everywhere while the world catches up to the capacity of the plant it has already constructed. Prices of Chilean bonds preclude public flotations of loans abroad. Any further depletion of gold reserves below present figures could not meet the need for exchange for long, and would be against the interest of both Chile and its creditors by draining the base of the country's currency and bank credit. Thus it is in the direction of a larger favorable balance of trade that the eventual solution of the problem needs be sought, emphasizing once again the fact that the basic remedy for disordered world finance is in the restoration of trade and of conditions that will promote it.

Deposit of pesos soon ceased, and the default of Chile became perfect, threatening to prove of more than temporary character.

CHINA

With the exception of loans secured on the maritime customs revenues, payment of interest and sinking fund on all obligations of *China* has been made irregularly and is in arrear.

ECUADOR

After a series of defaults and resumption of payments, *Ecuador* defaulted once more in August, 1914 and continued in complete default until July, 1918. In the following month, payment of coupons in arrear was begun, but payments have been small and were made irregularly.

In 1929, remittances abroad for service on certain of its external loans were discontinued, but were partially resumed in 1930. The bonds affected include the Condores 4 per cent loan, the 4 per cent Salt Bonds, and the Guayaquil and Quito First Mortgage 5 per cent Bonds. In August, 1930, the Council of Foreign Bondholders intervened, inviting deposits of the above issues, issuing Deposit Certificates therefor, properly negotiable. Discontinuance of debt service was officially said to be due to the fact that the Government was anxious to accelerate a debt settlement rather than to a complete lack of funds. The Council lodged a vigorous protest with the Ecuadorian Government which in January, 1930 replied that a decree by the Assembly prevented remittance of the debt service funds.

Costa Rica

On August 26, 1932, the *Costa Rican* Government announced that "due to existing very unfavorable economic and financial conditions in the Republic, including an acute shortage of foreign exchange," it will be necessary to suspend payments in respect of its 7 per cent External Gold Bonds of 1926, the 5 per cent Refunding Loan of 1911, and the 7½ per cent Railway Bonds of 1927, in each case for a period authorized by law No. 80. (It will be noted that some creditors are very meticulous about defaulting on contractual engagements. Nothing is done without enacting the necessary legislation). In the case of dollar bonds, this period will extend to and including November 1, 1935. In the case of the other two issues, the period of suspension will be of approximately equal duration. Interest is to be paid in 5 per cent Funding Bonds, the Republic agreeing to resume on November 1, 1935 full payments for interest and amortization, to increase the semi-annual payments required for the service of its external debt so as to accelerate the rate of retirement, and to make good by their maturity the deficiency in sinking fund payments during the period of suspension.

Germany

Under date of June 9, 1933, the *German* Government enacted legislation providing for the suspension of payments on contractual obligations. The legalized suspension of payments has been given the official designation of transfer moratorium, which became effective July 1, 1933, or only three months after the proclamation of the Third Reich under the Nazi régime. The decree permits the transfer of interest payments in full on the so-called Dawes and Young loans. Amortization payments on the Dawes Loan will also be transferred, but transfer of redemption sums for the Young Loan and all other amortization sums falling due will be omitted. The Reichsbank agreed to make payment in respect of interest due for six months to December 31, 1933, at the rate of 50 per cent of the amount due. It was further provided that a maximum interest of 4 per cent per annum would be paid. Amounts due by German debtors, but not transferred, are to be paid in marks into a conversion fund administered under the direction of the Reichsbank. They will be kept at the disposal of creditors with this distinction: Untransferred interest and dividends will put at the disposal of creditors negotiable bills, while untransferred amortization payments will be held by conversion funds for bondholders.

Commenting on Germany's default, Sir Arthur Samuel, prominent British statesman-economist, has this to say: "Germany will not be able to raise money again in Great Britain, France, or the United States during our lifetime. . . . Abuse of credit by foreign borrowers has developed into abuse of confidence, amounting to nothing less than vulgar dishonesty. We see the result: International commercial intercourse has become nearly impossible because the structure on which such commerce can be organized lies in ruins. . . . Cold and selfish disregard of post-war obligations by the Prusso-German authorities when they imposed the transfer moratorium upon those who trusted to their pledged faith shocked all honest men. . . . The arrogant trampling on the rights of others is all of a piece with the German mentality that led up to the World War and constitutes one of the worst cases of debt default."

GREECE

Greece defaulted with respect to contractual commitments in April, 1932, Premier Venizelos notifying the League of Nations Council that the 1933 budget contained no provision for payment of sinking funds on foreign or internal debts; that interest on external loans would be paid in drachmae in a blocked account in the Bank of Greece, and that interest on internal loans would be reduced 25 per cent. Default was authorized by Law 5456 of May 10, 1932, the law being retroactive to March 31, 1932. The International Financial Commission protested against violation of loan contracts, with the result that Greece agreed to pay interest on foreign engagements at the rate of 30 per cent in cash, the remainder to be taken care of in Greek currency deposited to the credit of bondholders in the National Bank of Greece, for transfer as and when conditions allow.

GUATEMALA

The default of *Guatemala*[3] involves in addition to direct loans of the Republic, interest payments on the International Railways of Central America, Zacapa-Salvador Extension, carried by the Government under the item "Current Deficit," and on the Los Altos Maintenance Contract.

JUGOSLAVIA

Beginning with January, 1926, *Jugoslavia* is paying with each coupon of the Montenegro 5 per cent Loan of 1919, one arrear coupon. In 1933, two coupons were still in arrears. Sinking fund payment on bonds was resumed in 1923 but discontinued in 1932.

Interest and sinking fund payments on all Jugoslav external loans defaulted in the Fall of 1932. In the following year, the Government proposed a plan to bondholders, providing for the payment of six coupons by either of two methods, at the option of holders, as follows:

---

[3] From Special Report No. 14, prepared by U. S. Commercial Attache Bohan at Guatemala City, under date of March 9, 1931.

1. Coupons to be paid in dinars, at the rate of 56.78 dinars per dollar, during a period of six months after their respective maturing dates.

2. Coupons will be paid to the extent of 10 per cent in U. S. dollars, and balance in 5 per cent Funding Bonds, due November 1, 1956.

Either of these alternative proposals may be accepted by bondholders in respect of any or all coupons.

LATVIA

The *City of Riga* has been in default since May, 1918. In June, 1930, a conference was held at Riga relative to a settlement of the municipal debt, and attended by representatives of the bankers, the Latvian Government, and the City. The bondholders apparently were left out. They are included, apparently, only when bonds are sold.

The *Wolmar Railway Company* has outstanding a 4½ per cent loan of £178,760 of an original issue of £179,880. The loan was sanctioned by the Russian Government in 1910, for the purpose of constructing a railway of about 71 miles, taking the entire capital stock of 560,000 rubles, paying for it in cash. Bonds have been in default since December, 1917. The issue was unconditionally guaranteed by the Council of Landowners of the Province of Livonia, while for twenty years from the opening of the railway for regular traffic, interest was unconditionally guaranteed by the Government of the Province of Livonia by virtue of the sanction of the Council of the Russian Government which reserved the right to purchase the railway at the expiration of the twenty-year period, by assuming all the liabilities of the company.

In January, 1922, bondholders were requested by the British Bank for Foreign Trade to submit their bonds on the basis of a cash settlement of £40 for each £100 par value, the price of £40 to cover accrued interest and sums payable in respect of bonds drawn for redemption. However, the Bank failed to carry out the agreement and, under a decision of the District Court of Riga, bondholders' claims were to be regarded as settled by the deposit of a sum in paper rubles in payment of the sterling bonds. This sum was equivalent to only £1,307. However, an appeal was made as a result of which the decision was upset and in December, 1927, the Latvian Senate handed down a final verdict in favor of the British bondholders.

MEXICO

Under date of July 25, 1930, an agreement was reached between the Government of *Mexico* and the International Committee of Bankers acting on behalf of holders of Mexican obligations. The agreement provides for the scaling down and funding of the Mexican Government so-called direct debt in 5 per cent bonds of a new issue. The direct debt includes the External 5 per cent loan of 1899, the External 4 per cent loan of 1904, the External 4 per cent of 1910 and the Treasury Bonds of 1913.

The new conversion bonds were to be secured by a first lien on the customs receipts of the republic and were to be divided into two series, A and B. The former was to be secured by a first lien on the pledged customs and was to be given to holders of the Mexican Government debt which enjoys the benefit of specific security. Series B, on the other hand, was to rank, in point of security, after the series A bonds and was to be exchanged for obligations of the Mexican unsecured debt. Interest rate on both series was to commence at 3 per cent per annum, rising gradually to 5 per cent, which figure series A was to attain by 1935, and series B one year later.

In the case of the Railway debt it was suggested that the bonds would also be converted into a new issue of 5 per cent obligations to be secured by general mortgage on the Mexican railway system. Interest was to be paid at a graduated rate attaining 5 per cent within five years from the commencement of payment.

With respect to interest in arrears covering the period 1922-25, bondholders were asked to forego such payments to a large extent. The holders of class A receipts were to receive 2 per cent of their nominal value and holders of class B receipts were to receive 1 per cent, while current interest scrip, cash warrants and coupons maturing prior to January 1, 1931 were to receive 10 per cent of the amount held. The agreement also provides for the creation of a special fund to be utilized for the redemption of these arrears. The Mexican Government agreed to provide annuities beginning with $12,500,000 in 1931 and gradually rising to $15,000,000 in 1936, at which figure they were to remain during the balance of the 45-year period stipulated for the entire redemption of the Mexican Government debt, including direct as well as railway obligations.

Due to the substantial decline in the Mexican exchange the agreement was not ratified. A supplemental agreement was entered into which postpones for a period of two years the annuities referred to above.

In the meantime however the Government agrees to pay to the Committee, or to the credit of the Committee, the required amounts on a silver basis, disbursements to be made to bondholders as and when excharge conditions allow.

Later developments in regard to the Mexican debt situation include a report, published in the Wall Street Journal on August 14, 1931 to the effect that President Ortiz Rubio had asked the Mexican Congress to prolong its present extraordinary session in order to take up the problem of liquidating the government's public debt, and that a bill establishing the means of handling the interior debt and drawn up in conformity with the report of the Interior Debt Commission, which was established in January, 1929, would be presented to Congress. The Lamont-Montes de Oca pact for payment on the foreign debt is still pending before the legislative body, but nothing definite was undertaken. Same applies also to the problem of the interior debt.

Of interest is also the following information published in the Wall Street Journal and based upon a special report from Mexico City in the summer of 1931: "Proposals for a ten-year moratorium on Mexico's foreign debt, intensification of the campaign for the consumption of national products, bringing in of select groups of foreigners for colonization purposes, abolition of the stamp tax, and construction of highways from production fields to railroads, will be taken up at the convention of the Confederation of Chambers of Commerce scheduled to convene in September." As was to be expected, nothing was accomplished, and the default continues as regards all Mexican obligations.

PERU

On March 1, 1931, *Peru* announced that she would no longer be able to take care of payment upon her external debts. It was also stated that the Republic fully acknowledges her contractual obligations, but continued payment of interest and sinking fund would jeopardize the economic life of the country, so that a new arrangement is sought on the basis of the nation's ability to pay.

RUMANIA

In connection with Rumania's financial difficulties and the country's inability to meet external commitments in accordance with provisions in original loan agreements, the following was prepared by the Rumanian Minister of Finance, Virgil Madgearu, and made public under date of September 30, 1933, by George Boncescu, Financial Counsellor of the Rumanian Legation at Washington:

Since the stabilization of her currency, Roumania made every effort to fulfill her foreign obligations scrupulously. Although in the last four years, the national income has been cut in half, due to the world depression and the increasing restrictions imposed by all the countries who normally import agricultural products and raw materials, Roumania continued to make enormous sacrifices in order to meet her foreign obligations punctually and in full.

Only at the end of last year and after all the agrarian countries ceased to meet in full their foreign financial obligations, has Roumania approached the foreign holders of Roumanian bonds (or bondholders), with the object of readjusting the service on her public debt to her present capacity of payment and transfer. On that occasion the Roumanian Government has requested a reduction of Lei 3,500,000,000 in the debt service for the fiscal (budgetary) year 1933-34; this amount was equivalent to the sums which had to be raised by extraordinary budgetary means during the preceding fiscal year, in order to meet the most pressing needs. However, in spite of these measures, the budget for that fiscal year showed a deficit.

The bondholders associations had agreed on February 18, 1933, to a postponement of the sinking fund payments, a saving of only Lei 1,016,000,000. This figure was raised to Lei 2,179,-000,000 thanks to the general postponement of war debt payments, suspension of sinking fund payments of certain commercial debts, and savings effected in the administration of the public debt service.

Under the circumstances, the Roumanian Government, on February 18th, stated definitely that in case the total revenue for the first five months of the fiscal year 1933-34 fell below the budgetary estimates or if the trade balance did not provide a sufficient amount of foreign exchange, it would be forced to make the necessary reductions in the public debt service for the second half of this year, in order to adjust this service to the situation. The actual steps destined to accomplish this adjustment were to have been presented previously to the representatives of the bondholders.

To this statement the holders replied that in case the contingencies foreseen in the declaration of the Roumanian delegation materialized and if the facts established by the experts of the Financial committee of the League of Nations warranted their cooperation, they would determine, together with the Roumanian Government, on September 1, 1933, whether an additional agreement providing for further reductions was necessary.

As the situation in the first three months of the current fiscal year proved the fears of the Roumanian Government to have been justified, on July 6 it notified the bondholders association and the fiscal agents of the Roumanian loans, and requested that

negotiations be started on August 15. The proposed date of the
meeting originally set for the 1st of September, under the agreement of last February, was advanced two weeks, owing to
marked deterioration of the foreign exchange situation, which
made the transfer of foreign currency on August 15, on account
of the instalment due October 1, impossible. In the invitation
addressed, on July 6, to the bondholders associations and fiscal
agents, it was therefore definitely stated at the same time that
due to the shrinkage of foreign trade for the last three months,
serious difficulties have compelled Roumania, as far back as
June, to request the fiscal agents to agree to a postponement of
the transfer of sums due at that time.

The associations of bondholders requested a postponement of
the negotiations until after the 1st of September, and the date
of September 5th was agreed upon. This, however, put the
Roumanian Government in a difficult position and as it was
materially impossible to execute the August 16th transfer, on
account of the payment due October 1st, it was compelled to
decree a transfer moratorium on all Government payments
abroad.

This step, made unavoidable by circumstances beyond the
control of the Government, was not a unilateral irrevocable
measure, inasmuch as all payments due prior to October 1st
were made, and, therefore, the October 1st instalments could
have been discussed during the negotiations scheduled to begin
September 5th. This decision was taken as a measure of preservation and elementary foresight. This fact is undeniable, as
Roumania has always made every effort to respect her promises
and to fulfill her obligations abroad, going as far as to postpone, during the years 1931-32, the payment of the pensions
due Government employees and firms supplying the Government, in order to meet in full the service on the public debt.

The Roumanian delegates arrived in Paris on September 5th
to start the negotiations. The associations, however, refused to
begin conversations, putting, from the outset, conditions which,
normally, would have constituted the very objects of the nego-

tiations themselves. These were clearly stated in the declarations
when the agreement was signed in February. Now they are
being put as conditions to be fulfilled as a preliminary to all
negotiations.

In fact, the first condition was the cessation of the transfer
moratorium. But the lack of an adequate amount of foreign
exchange, one of the main reasons justifying fresh reductions
in the foreign debt service, was a well known fact of which the
fiscal agents were notified in June, and the bondholders associations by the letter of July 6, and, on the other hand, the payment
of the sum on account of which the transfer was to be effected
on August 16, was due on October 1. To ascertain the lack of
foreign exchange and discuss the consequent transfer problem
of the sums due in October, was precisely one of the objects of
the negotiations, in which the bondholders refused to participate.

The second condition was an investigation of the financial
situation of the Country by League of Nations experts. But as
early as July 6th, I pointed out that, due to conditions beyond
the control of the government, the appointment of the League
of Nations experts had not been possible, and suggested that, in
order to avoid any cause for postponement of the negotiations,
the report of Mr. Aubein, who was entrusted by the League of
Nations to supply information concerning the situation in Roumania until the agreement signed with the League of Nations
for technical collaboration could be carried out, be used as a
basis for the present negotiations. As a matter of fact, until
August 29th no objections were raised in this respect, and, in
the meantime, Mr. Aubein has made and published his report.

As only the representatives of the Czechoslovakian Bondholders Association appeared at the meeting of September 6th,
the Roumanian Delegates informed the associations of bondholders that they would remain in Paris until September 2?,
in readiness to begin conversations. However, as until that date
the associations have not shown any willingness to negotiate,
the Government, in view of the instalment due on October 1st
and of the failure of the bondholders associations to make any

proposals towards reaching an agreement, but wishing to prove its willingness to make every possible effort to fulfill its obligations, is obliged to appeal direct to the holders of Roumanian bonds.

In order to realize in the fiscal year 1933-34, i.e.: until April 1, 1934, the total saving of Lei 3,500,000,000, as requested last December, and as a further reduction of Lei 1,303,000,000 is therefore necessary, the Roumanian Government offers to the bondholders the following mode of payment of interest due in the second half of the year:

20% in cash, transferable in foreign exchange; and

80% in bonds of the Caisse d'Amortissement de l'Etat, bearing interest at the rate of 4% per annum, beginning April 1, 1934, redeemable in two half-yearly installments during the fiscal year 1936-37. These bonds will be issued in lei, and their exchange value will not be transferable until the dates above-mentioned; during this period, they can be negotiated and the proceeds invested in Roumanian mortgage bonds.

Without prejudging the execution of this offer, the Roumanian Government is ready to reach, on this basis, with the bondholders associations, the agreements imposed by unavoidable circumstances, keeping in mind that the Government has paid in full the interest in foreign exchange due in the first half of the year, and in the second half it will pay to the extent of 20%, also in foreign exchange. Therefore, during this year the holders of Roumanian bonds will have received, in spite of the seriousness of the crisis, 60% of the interest in foreign exchange and only the remaining 40% will have been paid in bonds.

RUSSIA

By virtue of a decree promulgated under date of February 3, 1918, *Russia* announced to her creditors that she would no longer meet the service on the country's obligations. Thus far, the decree has been very faithfully adhered to. A detailed analysis of the Russian indebtedness is given in the following table:

SUMMARY OF DEBTS CONTRACTED BY CZARIST RUSSIA

A—Pre-war debt.........................	$ 4,623,849,300
Accrued interest.....................	3,050,100,000
Total Pre-War Debt................	$ 7,673,949,300
B—External war loans..................	$ 75,000,000
Accrued interest.....................	50,125,000
Advances from Allies................	3,854,644,750
Accrued interest.....................	2,500,000,000
Total External War Debt..........	$ 6,479,769,750
Internal war loans...................	$ 8,500,000,000
Accrued interest.....................	5,335,000,000
Total Internal War Debt...........	$13,835,000,000
Total War Debt..................	$20,314,769,750
TOTAL DEBT.....................	$27,988,719,000

Of the above total, the debt to the United States, exclusive of private investments, aggregates $601,-853,750, distributed as follows:

	Principal Amount	Interest in Arrears	Total
Pre-war loans.....	$ 25,000,000	$ 12,750,000	$ 37,750,000
External war loans.	75,000,000	46,000,000	121,000,000
Advances from United States Government....	187,729,750	101,374,000	289,103,750
Internal war loans.	100,000,000	54,000,000	154,000,000
Total........	$387,729,750	$214,124,000	$601,853,750
Private Investments......	$110,000,000	$ 88,704,000*	$198,704,000

* Computed on basis of 6 per cent interest per annum.

TURKEY

In December, 1932, an Agreement was signed by the *Turkish* Government and representatives of foreign creditors, providing as follows:

1. The issue of a 7½ per cent Turkish National Bond, redeemable in 50 years, to replace the Turkish portion of the Ottoman Bonds, involving a reduction of the nominal capital of the Turkish share of the debt to about 890 million French francs.

2. The exchange of new bonds for old is to be effected during the first 10 years, and the ratio of new bonds to be allotted to existing loans is to be established after consultation with an expert.

3. An annuity of 700,000 Turkish pounds (gold), covering interest, redemption and expenses, to be transferred by the Government, payable in French francs or in another currency to be chosen by the Debt Council.

4. Customs revenues are pledged, but no agent of the Council is to be appointed for their supervision.

Ratification of the Agreement will necessitate the revision of the table exhibiting in detail the status of Turkey's external commitments in default.

America's Imperfect Record

In discussing defaults of governments or political subdivisions, attention must be directed to the suspension of payments by a number of States in the Union.

ALABAMA

During the period 1823-1826, *Alabama* acquired bank stocks to an aggregate amount of $8,000,000.

The banks collapsed in 1842, and the State was liable for their bills and most of their obligations. By 1861, this debt had been reduced by $4,555,000, leaving $3,445,000 still outstanding. The remainder of Alabama's debt arose from budgetary deficits and endorsements made and bonds issued on behalf of railroads. In 1871, the Alabama and Chattanooga Railroad Company defaulted in its interest, and, in 1873, other railroads followed suit. Thus, the State became liable for about $18,000,000 worth of railroad bonds, besides the State debt proper.

An agreement was reached in 1873, providing for the exchange of railroad bonds into State bonds on the basis of $4,000 par value of the former for $1,000 of the latter. The amount of new bonds created under this arrangement was $1,192,000. In 1876, a final settlement was made by the so-called Funding Act, as follows:

Issue	Original Amount	Amount Issued under Funding Plan	Purpose of Loan
Alabama 5's, 1866–1873....	$1,040,000	$1,040,000	To cover budget deficits
Alabama Educational Fund Loan, 1823–1826........	2,810,670	2,810,670	To purchase stock in State banks
Alabama Ordinary Loans, 1865–1873..............	7,416,800	7,127,709	To cover deficits and acquire stock in banks
Alabama Railway bonds,1873	1,192,000	596,000	In exchange for State Railway bonds
Alabama & Chattanooga Ry. Loan, 1867–1873........	5,300,000	1,000,000	......
Alabama & Chattanooga Ry. Loan, 1870.............	2,000,000	....	......
Alabama State Ry. Loans...	3,705,000	....	......

The interest which had accrued on the first three issues mentioned above was not recognized in the Funding Arrangement. The holders of the $2,000,000 issue of 1870 sold on behalf of the Alabama & Chattanooga Railroad became the recipients of the land of the latter, variously estimated from 500,000 to 1,200,000 acres.

ARKANSAS

Arkansas heads the list. The following comment on the early fiscal history of the State was made by the Honorable Robert J. Walker in 1864, in a brochure entitled "American Slavery and Finances":

In 1830, James Smithson, an eminent and wealthy citizen of London, in the Kingdom of Great Britain, died, bequeathing, by his last will and testament, the whole of his property to the United States of America, in trust, to found at Washington, under the name of "The Smithsonian Institution" an establishment "for the increase and diffusion of knowledge among men." After some delay, the Congress of the United States, in 1836, passed an Act, accepting the trust and pledging the faith of the Government for the faithful application of the money to the noble purpose designated by the illustrious donor. Under this Act, Richard Rush, one of our most distinguished citizens, who had been minister to England and to France and had held the position of Secretary of State and of the Treasury at Washington, was sent by the Government to London to obtain from the Court of Chancery the fund, amounting to over $500,000. It is usual, in the proceedings of the English Court of Chancery, when funds, under circumstances like these, are bequeathed to trustees for scientific or charitable purposes, not to part with the money to the trustee except upon his filing in Court absolute security for the faithful fulfillment of the trust. In this case however the High Court of Chancery in

England, considering that to imply any laches or neglect of a trust so sacred on the part of the Government of the United States was an idea not to be entertained, did, by their decree, without any security, hand over all the money to the Government of the United States, to be appropriated to the purpose designated by the donor, receiving only the pledge given by the Congress of the United States for the faithful appropriation of the money. Now, if there ever was any obligation that would be considered sacred by the whole civilized world, it was this, and most faithfully has the Government of the United States executed this trust. Nay, it has done much more; it has granted forty acres of ground, belonging to the Government, in the City of Washington, gratuitously, for the erection of the buildings for this noble Institution, which grounds, with the buildings upon them, erected by the Government, are worth largely more than the whole bequest. Not only has the Government done this but, upon the whole fund received from Mr. Smithson, it has always punctually paid an interest of 6 per cent in gold upon the whole sum and pledged its faith for a similar perpetual payment. It has also largely aided the Institution by contributions to its museum, collections and library and by the gratuitous services of public officers in its behalf. Such was the Bill passed by Congress in 1846 and which has always been most faithfully executed. So that the Institution is now established upon a permanent basis and is fulfilling all the great and noble purposes proposed by the illustrious donor. Now, in 1837, this fund was received by the Government of the United States and invested by the Secretary of the Treasury, Mr. Woodbury, in the 6 per cent Bonds of the State of Arkansas at par, to the extent of over half a million of dollars. During the same year, Arkansas invested this money in a bank entitled "The Real Estate Bank of Arkansas" and of which the State was the great stockholder.[4] In 1839, this

---

[4] Bonds issued by the State during 1837 and 1838 to aid the Bank of the State of Arkansas and the Retail Estate Bank of Arkansas, aggregated more than 3½ million dollars.

Bank, having loaned out these funds to the citizens of Arkansas, became absolutely and totally insolvent and has never been able to pay one cent on the dollar to any of its creditors. In 1839, the State of Arkansas failed to pay the interest on its Bonds and from that day to this has never paid one dollar either of interest or principal on any of these most sacred obligations.

On the 4th of March, 1845, I became Secretary of the Treasury of the United States and having taken the deepest interest in this Smithsonian fund and in its faithful application to the noble purpose of the donor, and inasmuch as one of my predecessors had invested these funds in these Bonds, and the Government had made itself directly responsible for the faithful execution of this trust, I endeavoured to reclaim, as far as possible, this money from the State of Arkansas, and to induce Congress to appropriate its own monies to redeem the pledge of the Government and fulfill this trust. My first official action on this subject was as follows: By Act of Congress, 5 per cent of the net proceeds of the sales of the public lands in the United States in Arkansas was payable to that State, for certain purposes designated in the Act. There was also an Act of Congress in force, authorizing the Secretary of the Treasury, where there were mutual debts and credits between the Government and any other person, to offset any debt due by any creditor to the United States, against any debt, so far as it would go, due by the United States to such creditor. I interpreted this Act as authorizing me to withhold this 5 per cent fund from the State of Arkansas and appropriate it, as far as it would go, in payment of the interest which had accumulated on the Bonds of the State of Arkansas, in which my predecessor, Mr. Woodbury, on behalf of the Government, had invested the Smithsonian Fund; thus saving a small portion of the interest which had accrued on these Bonds. For this Act I was violently denounced by the Senators and Representatives of Arkansas in Congress, as also by the Legislature and Governor of the State and strenuous efforts were made, unsuccessfully, first to induce me to prevoke my action and, secondly, to have it overruled by the Government. But I adhered to it and declared openly that if such a breach of trust were consummated, and my action overruled in the premises, I would resign my seat in the Cabinet. My official action, however, was sustained by an almost unanimous public sentiment of Congress and of the country. Indeed, beyond the limits of the State of Arkansas and the circle of the repudiators of Mississippi, my course was sustained and approved.

In 1869, the State Legislature passed an Act by which the debt, as well as the interest in arrears, was to be funded, and, by January, 1873, new bonds to the amount of $3,050,000 were issued under authority of this Act. The same Legislature promulgated a decree under which bonds to the amount of $5,300,000 were issued on behalf of railroads. The latter, however, defaulted with respect to interest, in 1873. Default also occurred with respect to a loan of $2,000,000, floated for the purpose of building levees.

A rather peculiar settlement was effected in 1884 by an amendment to the Constitution passed in September of that year, and which declared that the General Assembly should have no power to levy a tax or to make an appropriation to pay the interest or principal of the bonds or the claims upon which they were based, including the so-called Holford bonds, the Railroad Aid bonds, and the Levee bonds. In this way, about $7,900,000 worth of bonds have been repudiated. In addition, the Supreme Court declared the acts under which the above bonds were issued as unconstitutional.

FLORIDA

The repudiated bonds of the State of *Florida* belong to two distinct periods of default, one dating from a score of years before the outbreak of the Civil War, and the other relating to bonds sold by the State a few years after the close of that conflict.

In 1835, $1,000,000 6 per cent bonds of the Territory of Florida were sold in England, chiefly through the investment house of Prime Ward & King (later James G. King's Sons) of New York and London, who, together with some other well-known New York firms, bought them from the Territory, $500,000 at 100½, and $500,000 at 101½.

The incorporation of the Union Bank of Florida, and the issuance by the Territory of bonds for the capitalization of the bank, were special subjects of consideration in 1834 by the United States Congress, which approved the authorizing Act without amendment. Although, in 1836, when a further issue of $2,000,000 Florida Union Bank bonds was proposed, Daniel Webster, Chairman of the Committee on Finance of the Senate, urged Congress to withhold its sanction, Congressional approval was again given, and, in 1838, two additional millions of these securities were sold on the London market. This second issue realized somewhat lower prices than the first million, being purchased by various London houses at prices ranging from 91 to par, but it is on record that even at these discounts, $1,306,000 of them disposed of in London in the first few weeks produced in Florida an amount equal to 107.41.[5]

---

[5] Senate Document 447, 26th Congress, 1st Session.

By the following year, the Union Bank was known to be no longer flourishing, and murmurs against the debt incurred for its capital became articulate, culminating in 1842 in the repudiation of that debt by the Florida Legislative Council, on the ground of unconstitutionality of the issues. The repudiation included not only the whole of the three millions of bonds sold in England in 1835 and 1838, but also $900,000 of bonds sold in England and in Holland in 1835 for two other financial enterprises of the Territory, viz: the Bank of Pensacola and the Southern Life Insurance Company—$3,900,000 in all.

In 1844, when Florida was asking to be admitted as a State of the Union, the European bondholders petitioned the United States Congress, protesting against any grant of statehood with the repudiation of the Territorial Debt written into the new State Constitution. This petition was ignored.

A more common attempt to exonerate the State in connection with the above repudiation is the mistaken statement that the bonds "were invalid for the reason that they were never sanctioned by Congress!"[6]

The question of the liability of the Federal Government was brought on behalf of the British bondholders before the Anglo-American Mixed Arbitration Commission in London, in 1853. The casting vote was given by the umpire, Joshua Bates, of Massachusetts (the American partner of Baring Brothers), who decided against Federal liability. He added, however: "The bondholders have a just claim on the State of Florida; they have lent their money at a fair rate of interest, and the State is bound by every principle of

---

[6] Congressional Record, United States Senate, Dec. 10, 1926, p. 206.

honor to pay interest and principal. It is to be hoped that sooner or later the people of Florida will discover that honesty is the best policy and that no State can be called respectable that does not honorably fulfill its engagements."[7]

The above pronouncement had no effect on Florida, but George Peabody, the well-known American London banker, was instrumental in nearly a million of the Union Bank bonds being bought by Florida planters and farmers from the English holders at about 50 per cent of their value, and used to pay off mortgages held by the bank in Florida. Mr. Peabody also, in 1869, donated $143,000 Florida Union Bank bonds, "amounting with coupons to about $384,000," together with several millions in cash, to his great philanthropic work for the South, the Peabody Southern Education Fund.[8]

Governor Harrison Reed of Florida, in his Message to the Legislature in January, 1870, asked that the Territorial debt and other "incumbrances" be "promptly, courageously, and patriotically met, and steps taken to redeem the State integrity and establish its credit and honor." He also appointed at that time a committee of three to inquire into the condition, liabilities and assets of the Union Bank of Florida, and as to the liability of the State or of the United States for the bonds of said bank, trusting "that some way

---

[7] Moore's "History and Digest of International Arbitrations," Vol. IV, p. 3612.

[8] These bonds donated by Mr. Peabody were at the dissolution of his Trust in 1914 given to and accepted by the University of Florida in trust, the ultimate proceeds to be distributed to the University, the Florida Women's College, and the Peabody College in Nashville, Tennessee.

may be found to dispose of this matter, so as to relieve the State and the people of further liability and inconvenience."

At the end of that year, 1870, S. W. Hopkins & Co. of New York and London, "Fiscal Agents of the State of Florida," applied to the Council of Foreign Bondholders in London, stating that they were prepared to make a proposition for the settlement of the debt, and requesting that a meeting of bondholders should be convened. A meeting was accordingly convened by advertisement in all the London daily newspapers, and held on the 14th of December, 1870, at the Offices of the Council. The fiscal agents offered on behalf of the State £10 per bond to each bondholder, plus a warrant for 500 acres of land to be gradually redeemed by lot at not less than $5 per acre. The arrangement was subject to its being ratified within six months by the Florida Legislature.

The offer was accepted by the bondholders present, and a good number of the bonds were consequently presented at the office of Dent, Palmer & Co., one of the original London distributing houses, and stamped, each holder receiving £2 per bond as earnest money from the State. The proposed arrangement was not ratified, however, by the State Legislature, and the question of these unpaid Territorial Bonds has apparently ceased to trouble any local conscience in office since that time.

In the year just mentioned, 1870, Florida sought to place nearly $4,000,000 8 per cent Railroad-aid Bonds, but with over two millions of her repudiated territorial bonds held in England, prospects were not bright for

their sale, in London; hence, the endeavor of the
State's fiscal agents to placate the British investor with
the proposed arrangement outlined above.

However, within ten days of the meeting held in
the offices of the Council of Foreign Bondholders in
London (i.e., on December 23, 1870), the sale of
$3,000,000 of the new State railroad-aid bonds had
been effected in Holland, to Messrs. Holje & Boisse-
vain, and A. J. & M. Milders of Amsterdam.

Within a year or two the railroads, viz.: the Jacksonville, Pensacola & Mobile Railroad, and the Florida
Central Railroad defaulted. To promote the sale of
the bonds among the Dutch, a part of the proceeds of
the sale to the Dutch investment bankers was retained
to meet the interest for a time as it matured.

As provided by law, the State took possession of the defaulting roads but was unable to sell them for a long time, due
to litigation. . . . In the course of a suit over the ownership
of one of the railroads the constitutionality of the railroad-aid
bonds was brought under review. The court pointed out that
certain bonds had not resulted in a benefit for the State and
therefore "neither the State nor her people are bound for the
bonds in the hands of those who hold them." Hence the State
was no longer pressed to continue its litigation and the railroad-aid bonds were thereafter omitted in any statement of
liabilities.

In the Circuit Court of N. D. Florida on May 31,
1879 (Federal case No. 17434), Mr. Justice Bradley
reviewed the evidence, showing that one of the Dutch
plaintiffs, who had come from Holland to attend the
case, had bought the bonds in Amsterdam, as also a
number of his friends, at prices which forbade the

suggestion that they were conscious of anything
wrong in the sale of the bonds, and that "a great many
widows, orphans, and charity institutions in Holland
had purchased them believing them to be a good and
safe investment." Mr. Justice Bradley stated that the
said bondholders were to be regarded as bona fide
purchasers and holders of the bonds, and that they
had parted with their money relying on the good faith
of the State and the companies.

The first mortgage lien on the Florida Central Railroad which was all the consolation which the Circuit
Court gave the Dutch bondholders in this case, was
worthless, despite the subsequent sale of the road,
owing to a large prior indebtedness of the road to the
Internal Improvement Fund of Florida, and the State
having repudiated its liability in 1875.

Florida's defaulted debt aggregates $7,000,000, of
which $3,900,000 represented bonds issued or endorsed
for banks in the years from 1834 to 1839, and the
balance bonds issued in aid of railroads in 1870, as
follows:

Union Bank of Florida......................	$3,000,000
Bank of Pensacola..........................	500,000
Southern Life Insurance & Trust Company......	400,000
Jacksonville, Pensacola & Mobile Railroad......	
Florida Central Railroad....................	4,000,000

After the failure of the banks in the 40's, the service of the bonds contracted on their behalf was thrown
upon the State.[9] The question of the legality of these
bonds was referred to the Judiciary Committee of the
territorial legislature, which passed the following resolution:

----

[9] William A. Scott, "The Repudiation of State Debts."

That the power of the Governor and Legislative Council of the Territory of Florida . . . does not extend to the creation of banks with exclusive privileges and franchises, nor to the issuing of bonds and guarantees in aid of such institutions . . . that such pledge of the faith and credit of the people of Florida is null and void.

GEORGIA

Aid extended to railroads during the years 1856-1870 by the State of *Georgia* in the form of loans and endorsements, totalled approximately $8,000,000. The issues repudiated by the State are presented hereunder:

	Amount	Date of Repudiation
Central Bank Loan of 1854	$ 375,000	1876
Currency Loan of 1870	2,102,000	1872
Brunswick & Albany Ry. Loan of 1870	1,800,000	....
Miscellaneous railroad loans, 1868-70	5,075,000	1872-75

In addition to the above, about $4,800,000 worth of bonds issued in 1866 are also understood to have been repudiated, bringing the total up to $14,152,000. The clause in the Constitution relating to the debt of the State of Georgia reads as follows:

The General Assembly shall have no authority to appropriate money, either directly or indirectly, to pay the whole or any part of the principal or interest of the bonds or other obligations which have been pronounced illegal, null and void by the General Assembly and the constitutional amendment ratified by the people on the first day of May, 1877.

With respect to the Currency Loan of 1870, it is of interest to point out that $1,000,000 par value bonds were issued by Kuhn, Loeb and Company, and Hallgarten and Company in Frankfurt and Berlin, at 104. The German portion of the loan was over-subscribed seven times. Two years later, bonds defaulted. Germany repaid Georgians half a century later, by selling them worthless or practically worthless German paper known in the early post-war period as bonds and currency.

LOUISIANA

By a special Act promulgated under date of January 24, 1874, the total debt of the State of *Louisiana*, aggregating about $42,000,000, was repudiated to the extent of $22,000,000, while the remaining $20,000,000 was scaled down to approximately $12,000,000. The reason for this action by the State resided in the fact that some parts of the debt were regarded as unconstitutional on the basis of the debt limitation act passed by the State December 15, 1870, by which the debt of Louisiana was limited to $25,000,000.

The debt which resulted from the above readjustment took the form of new bonds bearing interest at the rate of 7 per cent per annum. Inasmuch as many considered the rate too high, an amendment was passed to the Constitution in 1884, providing that interest on the bonds be fixed at 2 per cent for the first five years and at 4 per cent thereafter. It appears that interest on the entire debt, up to the date of repudiation, was promptly taken care of but, after that date, payments were made irregularly and were often in arrears. In 1884, the Legislature provided for the continuation of the payment of the interest on the consolidated debt.

MICHIGAN

In 1837, the State of *Michigan* contracted a loan to the amount of $5,000,000 to be used for construction of a system of public works. Bonds were to be sold through the Morris Canal & Banking Company, which turned over a certain portion of the bonds to the United States Bank of Pennsylvania. The latter is understood to have sold an appreciable amount of bonds abroad. While the bonds were still in the process of distribution the two institutions failed, Michigan having received only $1,387,000 of a total of $5,000,-000. The State maintained that it would not recognize bonds beyond the amount actually received. Nevertheless, the Act of February 17, 1842 provided for the payment of $302.73 in new bonds for every $1,000 old bonds, so that Michigan appears to have received only $277. From the standpoint of the bondholder, the settlement represented a scaling down of about $2,500,000. Interest payments were made on the fully paid bonds, and interest up to July, 1841, included in the settlement on the partially paid bonds.

MINNESOTA

Under an Amendment to the Constitution dated April 15, 1858, the State of *Minnesota* issued $2,275,-000 of 7 per cent bonds. The interest on the loan was to be paid by four railroads, resulting from an Act of Congress passed in March, 1857, by which a grant of land was made to the Territory of Minnesota to aid in the construction of the lines. The latter defaulted in 1859, whereupon the State foreclosed its mortgages, taking possession of about 250 miles of road, franchises, and about 5,000,000 acres of land.

In 1881, bonds were exchanged into a new 5 per cent loan on the basis of 50 cents on the dollar, the new issue being dated July 1, 1881. In this way, $1,137,-500 was repudiated exclusive of interest in arrears which, at the time of the settlement, aggregated about $1,751,750.

MISSISSIPPI

The default by the State of *Mississippi* refers to an issue of bonds made in 1838 to the amount of $5,000,-000, for the purpose of paying for 50,000 shares of stock in the Union Bank of Mississippi. In less than two years the Bank collapsed and, in 1841, the Governor recommended that bonds be repudiated by the State. In 1842 the Legislature denied that the State was either under legal or moral obligation to pay the bonds in question, presumably because the investment had turned out to be a complete loss to the State. However, the Government suggested that the reason for the repudiation was the unconstitutionality of a supplemental act promulgated for the purpose of creating the above bonds.

In addition to the $5,000,000 issue there was another of $2,000,000, floated in 1831 and in 1832 for the purpose of acquiring stock in the Planters' Bank which was chartered by the State of Mississippi in 1830. In 1839, interest defaulted because of the inability on the part of the Bank to meet the service and the State was naturally called upon to take care of the loan. No action was taken by the State in this matter, but at the elections in 1852 the question was submitted to popular vote, whether a tax should be levied for the purpose of paying the interest on the bonds. A majority of 4000 was returned against the imposition of such a tax, indicating that the people were in favor of repudiation and the Legislature of the State so interpreted the people's vote.

In 1875, the Constitution contained the following clause pertaining to the bank bonds of Mississippi: "Nor shall the State assume, redeem, secure or pay any indebtedness claimed to be due by the State of Mississippi to any person, association or corporation whatsoever claiming the sum as owners, holders or assignees of any bond or bonds known as the Union Bank bonds or the Planters' Bank bonds." In this way, repudiation of bonds was not only effected, but was given legal sanction. Interest has been in default apparently since 1841.

North Carolina

The bonds repudiated by *North Carolina* by virtue of an Act promulgated March 4, 1879, comprise the following issues:

Chatham Railroad Loan of 1863	$ 215,000
Chatham Railroad Loan of 1868–69	1,030,000
Williamstown & Tarboro Railroad Loan of 1868–69	450,000
Western Railroad Loan of 1868–69	1,320,000
Western North Carolina Railroad Loan of 1868–69	6,640,000
Wilmington, Charlotte & Rutherford Railroad Loan of 1868–69	3,000,000
Atlantic, Tennessee & Ohio Railroad Loan of 1868–69	106,000
State Penitentiary Loan of 1868–69	44,000

In addition to the above loans, there were also $913,000 worth of bonds issued for other than war purposes and made payable in "good and lawful money of the Confederate States" which the State failed to recognize.

Bonds recognized by the Act of 1879 comprised issues with an aggregate value of $18,892,645 which was to be funded into a new loan of a par value of $5,006,616. Thus, the scaling down represented about $14,000,000, exclusive of several million dollars of unpaid interest also repudiated.

SOUTH CAROLINA

The *South Carolina* debt comprised loans contracted in 1861 and 1863 for other than war purposes. The total, including war debts, amounted to $3,814,863. The exact amount of non-war debt is not known, due to confused records and the conflicting official reports. According to Scott, the State's debt amounted in 1871 to $20,827,608, to which must be added a railway debt of $6,787,608 and other items of $1,382,292, giving a total of $28,997,608. In 1873, the so-called Consolidation Act was passed, authorizing the exchange of outstanding bonds and stocks for new bonds on the basis of 50 per cent of the par value of securities surrendered. Under this act, $5,965,000 worth of bonds were repudiated on the ground that they had been fraudulently issued. Other bonds were repudiated at a later date, but the exact amount is not known.

On December 23, 1879 another act was passed, amended in February of the following year, by which the debt controversy was finally settled and the amount reduced to a figure within the capacity of the State to meet. At the end of 1879, the debt was officially given as $7,175,454, representing, according to estimates, a repudiation and scaling down of about $16,-000,000, with respect to $6,000,000 of which there seems to be no doubt.

TENNESSEE

The debt of the State of *Tennessee* originated during the period of 1833-1838 and appears to have been contracted in connection with the Union Bank and the Bank of Tennessee. Loans contracted between 1848 and 1860 were employed towards the construction of the Capitol. In 1852, an important Act was passed under the authority of which State bonds to the amount of $27,678,000 were loaned to railroad companies. In 1856, bonds were created for the Agricultural Bureau and the purchase of the old home of President Jackson.

In 1865, the interest in arrears on the State debt proper was funded and, three years later, another funding agreement was put through covering additional interest accruals. In 1869 and 1870, four Acts were passed by which the total debt was reduced from about $43,000,000 in 1870 to $28,000,000 in 1874. By virtue of an Act passed in March, 1873, all interest and bonds due up to January 1, 1874 were to be funded into a new loan. Under authority of an Act passed in May, 1882, the debt of the State and accrued interest thereon was funded into a new issue on the basis of $60 par value of new bonds for $100 face value of old bonds plus coupons in arrears, and resulting in the refunding of $12,000,000 of old debts, which apparently represented a scaling down of about $4,000,000.

The debt question was finally settled by the Act of

March, 1883, which divided the obligations of Tennessee into two categories, State Debt proper and Contingent obligations. The former, totalling $2,118,000, was to be scaled down from 20 to 24 per cent, and the new bonds to bear the same rate of interest as the old bonds, namely 5, 5¼ and 6 per cent. The issues affected include:

Capital bonds..........................	$493,000
Hermitage bonds.......................	35,000
Agricultural bonds.....................	18,000
Union Bank bonds......................	125,000
Bank of Tennessee bonds................	214,000
Turnpike Company bonds...............	741,000
Hiawassee Railroad bonds...............	280,000
Eastern Tennessee & Georgia Railroad bonds	144,000
Memphis & La Grange Railroad bonds.....	68,000

The above figures are exclusive of interest in arrears which up to July, 1883, aggregated about $1,000,000.

The Contingent debt was to be scaled down 50 per cent and the new bonds were to bear interest at the rate of 3 per cent per annum. The loans are detailed hereunder:

Ante-war Railroad bonds...............	$8,583,000
Post-war Railroad bonds...............	2,638,000
Funding Loan of 1866.................	2,246,000
Funding Loan of 1868.................	596,000
Funding Loan of 1873.................	4,867,000

The Funding Loan of 1882, amounting to $7,200,-000, was to be scaled down according to the above provisions applicable to the class to which they belong.

In all, the scaling down aggregated about $19,000,-000. The interest on the entire amount accruing from

1875 to the date of adjustment was not honored, with the exception of interest on the State Debt proper amounting to $2,118,000. The new Funding Bonds were payable in 30 years and redeemable at the option of the State in 5 years.

VIRGINIA

By the Funding Act of 1871, *Virginia* agreed to recognize about $31,000,000 out of a total indebtedness of about $45,000,000, claiming that the difference represented the share of West Virginia which, in 1863, had become a separate State. This Act was attacked in the following year by the Legislature of the State. By virtue of the so-called Riddleberger Act of 1882, the debt was scaled down to about $19,500,-000 on the ground that, at the time of the funding agreement in 1871, about $15,000,000 of the $45,000,-000 represented capitalized interest. Only about $14,-000,000 of bonds were presented for exchange and about $9,000,000 of new bonds were issued.

In 1892, the debt question was finally settled. The scaling down was again justified on the principles of the 1882 Agreement. Bonds were to be issued for a new 100-year loan bearing interest at the rate of 2 per cent for 10 years and 3 per cent for 90 years. The exchange was made on the basis of $280 par value of old bonds for $19 of the new loan. This operation represents a scaling down of about $9,000,000.

WEST VIRGINIA

The part of the debt assigned to *West Virginia* was recognized by the latter in 1919. The total principal and accrued interest was fixed at $14,562,867, of which $1,062,867 was paid in cash and the balance in 20-year 3½ per cent bonds which were duly delivered April 18, 1919, with the exception of $1,133,500 held in escrow by the State Board of Public Works pending the filing of the balance of the outstanding Virginia Debt certificates.

In addition to the defaults discussed in the preceding pages, a number of municipalities in the United States have defaulted with respect to interest and sinking fund on their obligations. The situation is especially distressing in Florida. A survey of the situation by the Barnett National Bank of Jacksonville, contains the following comment:

Many communities became convinced that they were faced by a hopeless task in the payment of their obligations and were encouraged in this attitude by a large crop of financial advisors and fiscal agents, most of whom were out for personal gain. There were formed various adjustments committees, bondholders committees, etc. Many of these agencies sought and secured publicity in responsible newspapers and magazines. The object of much of this publicity was to scare holders of Florida bonds into "dumping" them at sacrifice prices, so that they in turn might be resold at a profit or used in a profitable compromise with the city or county.

However, says the bank, "no criticism is intended of those bondholders' protective committees formed to take court action to establish legal liability and enforce payment of bonds. These are generally formed by dealers who handled the bonds, and deserve support."

"We take the position that these bonds should and will be paid," the Barnett National Bank comments.

"We know, of course, that extension of time is necessary in the case of many cities. This can be done by the exchange of refunding bonds for those maturing and should be handled through dealers or banks."

INDEX